A Journey of
Consciousness

THE WORLD
IS IN MY GARDEN

A Journey of
Consciousness

THE WORLD
IS IN MY GARDEN

by Chris Maser with Zane Maser
Illustrations by Leslie Edgington

White Cloud Press
Ashland, Oregon

Inquiries should be addressed to:
White Cloud Press, PO Box 3400, Ashland, Oregon 97520.
Website: www.whitecloudpress.com

First printing: 2005

Cover photo: Eric Alan
Cover design: David Ruppe, Impact Publications
Interior design: Christy Collins

Printed in the United States of America

Library of Congress Cataloging-in-Publication Data

Maser, Chris. The world is in my garden : a journey of consciousness / by Chris Maser. p. cm. Includes bibliographical references (p.   ). ISBN 1-883991-55-2 (pbk.)
1. Gardening--Philosophy. I. Title.
SB454.3.P45M372 2004
712'.01--dc22
                                    2003028215

DEDICATIONS

Although my wife Zane and I created our garden together, I have written this book, with her persmission, as though it is my garden simply because I did not know how to write it otherwise. Be that as it may, this dedication is from both of us: In loving memory of Bemmy, who graced our garden with his presence and forever enriched our experience of it.—*Chris*

To my Dad, Vernon Zane Evers, who in the last year of his life sat peacefully, contentedly in the sun by our pond and watched the goldfish. Now his spirit enhances our garden with his radiant love. Truly, where there is perfect love, there can be no separation.—*Zane*

ACKNOWLEDGEMENTS

IT IS WITH GREAT pleasure that I thank the following people (in alphabetical order) for graciously giving of their time to review the manuscript of this book and improve it with their numerous suggestions: Bernard Bormann (Research Forest Ecologist, USDA Forest Service Research Laboratory, Corvallis, OR), Tricia Bormann (Corvallis, OR), Sue Johnston (Albany, OR), Paula Minear (Research Assistant, Department of Fish and Wildlife, Oregon State University, Corvallis, OR), and Greg Paulson (Instructor of Horticulture, Linn–Benton Community College, Albany, OR). Excerpts from the article in Resurgence by David Orr are printed by kind permission of the author.—*Chris*

OVER THE PAST SEVERAL YEARS MY TEACHER, White Eagle, has gently guided me on the path of spiritual unfoldment, which includes the central discipline of meditation. The guided meditations in this book follow White Eagle's way of quiet inner attunement. I hope this style of meditation is a peaceful and renewing experience for you.—*Zane*

CONTENTS

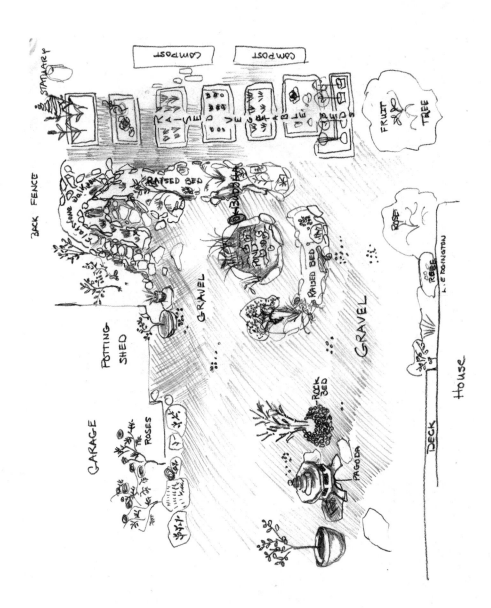

PREFACE

OVER THE MORE THAN twenty-five years that I have studied ecosystems in various parts of the world, I have often been overwhelmed by the sheer magnitude of the ecological and social problems with which I was dealing. "How," I used to ask myself over and over, "can I as one person affect anything?" And because I saw no way for me to change anything for the better, I often felt despair and helplessness. Then, a few years ago, I commenced gardening.

Now in my mid-sixties, I see that all the global problems with which I have for so long been wrestling (ecological, social, personal, and spiritual) are reduced to the size of personal awareness and understanding in ways that I could never have imagined as a younger man. Every conceivable problem is only a matter of scale and essentially the same, regardless of culture or language, and is played out again and again, whether I see it in the sub-arctic climate of Alaska, the deserts of Egypt or the American Southwest, the jungles of Malaysia, the Alps of Europe, the Rocky Mountains of Colorado, or the coast of Oregon.

The problems were not only repeated elsewhere but also occurred in my garden in one way or another. This is not surprising, when I think of it, because culture is a structure that is artificially imposed on people and consequently reflected in their gardens. While the specifics might differ, the principles are identical, and the scale of the problem in my garden is one I can understand, relate to, affect, and expand again to a global view.

On the other hand, "think globally, act locally" is much too abstract for most people to grasp even if they want to. "How," people ask me repeatedly, "can I as one person affect any change in the world? What can I do?"

For a long time, I had no good answer, but now I find that my garden is the perfect passageway to understanding the relationships among local action, global consequences, personal responsibility, and spiritual growth. This passageway is important because, as the South African author Nadine Gordimer discovered, the "facts" as we perceive them are always less than the reality of what happened. And yet, my garden is also an isle of solitude around which the increasingly hectic, time-diseased human world turns. I thus return again and again to its quiet confines, there to touch my spiritual ground while I confront my understanding of the overwhelming worldly problems outside of its borders. It is this link that I want to share with you, because it can inspire us as gardeners with a sense of personal responsibility and contribution to the welfare of our home planet.

In my garden, I find the spiritual and the material, the intuitive and the intellectual (including the scientific) coming together—not in the deadly grapple of today's outer world, but in a dynamic harmony that becomes ever clearer as I mature in both life and the art of gardening.

I offer these ideas with the hard-won realization that, of all species on earth, we humans are both blessed and cursed with the greatest of powers: the power consciously to change ourselves, to struggle towards an ideal of being, and frequently to fall short of that ideal. In struggling, however, we must understand and remember that anything worth doing well is worth doing poorly for a while.

I say this because we have control over what we choose to think and do—what we cause to be set in motion. The outcome (consequence) of our choice is therefore our responsibility. As such, it is within our creative power to change ourselves, one by one, from collectors of society's increasing psychological and technological garbage to trustees of one another's dignity, and it is within our power to transform the world from a growing toxic waste-dump back into a heavenly garden.

We are at this juncture because we humans have forgotten that we are an inseparable part of Nature, not a special case apart from Nature. Although this juncture originates as the thoughts and motives in our hearts and minds, it is manifested through our decisions and the subsequent actions we commit in our surrounding environments and on landscapes throughout the world.

With respect to landscapes, both human and otherwise, we, as a global society, stand once again, as I write in March 2003, at the precipice of a major war because we humans find it easier to fear than to love, easier to hate than to accept, easier to compete and hoard than to share, easier to accuse than to be responsible, easier to react than to respond, easier to kill than to live in peace with one another. What I have just described is a global problem, one almost beyond our comprehension and seemingly beyond our individual abilities to affect.

Nevertheless, at this, the beginning of the twenty-first century, it is imperative to remember the deeper values that make us human—the need for love, trust, respect, dignity, and the ability to safely share life's experiences in order to know that we exist and have value. It's these deeper values that are proffered in the giving of a flower or fruit that one has planted, grown, and harvested. The gift, be it a carrot, a head of lettuce, a bouquet of daffodils, or a single rose, holds within it the language of the heart and in so doing transcends the violence with which humanity so often besets the world.

It is with such a gift in mind that I now invite you into my garden to accompany me on a journey of consciousness, where we shall encounter the labyrinth of apparently competing values, such as the spiritual versus the material, and the intuitive versus the intellectual and the scientific. Our journey is a search for the centre of the garden in which all things coalesce.

As you wander my garden, remember that your sense of truth, like mine and even the history of people and events recorded in books, is a flight of fantasy on the wings of perception. This said, you can find facets of the ideas expressed in this book that you would revise through your own lens to fit your own sense of truth, facets of ideas that are missing, and some with which you just plain disagree. You are, of course, free to feel all of these things.

Because we have forgotten nature, there is a feeling of loss at the heart of modern people. We try to fill this inner gap with wealth and power, or with distraction, but this does no good at all. Each age has its own unique sadness. This, it seems to me, must be our own. Is it any wonder we have lost the meaning of our lives?

CHAPTER I

MY GARDEN AS METAPHOR

*The very best thing my garden gives me [is] a sense of
belonging to one special place.*
– Actress Juliette Binoch

I LOVE MY GARDEN because it is small, and I can physically care for it,
touch it, feel it, and smell it; whereas I can only love society, care for it,
and touch it through words on paper or in front of an audience or a TV
camera. But in my garden, I need no words.

My garden as an isle of solitude reminds me of an Eastern fable
about an emperor in a faraway land who built a palace, which he named
the House of the Singing Floors.[1] When the palace was completed, the
emperor looked at it and decided that he wanted some gardens planted
to accentuate the palace itself in the midst of an Earthly Paradise.

The emperor sent for the wisest and most skillful of his gardeners
and commanded him to create the palace gardens. The gardener, who
was very old and very wise, selected a place at some distance from the
palace and built for himself a simple chair, which he covered with a
canopy of branches as protection from the elements. There he quietly
seated himself.

Summer passed slowly and gently as the old man sat in silence,
watching. Autumn came. The leaves of the trees changed colors and
fell. Many of the birds departed as the north wind began to blow and
the storm clouds to gather. As the sky darkened, snow began to fall, and
winter lay upon the ground. But still the aged gardener sat in his chair
observing quietly.

The winds sent snow whirling and spinning across the land, sweeping the ground clear in one place only to bury it in another as the trees
now bent, now whipped back and forth under the fury of the gale. The
gardener, meanwhile, pulled about him his woolen cloak as he reached
for another bowl of hot tea.

Spring came. The snows melted. Little streams swelled. Birds began
returning, once again filling the warming breezes with song. Through
the spent stalks of last year's grasses and the limp, decaying bodies of

fallen leaves came the delicate heads of spring flowers. And still the old gardener sat watching in silence the mural of the seasons.

At last, summer came again. The gardener, having sat in his chair for a year, arose and entered into the presence of the emperor.

"I will now plant the garden," he said.

By the following summer, the Earthly Paradise was completed. On every hand bloomed rare plants. Strange and wonderful fishes added color to the ponds as shining native fishes swam in the streams. Birds, which migrated from afar, nested in the shrubs and trees, filling the garden with song. Little shrines reposed atop large rocks, and ancient stone lanterns enchanted pathways.

When all was in readiness, the old gardener requested an audience with the emperor, and led him onto the wide verandah of the palace.

"O Son of Heaven," he said, "my work is finished. In every season and with the passing of every year, this garden will retain its perfection. Each plant in its growing will become a living part of a balanced completeness.

"The fragrance of spring, hidden in opening blossom and unfolding leaf, will perfume the air with Heaven's own scent. The leaves of the trees will create an ever-changing dance of light and shadow as the flowers nod and the ferns and grasses sway in the breezes of summer. The falling leaves of autumn will form patterns upon the ground and in the ponds as berries ripen into hues of blue and orange and red. Through the leafless branches of late autumn shrub and tree you will see in vista grand the snow-capped mountains. With winter will the ponds and streams freeze in patterns bold and intricate, a perfect mix of composition and harmony. And with spring, the streams, released from winter's grip, will form ripples, eddies, and pools in their flowing, each perfectly attuned to the rest.

"It is for this reason that I sat for a year in meditation. There can be only peace here, for conflict cannot abide where Heavenly peace reigns. Each passing season will express itself in its own way. There will always be harmonious beauty in the gardens of your palace.

"As your majesty advances in years, your perceptions and tastes will change, but the gardens will grow and change also. You will thus find happiness in them as long as you live. And when at last you return to the sky from whence you came, those who follow after you will find themselves in this garden as you have found yourself. I have created a miniature world to reflect for you the mysteries of a far greater world.

This, O Son of Heaven, is a wise man's garden."

The fabled emperor is the *Self*, the garden one's life, and the aged gardener one's own wisdom with which one must build one's Earthly Paradise. But the mystery of this fable cannot be understood by reading the words; it can only be felt inwardly as a spiritual experience while gardening. By gardener, I do not mean one who just tends to the soil and the plants that grow therein, but rather one who consciously, purposefully tends simultaneously to the soil of the Earth and to the spirit of one's own being for only in their union can one flourish within the flow of the Universe.

In this sense, my garden reconciles me to my mortality within the scheme of things and binds me to the ever-changing great and small cycles of relationship, even while it reminds me of the Mayan term for human: "Those who bear the burden of time." My garden thus molds and transforms my worldview as it teaches me that my duty is one of respectful trusteeship of the environment *and* society for those who must follow.

Although my garden is still subject to the effects of Nature, when I stand therein, I am at the point of balance between a world of Nature and a world of culture. As a product of culture, it is therefore the quality of the compromise that I strike with Nature that is important, not the perceived correctness of my position or my act; for it is through the quality of the compromise that I assess the sensitivity of my connection with Nature.

As we tend the gardens of our lives, through the effects of our thoughts, motives, decisions, actions, and their outcomes, we struggle with concepts both for purposes of clarification and because change in our ever-evolving perceptions opens new vistas to explore. Each concept, such as *compromise*, is the seed of thought, which I cannot define in language. I cannot, therefore, approach anything directly or absolutely through language. Words are at best only symbols or metaphors for those things I cannot fully grasp or explain because they go beyond language to the center of the Universe, which encompasses all symbols, all metaphors—all words.

Lao-tzu, the Chinese philosopher, understood that no word can define the object of its focus; he wrote:

> Existence is beyond the power of words
> To define,
> Terms may be used
> But are none of them absolute.[2]

While most of us attempt to "cut the best deal" by trying to open the Universe to ourselves, Lao-tzu opened himself to the Universe. This is but saying that while we seek positions of outer authority from which to control our surroundings, Lao-tzu lived from a well of inner authority, through which he simply placed himself at the disposal of Universal harmony.

Although I have not yet achieved such harmony, in trying to "define" my inner Universe within the greater context of the outer, I have become a gardener. It is through gardening that I have struggled with such concepts as crisis, self-knowledge, experience, change, killing, death, and peace. And it is in struggling to understand these concepts that I daily refine the inner garden of my soul in thought, word, and deed and see it reflected in my outer garden through Nature.

As I mature, I find that each concept not only has been central to my life at one time or another but also has become a fascinating, ever-changing kaleidoscope of perceptions and illusions of the Truth. The latter has taken shape in the form of lessons that I needed to learn, lessons that ultimately brought me a little closer to the Truth. In this, as in the whole of life, whether we know it or not, whether we accept it or not, we all follow the same path, the path that leads to Truth.

Be that as it may, George Santayana, the American philosopher and poet, found that, "Truth is allowed but a brief interval of victory between the time it is condemned as falsehood and belittled as trivial." Nevertheless, it is the concepts with which we struggle that become the stepping stones of understanding along the way. We must, however, pay heed to these stepping stones lest we sleep-walk through life and live in the shadow of an idea without grasping it.

So it is that while working in my garden, I can, for a while, be untouched by the various wars (both those of ideology and those of physical weapons) that are raging in the outer world, or by the disease and hunger that ravage this country or that, or by the corporate greed that is destroying whole ecosystems and cultures, both at home and abroad. It is not that I don't care about what goes on in the outer world, but rather that my garden is at once the field of battle in which I struggle within myself to grow, an isle of solitude in a sea of worldly strife, and an entrance into a realm of reality beyond the material, much like the rabbit's burrow leading to Alice's Wonderland.

It is here, in my garden, that I personalize my perception of the world in a scale with which I can cope and to some degree affect. Here,

as the French painter Ingres says of art, "one arrives at an honorable result only through one's tears." Thus, in some small way, I can affect the world at the scale of my garden by consciously learning to understand and work with those physical, biological, and spiritual principles that govern the intrinsic wholeness of Nature—and myself as a quintessential part thereof.

As such, it is spiritual succor that I find in my garden when the burdens of the outer world grow too heavy for my shoulders. It is here that I kneel before the Eternal Mystery and find peace in turning the soil and in weeding. And it is while weeding that my inner vision shifts, and I often see my garden not as an infinitesimal place in the world, but rather the world as an infinitesimal part of my garden.

I say this because if my garden were encircled by a high stone wall in which there were four gates, one for each cardinal direction, I would name each gate by the element it brings to the inner unity of the circle wherein lies my garden. One gate would be named "Ecological Consciousness" in honor of the awe inspired by Nature, another "Social Consciousness" to commemorate the human struggle for just governance, the third "Personal Consciousness" to highlight the courage it takes to change and grow, and the fourth gate would be named "Spiritual Consciousness" to connote the unity of all things found within the garden, which is a reflection of the same unity found without.

Each gate would be perpetually open to anyone who wished to enter, and upon entering, one would merge with the Tao—the gateway through which we are constantly passing. It would matter not, therefore, through which gate you passed, for one is equal to another, and all paths merge in the center of the garden, in which lies the unity of all things. Knowing that the Well of Unity lies in the center of the garden is important because it is a safe harbor in life's sea of uncertainty.

It is interesting to see the reactions of those who come into my garden. The scientist clearly enters through the gate of Ecological Consciousness, whereas a State Legislator I once entertained found her way through the gate of Social Consciousness. Now and then someone enters through the gate of Personal Consciousness, but it is a rare person indeed who finds the gate of Spiritual Consciousness. There is, however, a commonality to almost all who enter; it is the peace they feel within the confines of my garden.

In our journey of consciousness, we shall experience the relationship of each gate to the divisiveness of the world outside of the garden in contrast to the unity of that within, beginning with the gate named "Ecological Consciousness." We begin with the gate of Ecological Consciousness not only because the concepts of this domain are the most concrete for many people to grasp but also because without these ecological underpinnings neither the garden nor we as human beings would exist.

The gateway is at once the end of one world and the beginning of another, which means we are in both worlds simultaneously when we stand in the gateway of the ineffable present between the past and the future. I say "ineffable" present because the gateway is like sitting alongside a large river of mild current in which that part of the river immediately in front of me represents the present, that which flows towards me a future dream, and that which is already by me a past memory. There is no stopping the flow of the river, so that grasping past and future in the fluidity of the present moment is the purpose of Tao—the gateway. "Though we travel the world over to find the beautiful," wrote Ralph Waldo Emerson, "we must carry it with us or we find it not."

Go, therefore, into your garden, and it will teach you everything you need to know about gardening, Nature, yourself, and the Way. These lessons are important because much of industrialized humanity is dangerously out of touch with the fact that we and the biophysical world in which we live are inexorably interwoven.

CHAPTER 2

THE GATE OF ECOLOGICAL CONSCIOUSNESS

BECAUSE THOSE WHO ENTER my garden through the gate of Ecological Consciousness are often "ecocentric" and out of touch with the soul of humanity, it is important to realize that humanity is an inseparable part of Nature. It is no accident, therefore, that ecology (which represents Nature) and economy (which represents humanity) both have the same Greek root *oikos*, a house. Ecology is the knowledge or understanding of the house. Economy is the management of the house. And it is the *same* house.

Although a house divided against itself cannot long stand, it has been the continuing assumption of our society that if we manage the parts right, the whole will come right. Yet, while evidence to the contrary now comes from all directions, our systems of knowledge, governance, and management are still structured around this assumption.

"Call a thing immoral or ugly, soul-destroying or a degradation of man, a peril to the peace of the world or to the well-being of future generations," wrote economist E. F. Schumacher, "as long as you have not shown it to be 'uneconomic' you have not really questioned its right to exist, grow, and prosper." Schumacher's words point to the untenable divisiveness that weakens the house inhabited equally by ecology and economy. The question, therefore, is how do we heal the current division in the house shared by ecology and economy in all its various scales from the personal to the global? The answer, I would suggest, can be found in gardening.

GARDENING CHANGED THE WORLD

Every new concept begins with a majority of one, including a garden.

Standing in the early morning sun, feeling its gathering warmth caress my body, I am surrounded by dancing colors as the flowers in my garden nod and sway in the teasing breeze of June. I love my garden

21

with its ever-changing combination of hues, scents, flavors, textures, and shapes.

Working in my garden gives me a spiritual ground. My garden is a place to keep the accelerating pace of life and its increasingly fragmentary activity in balance with the solitude required by my soul as I struggle to cope within a society that seems to be rapidly losing touch with its sense of morality. Was there, I wonder, also a time in the far-distant past when the tempo of life's flow and ebb seemed to pound with disquieting force on the gate to the heart of the primitive human being, in which is secreted the stillness of peace? Was that when the first flower was consciously planted in a particular place to commemorate the inner stillness that was being assaulted by the outer world? Did planting that first flower constitute the birth of gardening as a conscious act of human love that fulfilled a void in the human soul? Was it a practical act or the soul's need to create a small corner of beauty and harmony? If it was the latter, Ralph Waldo Emerson would have approved, because he counseled that we should "never lose an opportunity of seeing anything that is beautiful, for beauty is God's handwriting—a wayside sacrament."

With the planting of that first flower, I can in my mind's eye see the gentle touch of woman extending spiritual beauty and compassion into the dangers of a harsh world beyond the family fire. And because the first act of gardening altered how people participated with Nature, I wonder how gardening as a specific and practical activity got started. Perhaps it started with comets.

Although the ancient Chinese thought of comets as celestial brooms wielded by the gods to sweep clean the heavens of all evil, author Rebecca McClen Novick has another thought. She likens the 1997 comet, Hale-Bopp, to a time machine taking us back to 2213 BCE, the date of its visit before this one. As we gazed at the comet, we were sharing a common experience with everyone who stopped to watch something rare and beautiful 4,210 years ago.

To see a comet, writes Novick, "is to unite with the mythic history of humanity and …the genesis of life itself," for many scientists now believe that comets brought water to our world, creating the necessary conditions for the beginning of life. Hence Novick refers to comets as the "cosmic gardeners, tending the flower beds of the stars." When we view a comet, are we really seeing a celestial gardener who brought water to Earth and thus made possible the first garden on this tiny planet suspended in infinite space?

The First Garden

"In the beginning was the Word, and the Word was with God, and the Word was God," so begins the Gospel of St. John. And time passed, and the land began to break into pieces that drifted apart, and the land changed. And time passed, and plants took dominion of the land. Somewhere in time, animals began to consume the plants in an endless cycle of life and death and life, which augmented both the fertility and variety of the soils. Then came humans. And time passed.

Being ingenious and open to the opportunities of life, humans sought easier and better ways of getting food, ways that helped to ensure their survival. Perhaps one of the earliest ways of improving the chance of getting sufficient food was altering the vegetation of a landscape.

With this realization, they began consciously changing the dynamics and the design of every landscape with which they interacted. In doing so, they created a tension between their need for resources and their spiritual beliefs about Nature as they endeavored daily to survive. This seeming incongruity between exploitation and reverence was mediated and integrated through these early people's Nature-based spirituality, which dignified the necessary exploitation of that which they deified by transforming hunting, fishing, and gathering into sacred acts. By harmonizing their more mundane acts of living in a way that aligned them with their spiritual beliefs, the people not only created but also maintained the continuity of their psychic holism, rather than compartmentalizing their lives into isolating fragments of behavior by separating the two.

People, including our ancient ancestors, have never been totally in harmony with Nature, if for no other reason than because they had to kill in order to live. In addition, they altered their environment simply by living, often in ways locally detrimental to themselves, before they moved on. Although they were not enraptured with the concept of Nature, their spirituality encompassed the whole of their lives, including their economics, and that made all the difference.

It was ordained in the nature of things, however, that somewhere in the world, one of the most important technological events would sooner or later take place—the invention of the irrigation ditch. Just think, there actually was a time before ditches, a time when the distribution of water was dictated solely by Nature.

But then came the first ditch, which allowed humanity, plants, and animals to move into areas heretofore uninhabitable by those who needed water in close proximity. Ditches and the conscious, selective domestication and cultivation of plants and animals gave rise to agriculture and an illusory sense of control over Nature. With that sense came a greater degree of fidelity to a particular place, a conscious, personal relationship with the Earth, which may have led to the first true sense of gardening.

Gardening Is a Reciprocal Relationship

As previously mentioned, the tension created by ancient peoples between their need for resources, which often necessitated the act of killing, and their spiritual beliefs about Nature were a seeming incongruity between exploitation and reverence. This incongruity was for a time mediated and integrated through the people's spirituality, which guided their reciprocal relationship with Nature—a relationship that began to change with the first irrigation ditch.

Although Nature had long been objectified before I was born, I remember the small, diversified family farms of my youth in western Oregon with their personable fields. I also remember watching in helpless dismay as the family scale of farming gave way to the corporate scale, and in the process of this escalating social trance, I was taught to believe that I could never have enough or own enough to feel secure. I was also taught that security is synonymous with the word "mine."

Finally, there came the time I started working in *my* garden, which I own in fee simple. Although the connotation of ownership is control, I have learned, sometimes painfully, that I neither do nor can control my garden. Rather, gardening is a reciprocal relationship between me and the Earth. The soil is my medium of experimentation and everything thereon and therein is my teacher. As I treat Nature, so Nature responds in kind. If, for example, I am neglectful of the soil, it produces little of what I desire, but if I am mindful and nurture the soil, it produces in abundance what I wish. The reciprocity of which I speak is an outer reflection of an inner attitude of my being, which brings to mind a story about a Chinese priest in search of the Book of Knowledge.

The priest spent his entire adult life fighting dragons, thieves, armies, and demons of every kind that blocked his path to the Book of Knowledge, a path he followed without knowing where it was leading. Finally, after years of struggle, the path led him to the edge of the sea, and there, high atop a lava pinnacle, was a monastery.

With the last of his strength, for he was by now an old man, he climbed the narrow, winding stairs to the monastery, where he was welcomed by a monk. The monk bade him enter and told him to rest, for his way had been long and difficult.

After the priest had rested from his arduous journey, the monk came to him and said: "You have traveled from afar to this monastery following a path that led you knew not where. In so doing, you have shown the strength of your faith through your obedience to that which has guided you from within, and you have had your courage well tested along the way. I am the keeper of the Book of Knowledge, and, since you have earned the right, I give you leave to look within."

The old priest looked at him and asked: "What shall I find?"

Whereupon the monk replied: "Only what you bring with you."

With that, the old priest opened the long-awaited Book and found within a mirror, which reflected the image of his own face. And within that reflection was all knowledge contained, for it revealed the relative wisdom of what he had learned and thus become as a result of his trials and struggles and the choices he had made along the way.

He saw, for instance, the very moment in his life when he learned that discrimination of choice determines the path one's feet are destined to walk. He saw the far distant circumstance in which he had learned that a life without desires is the key to freedom from the prison cell of materialism. He saw, by contemplating the cumulative events of his life, that good conduct is the sole responsibility of the individual traveler and is not dependent on the behavior of another.

He now realized that all the demons along his path were only distortions in the house of mirrors, those disowned parts of himself that lived in the shadowland of his own soul. He suddenly understood that wisdom can neither be taught nor given away, that wisdom, the distillation of life's experiences, must be earned and that unconditional love, which asks nothing, overcomes all obstacles.

With ever-so-slight a sigh, he slowly closed the Book and reconciled himself to the fact that the sacred Book was in reality a mirror reflecting the opportunities and the choices he had made along his journey of incarnation, as well as the lessons he had learned—lessons presented to him by the Lords of Karma. In retrospect, he saw within the great Book the sum of his life.

Here you might ask what this story has to do with a book about gardening and reciprocal relationships? Well, as I work in my garden, I see those things that I did correctly and those I did not; they are reflected in the health of the soil and in the growth of the plants. I see where I made impatient choices with Nature, and the environmental, emotional, and sometimes physical cost of my impatience. I also see where I made decisions, out of a center of peace, and the resultant harmony I helped to foster by treating my garden with patience, kindness, and respect and how it reciprocated in health and beauty.

In short, my garden is, in many ways, the mirror in *my* Book of Knowledge, and in it I see myself reflected because I and the priest are one. And like his, mine is an inner journey, a journey without end, a journey without distance, a journey in which I am both in creation and creating. As I create so I am in creation and I am either freed by my creations—those born of love—or imprisoned by them—those born of fear.

The decision is mine, for I have free will, which means that each day, with a pen called imagination and an inkwell called choice, I write and rewrite, edit and re-edit my autobiography. And change is the vehicle with which I mold and remold my character, the image I will one day see in the mirror of my soul when I open my own Book of Knowledge. But until that final day arrives, I see myself reflected daily in the mirror of my garden.

I have learned, for example, that I can neither own the plants I grow or purchase, nor even the soil of my garden to which I hold legal title and deed, and thus I cannot manage them for predictable outcomes. Both plants and soil are born of Nature, as am I, and so they are my teachers, not my subjects. I say this because they are free to respond according to the manner in which I treat them, but not necessarily in the way I would wish.

I have learned that I do not and cannot own my garden, that my thoughts, motives, experiences, and behavior are all I own. I can, however, relate to my garden. Learning the loving heart of relationship is the purpose of life, be it a relationship with myself, another person, Nature, literature, science, or technology. Relationship is all there is because I must be in relationship with something and everything in order to exist.

When I treat each plant in my garden in a certain way, it responds to that treatment by conversing with me through the timing, duration, and vigor of its cycle of growth, bloom, and seed. Collectively, these cycles, mediated through my treatment of the soil and the apparent whims of Nature, produce in my garden an annual living poem of ever-changing colors, scents, textures, designs, and flavors.

A great blue heron flies overhead and peers down into my garden pond contemplating an easy meal of goldfish. The heron circles and glides in for a dawn landing. What a magnificent bird as it stands patiently at the edge of the pond. But I, too, want the fish, for I have come to love them as they grace the waters amidst the pink and yellow pond lilies. How empty of visible activity the pond would seem if the heron succeeded in securing its breakfast before departing to the next convenient neighborhood buffet.

This time, my cat detects the heron and alerts me. I race outside and shoo the heron away. It flies out of sight behind some trees to the west, where, unbeknownst to me, it sits and watches—waiting. After working in the garden for a half an hour or so, I enter the house, and in that instant the heron again swoops down to the edge of the pond. Zane, my wife, seeing it, calls to me as she runs out the back door. The heron leaves, and does not on this day return.

We purchase a fine mesh net in reaction to the heron's unexpected appearance and spread it over the pond to keep out the great bird. But alas, the net also keeps us out. We are now separated from the pond, held at arm's length in a way we have never before been.

Although the fish may be momentarily protected from the heron, the pond is also unavailable to us. We can no longer actively participate in its daily life except through the net's plastic mesh. We have unknowingly and unintentionally distanced ourselves from the pond in the same manner as we have intentionally distanced the heron.

This is brought home to me the next day as I gaze through the net into the water along the edge of the pond. There in the water is a damselfly slowly drowning because it cannot get out through the net no matter how hard it tries. The damselfly, the immature forms or nymphs of which are aquatic, is the first to emerge from our pond this year, which makes me realize that we cannot protect the fish from the heron without somehow closing our pond off to ourselves and seemingly to the Universe. We not only have kept the heron and ourselves out but also have trapped the damselfly within.

Just as we interact with the pond, so the pond interacts with the Universe, of which we, the heron, and the damselfly are inseparable parts. My feeling of separation from the pond becomes increasingly acute; until, after three weeks, I can no longer bear it and remove the net. Feeling an immediate and immense sense of relief, I reconnect with the pond and the pond reconnects with the whole of the garden, including the heron.

And so I learn that I can no more protect the fish from the marauding heron than I can keep the cabbage butterflies from laying their eggs on my vegetables, or the scrub jays from planting acorns and filberts amongst the flowers, or the robins from sowing holly trees seemingly everywhere through their droppings. Nor can I force the freezing north wind to bypass my garden in spring or bargain with the late frost to spare my plants while it kills those in other gardens. And I cannot stave off the lost, empty feeling each summer when the baby swallows, raised in the nest box on the north side of our house, fledge and join their parents as they navigate the winds.

As summer wanes, I realize once again how much the seasons differ one from another, both among themselves and among years. And I am different, for no year goes by during which I do not grow and see the world and my garden with a new and different perspective that of the world dimming outwardly with the aging of my eyes and that of the spirit growing inwardly ever clearer within my heart. Of late, the growing clarity of my inner vision causes me to wonder whether we as a species will ultimately end up with an environment compatible with our existence or hostile to our existence. But do we deserve any better in light of our current behavior? The answer will depend on the questions we ask, the decisions we make, and the actions we take while gardening, for as we treat our gardens, so we treat the larger world.

Gardening Makes Ecosystems Increasingly Fragile

Gardening is the act through which spirituality and art merge into the context of Nature's landscape. It is where we use the form and function of Universal Laws to transpose into graphic symmetry the cultural beauty and spiritual harmony of our inner landscapes through the fluid medium of Nature's outer landscape. Gardening is the conscious marriage of cultural myth and Universal Laws of Being. To garden is to bring Nature, art, and our souls into harmony with one another in such a way that one cannot tell where Nature ends and art begins, and vice versa.

Whether we wish to admit it or not, contends ecological restorationist William Jordan, the world really is a garden that invites, even requires, our constant participation and habitation. In this sense, gardening the Earth means to negotiate a new reality with Nature, one that is based on Universal Laws and on our spiritual consciousness, because the patterns created on the landscape by a community or society are a true "pictorial" reflection of its collective spiritual attainment and ecological understanding.

An ecosystem, in turn, is an ecological community of plants and animals together with its physical environment, taken as a unit. An ecosystem is therefore an arbitrary convenience of the human imagination in that we delineate into "ecosystems" any portion of the landscape that we desire—from a huge forest, to a river flowing through the forest, to a swampy area bordering the forest, to a farmer's field, to my garden. We make such designations in our attempt to understand the dynamic interactions between the nonliving and living components of our world at scales we can comprehend.

Ecosystems are designed by the variability of natural phenomena, such as volcanoes, climate, fires, floods, and the cyclical nature of populations of organisms; they are not designed by the predictable averages of anything, which includes my garden. Of course, the type of variability that affects ecosystems normally depends on the size or scale of the ecosystem. For example, while climate obviously affects my garden daily at the macroscale, the cyclical nature of the plants and the soil organisms within my garden also affects it, but at the microscale.

All this means that ecosystems, including my garden, are designed by the simultaneous interactions of natural phenomena, which create novelty and uncertainty, not static surety. Ecosystems cannot be completely engineered and controlled by us humans, despite our most fervent desires and efforts.

Although the many incremental changes we make in an ecosystem in our attempt to engineer and control it may seem insignificant to us, and their effects for a time invisible (lulling us into the illusion of being in control), ecosystems operate on thresholds with unknown margins of safety. Consider these incremental changes, commonly called cumulative effects, in terms of fine vintage wine.

In my youth, I held the illusion that I wouldn't know the limits of sobriety *before* I crossed the threshold of no return by keeping careful track of the number of small swallows I took at intervals of a good wine. I found, however, that, while I could always determine the limits of sobriety, it was only *after* I had crossed the threshold and knew I had taken one swallow too many.

Subtle changes, such as the hidden, compounding effects of the alcohol in the wine, are similar to unsuspected ecological events brought about by the gathering tyranny of small, seemingly unrelated decisions. We find it difficult to become alarmed over potential change, even that with a high probability, because in today's society we expect someone to announce imminent ecological disasters, like earthquakes or hurricanes. If no one announces an impending disaster, we take little notice of the socio-economic decisions that cause comparatively minute and seemingly harmless alterations in our environment. Thus, we usually refuse to change our behavior, despite mounting evidence—even compelling evidence gathered over time—that change is necessary for the safety of the future.

Once a threshold is crossed (whether in drinking wine, in my garden, or in society at large), there is no going back to the original condition, such as instant sobriety, the recovery of a dead plant, or bringing a rare bird back from extinction by reversing an ill-advised, socio-economic decision. It is thus necessary to understand something about the relative fragility we humans cause when we simplify ecosystems (gardens, agricultural fields, and tree farms) to meet our cultural desires, as opposed to the robustness of complex, "wild" ones (marshes, grasslands, and forests).

Fragile ecosystems can go awry in more ways and can break down more suddenly and with less warning than is likely in robust ecosystems, because fragile systems have a larger number of components with narrow tolerances than do robust ones. As such, the failure of any component can disrupt the system. Therefore, when a pristine ecosystem is altered for human benefit, it is made more fragile, which means that it will require more planning and maintenance to approach the stability of the original system. Thus, while sustainability means maintaining the critical functions performed by the primeval system, or some facsimile thereof, it does not mean restoring or maintaining the primeval condition itself.

To the extent that we alter ecosystems, either in our gardens or across landscapes, we make them dependent on our labor to function as we intend them to. If we relax our vigilance, they regain their power of self-determined functioning, but usually in ways we do not want.

When Zane and I bought our present home, what had been the vegetable garden was a gigantic patch of weeds, and the lawn was a sorry sight. A few unkempt patches of forgotten flowers were inadvertently scattered here and there. If we had been content with this arrangement, it would have been relatively maintenance-free, except that the grass would have needed mowing if we had wanted it to function as some kind of a usable, attractive lawn.

If we had planned to live here for only a short time, like a family of hunter-gatherers, we would have invested little time and energy in the garden of our new home. Our intention is to be here for many years, however, and that knowledge breeds a sense of place and permanence, which gives us a vastly different outlook on the garden and its considerable potential.

With this feeling of "permanence" in our hearts, we redesigned the garden, but not with pencil and paper in minute detail. Instead, we spent some months sitting with, looking at, and walking in our unkempt patch of earth. Then we let the garden be born unto itself one piece at a time as our inner promptings dictated.

The lawn area was covered over with black plastic and committed to gravel, a purposefully functional yet attractive choice. The weeds were pulled in the vegetable bed, copious amounts of organic material were added, and the clayey soil was turned over many times to work the organic material into its matrix. Although this worked fairly well for the first year, the soil was so clayey that it still became hard as a rock in summer with any compaction from my tending the garden. So the second year I built raised vegetable beds of wood, which are splendid.

We constructed flower beds in unique configurations of lava, andesite, and other captivating rocks. We built one raised vegetable bed of large, rounded, smooth river rocks; a sizable bed for roses; and several smaller beds for other flowers. We added large pots planted with contorted filberts and Japanese maples. Having wanted for several years a pond with water lilies, goldfish, and the quiet laughter of water cascading over a rocky falls, we brought out the shovels and went to work. While our garden is now to us a beautiful and peaceful sanctuary, it becomes more complex culturally and more labor-intensive ecologically with each additional creation.

The more we groomed the garden, the more specialized the flower beds and vegetable beds became, the more fragile the whole manifested itself to be as an internally functioning ecosystem. As its fragility increased, so did the time and energy we had to commit to maintain the processes we originally disrupted by designing what was pleasing to our senses. But what, you might ask, did we disrupt?

By weeding, for example, I disrupted the cycling of organic material that nourishes the infrastructure of the soil and therefore the processes governing the relative biological balance among soil microorganisms. To fully understand the import of what I am saying you must first understand what a weed is.

A weed is a plant growing where you or I do not want it to grow, a plant considered by most to be worthless, and unsightly, troublesome, but growing in abundance. Consider a dandelion in your lawn. If you do not want it there, then it is, by definition, a weed. But I once knew a woman who loved to make dandelion wine. For this, she used only the best blossoms, and she needed a lot to make the amount of wine she wanted. To her, the dandelions in her lawn were not weeds at all, but rather the stuff of excellent wine to be nourished and encouraged in their growth, much as grapes in a vineyard.

Nevertheless, the weeds in my garden are an important source of organic material created out of sunlight, carbon dioxide, chemical elements, and water. When they die, this organic material is committed to the soil as dead plants, where it becomes part of the source of energy for the organisms in the soil that are needed to drive its processes and maintain its health. Because the weeds serve a vital function, which I eliminate when I commit the act of "weeding," I must consciously, purposefully put organic material into the soil of my garden in the form of compost to replace the processes performed naturally by the weeds that I eliminate to maintain my desired sense of order. Compost, in turn, is made of decomposing plants—even the very weeds that I pull.

So the more intensely I try to control my garden, the more intensely I *must* try to control my garden if I am to maintain that which I desire. This is the self-reinforcing feedback loop that I and every gardener creates to a greater or lesser degree.

L. EAGINGTON

Exercise In Conscious Awareness

If you are interested in experiencing what I mean when I say that gardening makes the ecosystem more fragile, more labor intensive, and more expensive to maintain, then select a small plot of ground, say nine square feet, and leave it alone for a whole year. During this year, watch what happens. Be mindful of what plants come into the plot of soil, how much of the soil they cover, when they bloom, when they die, and what succeeds them.

Observe that the invertebrates, such as slugs and pillbugs, which may be considered pests in your garden, are harmless to you in this plot of ground as they convert plant material into compost. Watch also as the plant material decomposes and disappears back into the soil.

You can chose to water the plot when you water the garden or be tough and just leave it alone. Regardless, something will grow in it. If you were to leave the plot alone for three or even two years, you would find that it would fill entirely with plant life. As the plants slow their growth in winter or lie dead upon the ground, they protect the soil from the constant pounding of winter's rain by breaking up the drops before they compact the earth. If, in late spring or early summer, you were to look at a sample of the soil under high magnification, you would be amazed at the life you would find therein.

At the end of a year, or longer if you so choose, convert the plot back to an active part of your garden. Be conscious of the work it takes to remove the "weeds," which these plants have once again become, and to prepare the soil. Plant the vegetables or flowers of your choice and observe how much weeding you have to do to control the unwanted plants, the seeds of which are secreted in the soil.

Note also that by removing the weeds, there is no vegetation—no biological capital in the form of organic material—to die and return as compost to the soil unless, of course, you purposefully incorporated it. Nor is there a cover of vegetation, either alive or dead, to protect the soil from rain.

Now, you must water your garden if it is to produce as you desire, and every slug and pillbug in the area is suddenly a pest that must also be controlled. And you must diligently repeat this labor, with all its time and expenses, year after year if you are to maintain the processes that keep the soil healthy and the plants you want producing the flower, fruit, or leaf of your desire. Thus is an ecosystem made fragile by gardening.

The Foundation of Gardening:
Soil, Air, and Water

Soil is the cradle of human evolution and survival, the stage on which the entire human drama is enacted. Destroy the soil—thus the stage—and the human drama will be an evolutionary tragedy. As we humans pollute the air, which, of necessity, is shared by everyone and owned by no one, we are not only committing indirect suicide but also genocide through suffocation. Water, in its turn, is a lesson in humility because it not only seeks the lowest level but also accepts without judgment whatever we do to it. In so doing, it is the conveyor of life or the bringer of death, depending ever more on the purity or the toxicity with which we humans endow it.

The Wonder Of Soil

"We belong to a mystery that will never belong to us," says poet John Daniel, "yet it is freely given to all who desire it. Though we distance ourselves and fail to see, it is granted everywhere and all the time. It does not fail us [although we may fail it]." Soil is a part of the vast mystery to which we belong. Losing our connection to the soil is to lose ourselves.

Many cultures have emphasized the trusteeship of the soil through religion and philosophy. The Biblical Abraham, in his covenant with God, was instructed: "Defile not therefore the land which ye shall inhabit, wherein I dwell."[3] The Chinese philosopher Confucius saw in the Earth's thin mantle the sustenance of all life and the minerals treasured by human society. And a century later in Greece, Aristotle thought of soil as the central mixing-pot of air, fire, and water that formed all things.

In spite of the durability of such beliefs, most people cannot grasp their profundity because they are intangible. The invisibility of soil is founded in the notion that it is as common as air and therefore, like air, is a birthright that can be taken for granted.

Although soil seems "invisible" to many people, it is at the same time thought to be divisible in the sense that one can carve it into personal boundaries of outright ownership. In reality, however, soil is a seamless whole, unknown in its complexity to virtually all people.

When you think about it directly, you realize that human society is inextricably tied to the soil for reasons beyond measurable riches, for in soil is the historical wealth of the Earth archived, a wealth that nurtures culture even as it sustains life, as illustrated by the following quotes:

(1) "The social lesson of soil waste is that no man has the right to destroy soil even if he does own it in fee simple. The soil requires a duty of man, which we have been slow to recognize." H. A. Wallace, 1938; and (2) "In the old Roman Empire, all roads led to Rome. In agriculture [forestry, livestock grazing, and gardening] all roads lead back to the soil from which farmers make their livelihood." G. Hambrige, 1938.

Although both of these statements are as true now as on the day they were uttered, it is the doom of people that they too soon forget. Having said this, however, I must acknowledge that few people know what soil really is. Soil, the very foundation of life, is a long time in the making and all too quickly profaned and depleted!

Kneeling in my garden, I scoop up a handful of fine clayey soil. It crumbles between my fingers when moist, is smooth and slick to my touch when wet, and becomes hard as a rock when dry. Going to a near-by river, I dig up some fine sandy soil to bring back and mix with that of my garden, thereby changing its consistency. Now there are tiny sparkling flecks of crystalline structure in the soil of my garden, each catching the glint of the sun and tossing it to me.

Picking up another handful of soil and examining it closely, I see minute grains of various colors and textures amidst the decomposing organic material. Something moves! Did I imagine it? No, there it is again!

Getting a magnifying glass, I examine the soil more carefully. It's alive with all manner of things, things I've never before seen and things I don't yet see. Amazed by the myriad life in my hand, I begin to wonder where soil comes from.

Soil, I discover, is the result of two opposing geological forces: construction and erosion.[4] The fiery volcanism that builds mountains and the erosive power of wind, water, and ice that works to level them are some of the agents of these opposing forces.

A volcano is a vent or opening in the Earth's crust through which gases and melted rock, called molten lava, are ejected. A volcano that is ejecting gases and molten lava is said to be active; it is in creation. On the other hand, a volcano that has "run its course" of activity is said to be extinct because the "life" has gone out of it.

A volcano is built from within by fire and is eroded from without by wind, water, and ice. It defies gravity in its growing and falls to gravity in its dying. A volcano is born and dies and is reborn as something else. This means that volcanoes, which form mountains, are not eternal, but come and go, are born and die in concert with all living things.

Consider that children, flowers, and grasses are living entities, which at given times grow almost fast enough to actually watch them increase in size. Trees grow more slowly. And some rock-dwelling lichens, which are a combination of a fungus and an alga, grow just a fraction of an inch in a century—so slowly that historians use their growth to date events.

And, yes, rocks also grow, but more slowly yet. At a rock's pace of growth the history of the Egyptian pyramids is a wink and that of the Rocky Mountains a yawn.

Rocks even have a cycle of birth and death and birth again. Some geologists estimate that since the Earth was born some four and a half billion years ago, its rocks have been through ten generations.

As mountains are born and die, as pieces of continents come and go like ships leaving and docking, the rock formed on the floor of the sea is raised to the tops of mountains only to be eroded and returned to the floor of the sea, where it once again begins its journey through the Earth. And in approximately 450 million years, the rock may reappear on the surface of the continent to begin a new life.

The constructional processes, such as volcanism, sedimentation, metamorphosis, and tectonics or deformation in the Earth's crust, are the physical and chemical methods by which discrete bodies of rock are formed, assembled, and given their physical and chemical characteristics. Igneous processes, in which rock is melted for example, may produce large bodies of homogeneous rock, such as a large flow of basalt or an intrusion of granite; whereas tectonic processes, those causing the deformation of the Earth's crust, would produce in the same area a large mass of heterogeneous rock.

In contrast, weathering processes (being exposed to the affects of weather) are those by which landforms are shaped by wind, water, and ice, as rock is broken down physically and chemically into smaller and smaller pieces that eventually become soil. I have watched, for example, as some of the rocks that I used to make borders around the flower beds of my garden become saturated when it rains. Then, on occasion, here in the northwestern United States, the north wind comes blasting out of the Canadian Arctic and freezes the rocks. Inside, the water expands about nine percent as it freezes. If water expands in a confined space, it can exert a pressure in excess of thirty thousand pounds per square inch, which far exceeds the strength of rock. Although I cannot see the rocks expand, I often find them split into several pieces when they thaw. Awesome indeed is the hidden power and effect of ice.

Soil, which is like an exchange membrane between the living and nonliving components of the Earth, is dynamic and ever-changing. Derived from the mechanical and chemical break-down of rock and organic material, soil is built up by plants that live and die in it. It is also enriched by animals that feed on plants, evacuate their bodily wastes, and eventually die, decay, and themselves return to the soil of their origin as organic material.

Soil, the properties of which vary from place to place within a landscape, is by far the most alive and biologically diverse part of a terrestrial ecosystem and thus of my garden.

I say this because over millennia there arose a mountain many miles to the south and east of my home, only to have its spine carved and eroded by glaciers and carried as pebbles, sand, and fine powder by rivulet, stream, and river from lofty heights down through little valleys into bigger valleys and finally to the sea. After centuries of travel, some of the grains of sand and specks of fine powder rested along their journey in the soil I dug from the river's bank. As I mix this soil into that of my garden, I am adding not only the shoulders of a mighty mountain many miles and centuries distant but also the history of a colossal battle between a volcano and a glacier.

Once soil is formed, I can enhance the availability of nutrients to the plants at the time of year when they require massive amounts if I understand the nutrient cycles in the soil of my garden and work to enhance those processes that are beneficial to the plants I want to grow. I can also enhance the retention of nutrients in the soil during those times of the year when the plants don't use them. But first I must have the humility to accept that I will never fully understand soil; only then will I have the necessary patience to protect the organisms that perform those functions through which the soil of my garden is kept healthy.

The decomposed organic material, which lends soil its dark color, is termed "humus," from a Latin word meaning "earth." Incorporation of organic material into the surface of the soil, where the dark layer of "topsoil" is formed, is rapid when considered in the scale of geological time but exceedingly slow when considered in the scale of a human lifetime. In addition, soil quite literally resembles a discrete entity, which lives and breathes through a complex mix of interacting organisms—from viruses and bacteria to fungi, to protozoa, earthworms, and insects, to moles, gophers, and ground squirrels.

The activities of all these organisms in concert are responsible for developing the critical properties that underlie the basic fertility, health, and productivity of soil. The complex, biologically driven functions of the soil, in which soil organisms are the regulators of most processes that translate into a soil's productivity, may require anything from decades to a few hundred years to develop, and there are no quick fixes if soil is extensively damaged during gardening, farming, or forestry.

These organisms perform various functions in the cycling of chemicals that are required as nutrients for the growth of green plants. Some of these functions are the: (1) decomposing (recycling) of plant material by bacteria and fungi; (2) improving the structure of the soil, which increases such things as the soil's capacity to hold water; (3) mediating the soil's pH; and (4) controlling disease-causing organisms through competition for resources and space. Without the organisms to perform these functions, our gardens would be sterile, and the plant communities we see on the surface of the Earth would not exist.

As the total productivity of a garden or an ecosystem increases, the biological diversity within the soil's foodweb also seems to increase. The greater the number of interactions among organisms that decompose organic material (decomposers), their predators, and the predators of the predators, the more nutrients are retained in the soil. It is only through the belowground foodweb in the soil that plants can obtain the nutrients necessary for their growth; without this foodweb, the aboveground foodweb—including us humans—would cease to exist.

With this in mind, I regularly add composted organic material to the soil of my garden to safeguard its health, which *cannot* be maintained solely through applications of commercial fertilizer. When commercial fertilizer is applied to agricultural row crops, for example, much may be lost as it leaches downward through the soil into the groundwater, which it then contaminates, because neither the soil nor the organisms in the soil's foodweb can retain the added nitrogen. And contamination of the groundwater through the use of fertilizers is a major problem with agriculture throughout the world.

In some cases, adding fertilizer even acts like a biocide, killing the organisms in the soil's foodweb, which further degrades the soil. It is much wiser, therefore, to work in harmony with the soil and the organisms that govern its infrastructure, because they are responsible for the processes that in turn provide those nutrients to the plants.

The development of soil in my garden, as in a forest or a grassland, relies on self-reinforcing feedback loops, where organisms in the soil provide the nutrients for plants to grow, and plants in turn provide the carbon—the organic material—that selects for and alters the communities of soil organisms. One influences the other, and both determine the soil's development and health.

The soil foodweb is thus a prime indicator of the health of my garden as in any terrestrial ecosystem. But soil processes can be disrupted by such things as decreasing bacterial or fungal activity, decreasing the biomass of bacteria or fungi, altering the ratio of the fungal to bacterial biomass in a way that is inappropriate to the desired system, reducing the number and diversity of protozoa, and reducing the number of nematodes (which are roundworms other than earthworms) and/or altering their community structure.

A model of a soil foodweb, composed of interactive strands, is enlightening because it shows there are higher-level predators in the system whose function it is to prevent the predators of bacteria and fungi from becoming too abundant and so altering how the system functions. In turn, these higher-level predators serve as food for still higher-level predators.

In this way, mites, predatory roundworms, and small insects are eaten by organisms that spend much of their time aboveground. So predators in the third, fourth, and fifth upper strands of the foodweb are eaten by spiders, centipedes, and beetles, which in turn are eaten by salamanders, birds, shrews, and mice, and they in turn are eaten by snakes, still other birds, weasels, foxes, and so on.

If, therefore, part of the biological diversity of the belowground organisms is lost, the soil as a system will function differently and perhaps not to our human liking. If the predators in the soil are lost, which disrupts the governance of the soil, the mineral nitrogen in the soil may be lost, and the plants suffer. Conversely, too many predators can overuse the bacteria and fungi, which results in slower decomposition of organic material. A reduction or loss in any part of the foodweb affects at least two strands of the web at other levels.

Keep in mind that as the gardener, you and I not only design beds of vegetables and flowers with spade and trowel, wood and rock but also determine the presence or absence of plants and animals in a particular place and time, both above ground and below. If we, as individuals, poison the soil directly, for whatever reason, or otherwise damage its delicate infrastructure through the act of gardening, or if we damage the soil indirectly by condoning the pollution of our air and water, we help to destroy the stage on which the enactment of life depends.

An Ocean Of Air

The wind is the breath of the world. It carries the fragrance of south sea islands to the polar ice, the dankness of steaming jungles to the baking deserts. Wind caresses the land and buffets it, moistens the land and parches it. Wind, the divine messenger, is never still. It follows the sun westward, then leads the sun eastward. It pushes spring northward, then pulls winter southward. Free since the birth of the Universe, wind has blown through all the eons—never to be still. And in its blowing, the ocean of air flows through my garden for better or ill.

It is late afternoon on a clear, warm, sunny September day. I am sitting in my garden watching a tiny spider climb the stalk of an aster until it reaches the uppermost tip of the tallest flower. It pauses for an instant, and then raises its body into the air, almost standing on its head.

From spinnerets on the tip of its abdomen, it ejects a mass of silken threads into the breeze. Suddenly, without visible warning, the spider is jerked off the aster and borne skyward to join its relatives riding the warm afternoon air flowing up the valley, all casting their fortunes to the wind. Like their ancestors in centuries past, the spiders float in an ocean of air, riding the currents from the far reaches of the Earth. Who knows, some may become the first inhabitants of a newly formed island somewhere in the South Seas.

Spiders are not the only things borne aloft on air currents. In 1883, Krakatoa, a small Indonesian island between Java and Sumatra, was virtually obliterated by explosive eruptions that sent volcanic ash high enough above the Earth to ride the world's airways for more than a year. This changed the climate by reducing the amount of sunlight reaching the Earth, which in turn cooled the climate and affected all life. Just as it carried the volcanic ash of Krakatoa, air also carries the reproductive spores of fungi and the pollen of various trees and grasses, as well as dust and microscopic organisms. And the currents of air carry life-giving oxygen and water as well as death-dealing pollution—the fatal legacy of human society.

Air can therefore be likened to the key in a Chinese proverb: To every man is given the key to the gates of heaven, and the same key opens the gates of hell. In this case, air is the key that opens us to both life-giving oxygen and death-dealing pollution, and as pollution increases, the quality and utility of the air decreases.

Although I cannot often see visible signs of pollution in the air I

40

breathe or in the air that moves in silence throughout my garden, I can smell the stench of the paper mill some twenty miles away when sitting amidst my flowers as the wind blows out of the northeast. And so I am reminded of the pervasiveness of air pollution, which affects water in all its forms both within and without the boundaries of my garden.

WATER SEEKS THE LOWEST LEVEL

Water is both a physical necessity of life and perhaps the most important ingredient when it comes to gardening. A gardener's supply of quality water is therefore precious beyond compare.

True, it is common knowledge that water is derived from the combination of two atoms of hydrogen with one of oxygen. But for most of us, this is such an abstract thought that we have trouble comprehending it. Thus it is that most gardeners probably do not think beyond turning the handle on a faucet to obtain water. If they were to think beyond the faucet, they might conceive the source of water to be the city's utility department, or perhaps some reservoir or other, or maybe even a particular river. But in a practical sense, where does water really come from?

A community's water originates far from the tap you turn to fill a glass with this most precious of liquids. Water is stored on our home planet of Earth in four ways: (1) in the form of snowpack, which is a winter's accumulation of snow above ground, (2) in the form of water penetrating deep into the soil, where it flows slowly over months and years below ground, (3) in belowground aquifers and lakes, and (4) in aboveground reservoirs, lakes, ponds, streams, and rivers.

Most water used by communities and gardeners in the temperate and northern latitudes comes first in the form of accumulated snow (snowpack), either at high elevations or northern latitudes, which subsequently feeds the streams and rivers that eventually reach distant communities and cities—rivers like the Columbia, Snake, Colorado, Missouri, Mississippi, and so on. Snowpack is aboveground storage, which, under good conditions, can last as snowbanks late into the summer.

How much water the annual snowpack has and how long the snowpack lasts depends on five things: (1) the timing, duration, and persistence of the snowfall in any given year; (2) how much snow accumulates during a given winter; (3) the moisture content of the snow; wet snow holds more moisture than dry snow; (4) when the snow begins melting and the speed with which it melts; the later in the year it begins melting and the slower it melts, the longer into the summer its moisture is stored aboveground; and (5) the health of the water-catchment (which is an area of the land that catches water in the form of rain and/or snow and stores it in the soil, often thought of as a "watershed").

Although the first four points seem self-evident, the last one requires some explanation. People seldom realize that drinkable water comes predominantly from forested water-catchments. A curious thing happens, however, when water flows outside the forest boundary: we forget where it comes from. We fight over who has the "right" to the last drop, but pay little attention to the source of our supply—the health of the forested areas that catch and store water.

There are two divergent options in how we use water: one is to protect the availability of the long-term supply by disciplining ourselves to protect the water-catchments and to use only what is necessary in the most prudent manner. The other is to take water for granted by ignoring the health of the water-catchments and by using all the water we want with no discipline whatsoever.

In the first scenario, consider what I as a gardener might do to conserve water while gardening. Zane and I have a plastic tub in our kitchen sink over which we rinse vegetables and our hands and into which we put any other reusable water. We then use it to irrigate the garden. We also use plastic tubs to wash dishes—one for washing and one for rinsing. Since little soap gets into the rinse water, we let it cool and use it to water our garden. Zane also catches at least a gallon of cold water in a plastic jug each time she turns on the hot water tap and must wait for the hot water to arrive. This water, too, is used in the garden.

In the garden itself, I find that my raised vegetable beds are efficient to water with a spray nozzle, and use less water than a regular garden plot. For large, widely spaced individual vegetables, such as eggplants, peppers, tomatoes, broccoli, and cauliflower, I make seamless collars out of one- and two-gallon black plastic flower containers (with the bottoms cut out). I put the containers around the plants when they are small. With these vegetables growing up inside the plastic collars, which I have pressed part way into the soil, I can water each plant within its collar and thereby contain and conserve water.

I also mulch some of the beds and around each plastic collar with grass clippings from my neighbor's lawn, since I have none of my own. Grass clippings not only slow the evaporation of the water from the soil but also add valuable organic material to it. Wood shavings also work well, as does mushroom compost. In addition, I have installed several drip irrigation systems, which prevent water from being lost to evaporation while at the same time watering many of the plants individually, such as our roses.

If, on the other hand, I were simply to use all the water I wanted in a totally undisciplined, unconscious manner, I would be insensitive not only to the productive capacity of the water-catchments that supply the water but also to everyone else's share of usable water, which is a limited resource. As with any problem, however, there are solutions, but we tend to look for them only when and where the symptoms are obvious.

To illustrate, many years ago, I lived in an old mobile home. You know the kind. It leaked immediately every time a dark cloud appeared on the horizon. Finding where the leak ended, over my desk or my pillow in bed, was no problem, but finding the source of the leak was often so difficult that I had to repair the entire waterproof coating on the roof—and then hope.

The only responsible solution to the problem of dwindling supplies of available water, as I see it, is an environmental one: protect the health of water-catchments on a landscape scale that first and foremost nurtures the health of air, soil, and water, lest everything else becomes unhealthy. With the growing realization of the ecological interdependency among all living forms and their physical environments, it can hardly be doubted that even "renewable" resources show signs of suffering from the effects of society's unrelenting materialistic demands for more and more, which degrades the renewability of resources in both quality and quantity. In the last analysis, soil, air, and water form a seamless whole, the thin envelope we call the biosphere, which is all we have in all the Universe.

Oddly enough, it is precisely this partnership between humanity and water that has by and large determined how people participate with the known world. In the beginning water limited where people could live. Then people learned how to manipulate water, create gardens, and take more control of their destiny. Now people are polluting water to such an extent that we are committing indirect suicide throughout the world, just as we are through pollution of the air, which circulates around the globe and brings the world into my garden.

Exercise In Conscious Awareness

Get a small tub, such as one for rinsing dishes, and a clear drinking glass. Fill a tub with cold water. Invert the glass so the mouth is about an inch over the surface water. Then, slowly, push the glass under the surface of the water and notice that the air trapped inside the glass prevents the water from gaining an entrance, which means that air takes up space and holds it. As you observe the air trapped in the glass, visualize air as one of the three major components of your world and mine. The other two are water and soil.

Air belongs to everyone because its currents, bearing such names as "Trade Winds," "Nor'easter," "Sou'wester," and so on, continually circumnavigate the globe, and in their passing not only ventilate your body with life-giving oxygen but also blow through your garden. To get a sense of just how much you depend on air, exhale all the air you can from your lungs. Hold that position as long as you can and consciously feel what it is like to be deprived of air as your body tells you that air is more real than any human-derived boundary, be it country, state, county, city, or that of your own personal property. Relax, breathe normally, and, if you wish, describe your feelings on paper.

Now, inhale as deeply as you can and hold your breath as long as you can. Again, consciously examine what you are feeling while deprived of breathing. How long can you hold your breath? What does it feel like? Again, relax, breathe normally, and describe your feelings on paper.

Next, go outside and start your car. Once the engine is running, engage the emergency brake, put the gears in neutral, and get out of your car. Go around to the tail pipe, put your nose as close to it as you comfortably can, and take a breath—but only for a couple of seconds. As you do so, notice the odor of exhaust, which contains the life-threatening carbon monoxide, spewing into the air—the air we *all* breathe *all* the time. Record on paper how it feels to breathe such pollution. Does it make you want to walk or ride your bike more and drive your car less?

Now ask yourself what you would do if you had that odor, or a worse one, in your nose all the time and it was telling you every minute of your life that the air you were breathing was so polluted that it was poisoning you a little bit with every breath you took. How would you feel? How would you live? What would you do? What *could* you do? Would you exhale and never breathe in the polluted air again? Would you inhale deeply once, and forever hold your breath? How do you think the plants and animals in your garden feel? After all, they must use the same air you do—or die.

How many *unnecessary* trips by automobile do you think you make a week, a month, a year? How much pollution do you think we can really afford to have belching into our air every second of every minute of every day, month, year?

Have you ever been out after a cleansing rain storm and declared to yourself: "Wow, the air smells so fresh and clean?" The air smells so fresh and clean because the rain has scrubbed the pollution out of it. Now think about all the falling rain—and snow—cleaning the millions of tons of pollutants out of the air every day. Where does it all go?

Well, most of it goes into the soil, where it affects the plants and animals living there as they take at least some of the dissolved pollutants into their bodies through the act of living. Remember, some of those plants are the vegetables you think of as pure and healthy because you are growing them organically in your own garden. Well, think again. Nothing in the world today can be totally organic simply because of air pollution, which invades all we do, to the farthest reaches of the world. This means that you drink pollutants in your household tap water and you eat them in your food, regardless of where it comes from—even your garden. However, the food from your garden may be the cleanest you will ever eat.

Now, consider that the water falling as rain or snow cleans the air of pollutants in its descent to Earth, where most of it enters the soil only to pass through the soil and exit into ditches that enter streams that enter rivers that enter estuaries that enter the ocean—always carrying a certain amount of pollutants with it. Next consider that we humans, through industry, dump millions of tons of pollutants not only into the air but also into the rivers all of the time. This is safe, says the corporate America, because the rivers can flush themselves. Although they can to some extent, what about an ocean?

It cannot flush itself because there are no outlets, so all of the pollutants that are both toxic and nonbiodegradable are concentrating in the oceans of the world. On top of all this, pollutants are being dumped by the millions of tons annually directly into the estuaries and oceans. Is it any wonder that the seafood you perhaps love is so polluted?

So the questions become: What can I do in my personal life to reduce pollutants in the air, which ultimately end up in the soil of my garden, where I grow vegetables and flowers? Can I curtail unnecessary driving by planning to do several errands in a given trip instead of one errand at a time? Can I walk or ride my bicycle at least part of the time? What can I do directly to protect the health of the soil in my garden? Can I become more consciously aware of the consequences of what I introduce into the soil or withhold from it?

With these questions in mind, go and sit down in your garden and close your eyes. Imagine the wind blowing from the nearest industrial center directly over your garden. Imagine, too, a cloudburst, and watch the falling rain picking particles of pollution out of the air and depositing them in the soil of your garden. Now, follow the water, which has dissolved the pollution into itself, as it moves around and through the particles of soil.

Look, some of the water is evaporating back into the air, leaving its pollutants behind, where they concentrate in the remaining water. See, some of the dirty water is being taken up into the roots of the plants you will eat, which means that you will ultimately eat the pollutants. Now, watch as the rest of the polluted water passes through the soil, where it picks up other elements, which you introduced as fertilizer, and carries them downhill toward the nearest ditch.

Finally, arise and leave your garden. Go to the nearest ditch and look at it closely. Breathe in consciously and smell the odors in the air and contemplate the pollution they may represent. Study closely the human garbage strewn along the ditch's bottom and sides. Follow the ditch for a ways and see if there is any place from which you would dare to drink the water and feel safe in drinking it. Remember, some of that water has come from someone's garden, be it a backyard plot of soil, such as your own, or a farmer's field—and someday, somehow, you will drink it in one form or another. Can you think of a more sobering thought? Does this give you a new perspective? What feelings are you aware of now?

L. Edgington

I PARTICIPATE WITH THE WHOLE WORLD WHILE WORKING IN MY GARDEN

I am affected by the world as a whole while working in my garden, so I in turn affect the world as a whole. This is a given. But how I affect the world is my choice, which in gardening is mediated through the way in which I treat the soil.

Air pollution directly affects vegetation by altering the quality of the soil and water as well as the quality and quantity of the sunlight that drives the plant/soil processes. The chemicals we spew into the air also alter the climate and thus the environment in which the vegetation grows.

Soil, which is the main terrestrial vessel, receives, collects, and passes to the water all air-borne, human-caused pollutants. In addition, such pollutants as sewage, excess chemical fertilizers, pesticides, and so on, are added directly to the soil and through the soil to the water. At times, such pollutants make their way into the air as dust, and hence are re-distributed more widely over the planet's surface through strong winds, which carry aloft the topsoil following deforestation, desertification, and ecologically unsound practices of farming and gardening, which ultimately affect water.

In the western United States, for example, most of our usable water, which is a captive of gravity, comes from snows high on forested mountain slopes. When snow melts, the water percolates through the soil. It is purified when flowing through healthy soil; it is poisoned when flowing through soil stripped of Nature's processes and polluted with artificial chemicals. The same is true for rain. Therefore, if humanity continues destroying the water-catchments of the world, all nations will ultimately be equal in poverty.

Water, the great collector of human-caused pollutants, washes and scrubs the pollutants from the air by rain and snow; it leaches them from the soil, and it carries them in trickle, stream, and river to the point where we consume them in our drinking water. We protect ourselves from pathogens by adding chlorine to the already-polluted water to "purify" it before we drink. This same water we put on our gardens, perhaps after adding commercial fertilizers and pesticides, which then leach into the soil and are eventually concentrated through stream and river in the ultimate vessel, the combined oceans of the world.

As I mentioned, in my pond are not only aquatic plants but also fish. Each time in summer that I add water to the pond from my garden hose, I must add additional chemicals to counteract the chlorine in the water lest it kill the fish.

So chemical pollutants come from the outer world into my garden riding the currents in an ocean of air as the medium of transport. They also come through technology as mundane as my garden hose and lumber treated with chemical preservatives. As they are deposited in my garden, I may, if I so choose, add to them through fertilizers and pesticides and then help them on their way with irrigation water from my garden hose as the medium of transportation. And on their journey to the Pacific Ocean, which takes them through the soil of my garden, they will alter its governance, often to the unseen detriment of that which I have created and hold dear.

My garden is thus like the narrow, central portion of an hourglass. It collects pollutants from as far away as the winter storm winds blow and disperses them as far away as the waters flow. So I, as a gardener, affect the health of the world by how clean and healthy I keep the soil of my garden. The healthier the soil, the cleaner is the water leaving my garden, the cleaner and healthier by that measure is the soil through which the water passes outside of my garden, and the cleaner and healthier are the streams, rivers, estuaries, and ocean into which it flows. But first it is likely to enter a ditch.

Did you ever think about a ditch, say a humble roadside ditch, and wonder how the practice of ditching got started? Most people probably don't even notice them, much less think about them. Nevertheless, there was actually a time in the world before ditches, a time when water itself decided where humanity would dwell. Then the ditch was invented as a way to purposefully channel water to a given place for a particular reason, and that changed everything.

The first ditch was likely an idle scratch in the surface of the ground made by some child playing in a puddle after a rain storm or perhaps along a stream in the land of far memory. That first child's play—of leading water from one place to another—on that faraway afternoon, has continued through the millennia.

A ditch in the beginning is just a naked furrow in the skin of the Earth until Nature takes over, molding and sculpting the furrow with erosion, using wind and water and snow and ice as implements. Slowly the raw wound begins to round and crinkle as flowing water moves jousting grain and shifting pebble here and there. Little by little the ditch bottom loses all sign of human tool, and the once raw wound becomes a labyrinth of nooks and crannies, each with a pair of eyes silently watching the world.

As the ditch's bottom transforms, Nature plants seeds of grasses and herbs along its banks. Each seed, be it as large as a giant lima bean or as small as a gnat's eye, has locked within it the secret code of shape and color for leaf and flower, the height of stem and the depth of root, the season of bloom and the season of fruit. Each seed, millions of years in the making, is a crowning achievement in an unbroken chain of genetic experiments that began when life was born.

Now a dandelion seed drifts ditchward, suspended from its gossamer parachute. Where will it land? Will it germinate? If it germinates and grows, will it be eaten by a grasshopper, or a mouse, or will it mature and add its encoded link to the genetic chain? Of the thousands of seeds that fall on the fertile soil of the ditch's banks, each is an open question.

Relatively few will survive to maturity. The rest will disappear from whence they came, back into the Eternal Mystery. So Nature creates a backdrop of swaying grasses and brightly-colored flowers, of protecting shrubs and stately trees. On this stage unfolds her play enacted with the animals that live along the ditch, that burrow in its banks, and visit with the seasons.

Somewhere in time that first ditch became a conscious thought that translated into a conscious act. As the one ditch became the many ditches, humanity and plants and animals moved into areas hitherto uninhabitable by those who needed water in close proximity, and thus was expanded the human sense of place.

The first ditch irrevocably altered humanity's sense of itself, its sense of society, and its ability to manipulate Nature. Although the ditch itself is a simple invention, it nonetheless is an integral but un-recognized and ignored part of the land's arterial system of streams and rivers, and as such connects my garden to the Pacific Ocean and all the connected oceans of the world.

How, I wonder, can we learn to care for the health and ecological in-tegrity of streams, rivers, and oceans until we learn to care for the health and ecological integrity of the ditches that feed them? The answer, of course, is that we cannot!

Consider, for example, that the chemicals I put in my garden are leached from the soil through which the water flows and ultimately end up in the oceans of the world, where they concentrate over time because oceans have no outlets. Oceans lose their water through evaporation, which concentrates the remaining chemicals because there is no way to dilute them in a system that cannot be flushed.

Today, say Dutch scientists, human-caused pollution, such as poly-brominate chemical compounds are being found in the bodies of minke and sperm whales that wash up dead on Dutch beaches. These whales feed at depths of 3,000 feet below the surface of the ocean, which, according to Jan Boon of the Netherlands Institute for Marine Research, shows just how far toxic pollution has spread into the ocean's food chain—much further than previously thought.[5]

Like the ocean, the pond in my garden has no outlet, which causes the chemicals in the water to concentrate throughout the summer as I replace water lost to evaporation, much as in an ocean. This concentrating effect happens because the chemicals, including industrial chemicals, which were leached from the soil before the water entered the city's water system, are inherent in the water I get through my garden hose.

Fortunately, in winter I once again balance the chemicals in the pond. I can do this because it rains so much where I live that my pond has some on-again, off-again overflow almost all winter long. Rainwater, which does not pass through the soil but enters directly into my pond, does not bring with it the same concentration of chemicals. Rainwater instead dilutes the chemicals in my pond, and the overflow acts like an outlet, which flushes the system—a luxury oceans don't have.

Consequently, we must learn to care first and foremost for the health of humble things in our environment, such as the soil of our gardens through which water passes and the ditches that carry the water to the streams. Only then can we learn how to care for the mighty things in our environment, such as a river or an ocean.

Defile the ditch and we defile the stream, river, estuary, and ocean; protect the ditch and we protect the stream, river, estuary, and ocean, because it is ordained in the nature of things that water always knows where it is going—back to the sea. Whether it takes days or years makes no difference. Thus is Nature's lesson taught, a lesson that begins when we are children in the community of our gardens and in the gardens of our community.

If, therefore, every gardener made it his or her sacred duty to clean and protect the soil of his or her garden, the world, through the humble ditch, would be cleaned in like measure. In the collective consciousness and choices of individual gardeners lies a great power to heal *or* to sicken the Earth that supports us. To heal the Earth, we must reinvest in the health of the soil, which brings us to a clear connection between ecology and the choices a given society makes.

Exercise In Conscious Awareness

I wrote in the text about the way in which my garden is influenced by the whole world through air pollution and how I in turn influence the world based on the care I take of the soil in my garden, which can, if it is healthy, cleanse the water flowing through it. But there is another way in which we participate with the world while gardening, a way you can determine for yourself.

Get some paper and a pencil. You are going to make an inventory of all the things you use in caring for your garden, but first you need to know what kind of information to record. The following information is a partial list; you can fill in the rest if you wish: (1) Name the item, (2) Where was it made, if an implement, or grown, if a plant or seed? (3) Where did you purchase it? (4) Where did the store get it from? (5) When and where was the item invented? Who made it? (6) Where did the different components come from, such as the wood and/or the metal and/or the plastic, etc.? (7) What kind of wood is it? Where did it grow? How old was the tree? Who cut it? Who milled it? (8) What kind of metal is it? Where did it come from? Who mined it? Where was it smelted? Where was it formed? Where was it fitted together into the item you are now using? (9) Where did the plastic come from? What is it made out of? Where did the components in the plastic come from? (10) How did you earn the money with which you purchased the item? Where did the money come from? How many other people had used the money to purchase what they wanted before you got it to buy what you wanted for your garden? (11) Where does the water come from that you irrigate with? Where is the water-catchment? Does the water come into the water-catchment as rain and/or snow? Where does the rain and/or snow come from? The list is endless if you wish to make it so.

Now, take your inventory and experience your garden filling up not only with the natural resources of the world but also with human experiences from around the world in mining the metal; cutting, transporting, and milling the tree; making the implements; loading them onto trucks, trains, and ships; unloading them into stores; and the experience you have with the salesperson who helps you with your purchase. This is but one way in which the world is in your garden.

We must Reinvest in Nature
even as We do in Business

*I must always give something in gratitude for what I receive; for it is the law of
the Universe that I receive with the same abundance that I give. Therefore,
if I want to continue receiving a bounty of vegetables and flowers from
my garden, I must freely and joyfully reinvest in the health and
productivity of the soil that midwifes my abundance.*

There was a time when all of humanity participated with Nature in an open cycle of receiving and giving, a cycle governed on the human side by the spirit of gratitude and humility. That was before Nature was relegated to an objectified abstraction by an ever-increasing majority of humans who think that technological advances will free them from physical-biological restraints. This notion not only is erroneous but also is starving the soils of the world, including that of my garden if I am not diligent.

Human survival is predicated on the humility to admit and the courage to accept the fact that we humans do not and cannot manage Nature, that ultimately we are not in control. Rather, we treat Nature in some way, and Nature responds to that treatment, which may be what caused gardener Henry Mitchell to say, "Compared to gardeners ... others understand very little about anything of consequence." This is to say that if we honor Nature, we can find the place where culture and Nature meet and both are more nearly sustainable, but this requires a reassessment of the economic concept of waste.

The economic concept of waste says in effect that anything not used directly by humans is wasted. In a biological sense, however, there is no such thing as waste in a forest, an agricultural field, or my garden.

Consider that a tree rotting in a forest—composting as it were—is a *re*investment of Nature's biological capital in the long-term maintenance of soil productivity, and hence of the forest itself. Biological capital includes such things as organic material and biological and genetic diversity. And to *re*invest means to invest again.

In a business sense, one makes money (economic capital) and then takes a percentage of those earnings and reinvests them, puts them back as a cost into the maintenance of buildings and equipment, so as to continue making a profit by protecting the integrity of the initial investment over time. In a business, one reinvests economic capital after the fact, after the profits have been earned. It is different, however, with biological capital, which is the capital of all renewable natural resources. Biological capital must be reinvested *before* the fact, before the profits are earned.

Neither a forest, an agricultural field, nor my garden can process economic capital; biological capital is required. In a forest, one reinvests biological capital by leaving some proportion of the merchantable trees—both alive and dead—in the forest to rot and recycle themselves into the soil and thereby replenish the fabric of the living system.

Such biological reinvestment is necessary to maintain the health of the soil, which in large measure equates to the health of the forest. The health of the forest, in turn, equates to the long-term economic health of the timber industry and therefore of some human communities.

Planting and fertilizing tree seedlings is no more of a reinvestment in the soil of the forest than is planting and fertilizing wheat a reinvestment in the soil of a farmer's field or planting and fertilizing lettuce in my garden. All are investments in the next crop. As such, they are investments in a potential product, not in the biological sustainability of the living system that produces the products.

As a society, we fail to reinvest in maintaining the health of biological processes because we focus only on the commercial product. We fail to reinvest because we insist that ecological variables, such as the biological health of the soil, are really constant values in the economic sense, which can be discounted and therefore need not be considered when it comes to reinvesting economic capital.

But economic capital notwithstanding, all things in Nature are neutral when it comes to any kind of human valuation. Nature has only intrinsic value, be it in a forest, a farmer's field, or my garden. So each component of the forest, whether a microscopic bacterium or a towering eight hundred-year-old tree, is thus allowed to develop its prescribed structure, carry out its prescribed function, and interact with other components of the forest through their prescribed interactive, interdependent processes. No component is more or less valuable than any other; each may differ in form, but all are complementary in function.

The forest is an interconnected, interactive, organic whole defined not by the pieces of its body but rather by the interdependent functional relationships of those pieces in creating the whole—the intrinsic value of each piece and its complementary function. These processes are all part of Nature's rollover accounting system, which includes such assets as large dead trees, genetic diversity, biological diversity, and functional diversity, all of which count as reinvestments of biological capital in the healthy growing forest.

Intensive, short-term tree farms, which constitute traditional forestry, disallow reinvestment of biological capital in the soil because such reinvestment has come to be erroneously seen as economic waste. Traditional forestry, which has its root in agriculture and hence in gardening, began with the idea that forests, considered only as collections of trees, were perpetual economic producers of wood. With such thinking, it was necessary to convert a tree into some kind of potential economic commodity before it could be assigned a value. In assigning an initial economic value to timber, the health of the soil was ignored. And today, even with our vastly greater scientific knowledge, the health of the soil is not only ignored but also discounted.

And what about a farmer's field? Where is its reinvestment of biological capital? In the early days, farmers let fields lie fallow for a time, which allowed those plants normally called weeds to take over and add their organic material to the soil. Then, prior to planting the cash crop, the farmer would plow the weeds under, adding more organic material to the soil.

Today, however, it seems that society is in too much of a hurry to work in unison with the land, so instead of the old way of reinvesting in the soil, there usually is a large infusion of commercial fertilizers, many of which require tapping the finite supply of fossil fuels to make. But even today, a farmer can reinvest in the soil through organic farming, which does not require the excessive use of commercial fertilizers.

In areas conducive to growing vegetation in winter, for example, a farmer can plant a nitrogen-rich cover crop, such as crimson clover, after the autumn harvest, let it grow throughout the winter, and then plow it under in spring prior to the maturation of it seeds and prior to planting the cash crop. An alternative for areas where winters are long and cold is to leave the remains of the cash crop in the field, such as the stubble of wheat or corn, and plow it under in spring prior to planting the next cash crop. A third alternative might be to obtain, even purchase, manure from a dairy and work it into the field, rather than commercial fertilizer.

I work composted plant tissue into the soil of my garden as a reinvestment of organic material, both in spring and autumn. If I cannot supply enough compost from my kitchen middens and the trimmings from my garden itself, I augment it with manure from a nearby dairy barn and autumn leaves from the trees growing along the streets of my neighborhood. Use of commercial fertilizers is both unnecessary and undesirable.

Even though protection of soil and its fertility can be justified economically, our human connection with soil escapes most people. One problem is that traditional, linear economics deals with short-term, tangible commodities (such as fast-growing row crops) rather than with long-term intangible values (such as the future prosperity of our children). But when we recognize that land, labor, and capital are finite and that every ecosystem has a carrying capacity whose needed support in terms of labor and energy depends on its degree of fragility, then we begin to see that the traditional, linear-economic system is not tenable in the face of biological reality.

In the late eighteenth century, Thomas Malthus, an English economist, proposed that the human population would grow faster than the soil's ability to sustain it, but agronomic advances in the last century led many short-sighted leaders to dismiss this idea as simplistic and overly pessimistic. Today, however, Malthusian theory seems prophetic when one considers the following: (1) trends in the pollution of air and the reliance on chemical fertilizers, both of which poison soil and destroy its biological infrastructure; (2) overgrazing by livestock, which exacerbates the growing desertification; (3) global deforestation, which causes the loss of the soil's protective cover of vegetation and adds substantially to global warming through release of the greenhouse gas, carbon dioxide; and (4) the exploding human population with its ever-increasing demands on the Earth, including the loss of agricultural land to urban development.

In addition, those who analyze the soil by means of traditional, linear-economic analyses weigh the net worth of protecting the soil only in terms of the expected short-term revenues from future harvests, and they ignore the fact that it is the health of the soil that produces the yields. In short, they see the protection of the soil as a cost with no benefit because the standard method for computing soil, expectation values commonly assumes that the productivity of the soil will either remain constant or increase—but never decline.

Given that reasoning, which is both short-sighted and flawed, it is not surprising that those who attempt to manage the land seldom see protection of the soil's productivity as cost effective. But if we could predict the real effects of this economic reasoning on long-term yields, we might have a different view of the invisible costs associated with ignoring the health of the soil.

One of the first steps along the road to protecting the fertility of the soil is to ask how the various ways humans treat an ecosystem will affect its long-term productivity, particularly that of the soil itself. Understanding the long-term effects of human activities in turn requires that we know something about what keeps an ecosystem stable and productive. With such knowledge, we can turn our often "misplaced genius"—as soil scientist David Perry rightly calls it—to the task of maintaining the sustainability and resilience of the soil's fertility. Protecting the soil's fertility is buying an ecological insurance policy for our children.

After all, soil is a bank of elements and water that provides the matrix for the biological processes involved in the cycling of nutrients, which are elements under the right conditions of concentration and availability to plants. In fact, of the sixteen chemical elements required for life, plants obtain all but three, carbon, hydrogen, and oxygen, from the soil. The soil stores these essential nutrients in undecomposed litter and in living tissues and recycles them from one reservoir to another at rates determined by a complex of biological processes and climatic factors.

If we are concerned with the health of the topsoil, we need to accept the lessons of history. Consider, for example, that the birth of agriculture caused civilizations to rise, whereas abusive agricultural practices—based on flawed, linear-economic thinking—destroyed the topsoil and thus fostered the collapse and extinction of some of those same civilizations. And yet, with all the glaring lessons of history spread before us around the world, with all our scientific knowledge, and with all our technological skills, we insist on walking the historical path of agricultural ruin and impending social collapse.

The supreme irony is that, even as we work to rid ourselves of nuclear weapons on Earth and to establish a lasting peace among nations, we continue to commit genocide by progressively destroying the sustainability of our environment on which we all depend for life itself. Through rain and snow, air-born pollutants reach the entire Earth—from the tops of the mountains piercing the clouds down into the soil and the deepest recesses of the sea.

Soil scientist W. C. Lowdermilk addressed this point in 1939 when he wrote, "if the soil is destroyed, then our liberty of choice and action is gone, condemning this and future generations to needless privations and dangers." To rectify society's careless actions, Lowdermilk composed what has been called the "Eleventh Commandment," which demands our full and unified attention and our unconditional embrace if human society is to survive:

Thou shalt inherit the Holy Earth as a faithful steward, conserving its resources and productivity from generation to generation. Thou shalt safeguard thy fields from soil erosion, thy living waters from drying up, thy forests from desolation, and protect thy hills from overgrazing by thy herds, that thy descendants may have abundance forever. If any shall fail in this stewardship of the land thy fruitful fields shall become sterile stony ground and wasting gullies, and thy descendants shall decrease and live in poverty or perish from off the face of the earth.[6]

History is replete with lessons pointing out that soil, once destroyed or lost (such as the deserts of the world, which are growing at an exponential rate due to a loss of topsoil from abusive livestock grazing in their surrounding landscapes) takes many human lifetimes to replace. Yet we plan to exploit totally any part of the ecosystem for which we see a human use, and we either ignore, disdain, discount, or even plan the elimination of any part of the ecosystem for which we cannot see such an immediate use.

With this myopic view, we eliminate the diversity of Nature through our self-centered stinginess, which inevitably leads to biological extinctions of species and their functions, whether we are "managing" a forest, the soil of a farmer's field, or the soil in the gardens of our own back-yards. But this myopic view is only a choice about control, and we can always choose to choose again.

Exercise In Conscious Awareness

If you assume that the fertility of the soil is inexhaustible, you are in for a rude awakening. Different plants use different soil elements in varying amounts, thus rotating crops of vegetables allows a variety of elements to be withdrawn from the soil bank for some period of time, even without a reinvestment of organic material as biological capital. True, you can counter an immediately declining yield with an application of commercial fertilizer, but the true fertility of the soil will still become exhausted if organic material—the reinvestment of biological capital—is withheld. Such exhaustion of the soil may take a fairly long time, but it will inevitably occur and someone must then pay the price of rebuilding the biological capital in the soil and the soil's fertility with it.

Therefore, if you want to experience what happens to soil that is not nurtured for its own sake, plant broccoli or cauliflower in the same area for two or three successive years—without adding any organic material or commercial fertilizer to the soil. To determine the results, measure the height and breadth of your plants each year, as well as the diameter of their stems at the thickest point. In addition, weigh the cumulative yield you get off of each plant. At the end of the season add the weights together so you can compare annual totals. A declining yield *is* a sign of growing soil infertility.

To reverse the trend, add compost (the reinvestment of biological capital) to the soil without rotating your crops as one part of the experiment and simply rotate your crops in another area as the other part of the experiment. Again, measure your plants for the same period of time and compare the results.

What have you learned about the variability of soil fertility? What have you learned about the necessity of biological reinvestments in renewable natural resource systems? How might this lesson from your garden relate to the rest of the world's ecosystems? With these questions in mind, let's enter the gate of social consciousness.

CHAPTER 3

THE GATE OF SOCIAL CONSCIOUSNESS

HAVING JUST PASSED through the gate of Ecological Consciousness, we are now ready to enter the second gate—Social Consciousness. Because those who enter my garden through the gate of Social Consciousness are often estranged from Nature, it is paramount for them to realize that we are all inseparable from Nature. In fact, our entire lives are spent in an unending study of and practice of our relationship with Nature in one way or another, which—in the best of all worlds—includes a deep and abiding sense of community.

Before proceeding through the gate of Social Consciousness, however, be prepared for a softer and less well defined path than that leading through the gate of Ecological Consciousness. While ecological understanding is intellectually based on the scientific study of relationships, social issues are based on the emotional, philosophical, and moral interpretation of many of those same relationships.

To further illustrate, close your eyes and visualize a path leading uphill through a meadow with three huge boulders on the immediate right and two on the left. It is three o'clock in the afternoon of a bright sunny day, and the shadows cast by the boulders are crisp and clear, which makes the size and shape of the boulders not only readily discernible but also catching to the eye. This image of the meadow is analogous to the gate of Ecological Consciousness through which you have already passed.

Now visualize the same path on a bright moonlit night. Again, look at the five boulders. They are not so crisp in their outlines; they are more difficult to discern with absolute clarity. Yet their relationship to the meadow as a whole is perhaps easier to see because the background is closer to being within the same depth of field. This softer view of the boulders fits more easily with the fuzzy edges of social philosophy, which more often than not has an abundance of questions and a dearth of concrete answers.

As you will see when reading this chapter, the fuzziness, the lack of discrete boundaries, the seamless relationships between and among social issues carries over to the path leading through the gate of Social Consciousness. Unlike ecological decisions and consequences, which seem to have relatively discrete cause and effect relationships that simply are as they are, regardless of whether we understand them, social issues are difficult to discuss as discrete entities because they ooze endlessly in amoeboid fashion one into another.

With this in mind, let's proceed into my garden through the gate of Social Consciousness. In so doing, be prepared to discover, as I have, that there is seldom, if ever, a clear-cut "right" answer to any question I or you may pose. Rather, the "rightness" of each answer is a matter of personal consciousness, which lends credence to a claim found in *The Old Farmer's Almanac* of 1850, "Gardening . . . may, in some sort, be regarded as the test of civilization."

COMMUNITY BEGINS IN A GARDEN

True community is founded on a sense of place,
history, and trust through sharing.

As a community is rooted in a sense of place within the larger context of a surrounding landscape, so I, as an individual, am rooted in a personal sense of place in my home within the larger context of my surrounding garden. As a community has a collective history, so I create a personal history in my home and garden with the first vision of future possibility, the first squeaky door I oil, and the first soil I turn in cultivation. As a community is built on trust, so is my relationship with my neighbors, which coalesces around the mutual sharing of produce from our gardens as the hub of our immediate community—much like the common well in the villages of old.

My garden is the point around which my commitment to community revolves. By community, I mean my neighborhood, where we all have a sense of place and personal commitment. I say this because my hometown has grown too large and too transient to be considered a community in and of itself any longer in the intimate sense, and it is the intimacy of community that I crave.

As the world changes in ways both violent and socially unjust, I find my home, my garden, and my neighborhood becoming ever more important. They are the relatively known and predictable environment from which I venture into the unknown of the outer world and to which I return and search inwardly for my place in the scheme of things.

That is all fine, you might say, but what is community? To explore the meaning of community in the social sense, I will have to leave the confines of my garden and go into the outer world of larger vistas. If you will be patient with this part of our journey of consciousness, I will bring you back once again to the scale of my garden.

THE CONCEPT OF COMMUNITY

Community is a group of people with similar interests living under and exerting some influence over the same government in a shared locality. Because they have a common attachment to their place of residence, where they have some degree of local autonomy, they form the resident community.

People in such a community share social interactions with one another, with organizations beyond government, and through such participation are able to satisfy the full range of their daily requirements within the local area. The community also interacts with the larger society, both in creating change and in reacting to it. Finally, the community as a whole interacts with the local environment, molding the landscape within which it rests and in turn is molded by it.

Community is rooted in a sense of place through which the people are in a reciprocal relationship with their landscape. This relationship is well expressed in the Hupa word "Natinook," which means: "Land where the trails return." (Hupa is the name of a tribe of indigenous Americans in northwestern California.)

As reciprocal relationship implies, a community is a lively, ever-changing, interactive, interdependent system of relationships, not a static place within a static landscape. Because community is a self-organizing system, it changes its environment as well as incorporating information. Further, as the community in its daily living alters the landscape, so the landscape in reaction alters the community.

Reciprocity is the self-reinforcing feedback loop that either extends sustainability to or withholds it from a community and its landscape. We humans therefore create trouble for ourselves when we confuse order in a community with control. Although a degree of freedom and order are partners in generating a viable, well-ordered, autonomous community, a community is nevertheless an open system that uses continual change to avoid deterioration.

A community also has a history, which must be passed from one generation to the next, if the community is to know itself throughout the passage of time. History, by which we decide what is true or false, is a reflection of how we see ourselves and is the very root by which we give value to things. Our vision of the past is shaped by, and in turn shapes, our understanding of the present and our projection into the future.

There are people in Newfoundland, for example, who continue to remain in tiny, isolated coastal communities, where, says Canadian author David Suzuki, their ancestors lived and fished for centuries. As David says, this is not foolish nostalgia, but rather a spiritual relationship with their homes and communities of historical proportions that in sum have far greater personal value than standard economic theory could ever account for.[7] In this connotation, houses can be rebuilt, but many of the personal objects cannot be replaced, especially those of antiquity within a family. These things contribute to an individual's sense of identity and often form an irreplaceable thread of continuity with one's historical context of a sense of place.

When the continuity of its history is disrupted, a community suffers an extinction of identity and begins to view its landscape not as an inseparable extension of itself but rather as a separate commodity to be exploited for immediate financial gain. When this happens, community is destroyed from within because trust is withdrawn in the face of growing competition, which breeds distrust and intolerance.

It seems clear, therefore, that true community literally cannot extend itself beyond local place and history. Community, says Wendell Berry, "is an idea that can extend itself beyond the local, but it only does so metaphorically. The idea of a national or global community is meaningless apart from the realization of local communities."[8]

For a community to be founded in the first place and to be healthy and sustainable, it must rest on the bedrock of trust.

> ...a community does not come together by covenant, by a conscientious granting of trust. It exists by proximity, by neighborhood; it knows face to face, and it trusts as it knows. It learns, in the course of time and experience, what and who can be trusted. It knows that some of its members are untrustworthy, and it can be tolerant, because to know in this matter is to be

safe. A community member can be trusted to be untrustworthy and so can be included. But if a community withholds trust, it withholds membership. If it cannot trust, it cannot exist.[8]

Trust, according to the *American Heritage Dictionary*, is firm reliance on the integrity, ability, or character of a person or thing; confident belief; faith. But trust cannot really be defined because it is based on faith that this person or that is "trustworthy" or faithful to his or her word. Trust can only be lived in one's motives, thoughts, attitude, and behavior. Trust and love go together because, according to Greek dramatist Euripides, "love is all we have, the only way that each can help the other."

Trust versus mistrust is the psycho-social crisis in the first of psychologist Erik Erikson's eight stages of human development.[9] Trust versus mistrust is the dominant struggle from birth to age one year. Erikson assigned hope as the virtue of this stage in which the mother-baby relation lays the foundation for trust in others and in oneself. But as everything has within itself the seed of its opposite, this stage also presents the challenge of mistrust in others and a lack of confidence in oneself.

Hope, as the virtue of trust, is the enduring belief that one can achieve one's necessities and wants. Trust in human relationships is the bedrock of community.

If trust is not developed, none of Erikson's other stages of subsequent development can take place: *autonomy* versus shame and doubt, *initiative* versus guilt, *industry* versus inferiority, *identity* versus identity confusion, *intimacy* (relationship) versus isolation, *generativity* versus stagnation, and *integrity* versus despair—all of which are part and parcel of community. Community is the melding of both how people in different developmental stages relate to themselves as individuals within a community and with others as a community. *In a tolerant community, spirituality is possible; in a spiritual community, tolerance is possible.*

In sum, community is relationship, and meaningful relationship is the foundation of a healthy, sustainable community. American psychologist William James said it thusly: "Wherever you are, it is your own friends who make your world."

Community also reminds one that the scale of effective organization and action has always been small local groups. As anthropologist Margaret Mead admonished: "Never doubt that a small group of thoughtful, committed citizens can change the world; indeed it is the only thing that ever has."

"Community" is a deliberately different word from "society." Although it may refer to neighborhoods or workplaces, to be meaningful it must imply membership in a human-scale collective, where people encounter one another face to face. Community must nurture a system wherein quality, human-scale relationships are the norm, a system of relationships within which people can feel safe and at home in a particular place to which they feel a measure of fidelity. And it is precisely this sense of safety in and fidelity to a particular place that is being called into question as the face of community is being redefined—both politically and economically—in a more worldly context, where the scale of reference to community is extended well beyond that intimate scale of people living together in a local place in which they share a goodly dose of autonomy.

COMMUNITY MUST BE HUMAN IN SCALE

Contrary to what I hear spoken and see written today, community does not come in a variety of scales, from the local to the global, because community can exist at only one scale—the human scale, which is both local and resident. Here it is instructive to consider communities of birds in a given area as ornithologists think of them. First, there is the resident community, which is that group of birds inhabiting the area to which they have a strong sense of year-round fidelity, such as the scrub jays in and around my garden. In order to stay throughout the year, year after year, they must be able to meet all of their ongoing requirements for food, shelter, water, and space. These requirements become most acutely focused during the time of nesting, when young are reared, and during harsh, winter weather.

Then there are the summer visitors, which overwinter in the southern latitudes and fly north to rear their young, such as the violet-green swallows that raise their annual brood in the nest box on the north side of my house. They arrive in time to build their nests, and in so doing must fit in with the year-long residents without competing severely for food, shelter, water, or space—especially for nesting. If competition is too severe, the resident community declines and perhaps even perishes through overexploitation of the habitat by the summer visitors, which have only a seasonal commitment to a particular place.

There are also winter visitors, that spend the summer in northern latitudes, where they rear their young and then fly south in the autumn to overwinter in the same area as the year-long residents, but after the summer visitors have left, such as the yellow-rumped warblers that sustain themselves throughout the winter on the suet that I hang from the pear tree in my garden. They, too, must fit in with the year-long residents without severely competing with them for food, water, shelter, and space during times of harsh weather and the periodic scarcity of food. Here the resident community can once again decline and perhaps perish if overexploitation of the habitat through competition was too severe. And like the summer visitors, the winter visitors are committed only seasonally to a particular habitat, thereby using the best of two different habitats, one in summer and the other in winter.

On top of all this are the migrants, which come through in spring and autumn on their way to and from their summer nesting grounds and winter feeding grounds, such as the Canadian geese that fly over my garden on their way to the farmer's fields to graze on newly sprouted vegetation in early spring and leftover grain in late autumn. They pause just long enough to rest and replenish their dwindling reserves of body fat by using local resources to which they have only a passing fidelity necessary to sustain them on their long journey.

The crux of the issue is the carrying capacity of the habitat for the year-long resident community. If the resources of food, water, shelter, and space are sufficient to accommodate the year-long resident community, as well as the seasonal visitors and migrants—then all is well. If not, then each bird in addition to the year-long residents causes the area of land and its resources to shrink per resident bird. This, in turn, stimulates competition, which under circumstances of plenty would not exist. If, however, such competition causes the habitat to be overused and decline in quality, the ones who suffer the most are the year-long residents for whom the habitat is their sole means of livelihood.

How might this idea of a resident bird community be related to a human community? It has to do with the statement previously made by Wendell Berry, that true community can extend itself beyond the local, but *only* if it does so *metaphorically*. This means, if the resident community is rendered nonsustainable, the trust embodied in the continuity of its history dissolves, as does the self-reinforcing feedback loop of mutual well-being between the land and the people.

Having lost the cohesive glue of trust embedded in its fundamental values, the community loses its identity and is set adrift in the ever-increasing competition both within and without, where "growth or die" becomes the economic motto driving the cultural system. Such vision-less competition inevitably kills the sense of community.

And it is precisely this visionless competition that is destroying not only the living system of the Earth but also my hometown. If my home-town is to be sustainable as a community within a sustainable landscape, the requirements of my hometown as a community must be met before any other considerations are taken into account. If this does not happen, no other endeavor will be sustainable.

Community begins with one person sharing with another a necessity of life, such as relationship, food, or help, which in an agrarian culture is perhaps more often than not focused around a garden, as in my case.

When Zane and I moved into our house and began fixing it to meet our notion of harmony, I felt a growing fidelity to the wooden structure with its concrete foundation that was gradually becoming home—the first I had ever really known, because this time we made a conscious decision to settle in for what we hope to be the rest of our lives. Always before, I knew that one day I would move on.

During our first autumn and winter, we, being true introverts, worked inside, out of view of our neighbors, and thus did not get to know them to any discernible degree. Early in our first spring, however, we started working outside.

At that point, we could be seen by our neighbors, who started coming over to watch and share in the progress as the patch of weeds was trans-formed into a garden. Then came the sharing of tools, labor, and ideas. We helped one another build fences; chop and pile wood; get manure, mulch, and much-needed topsoil.

As spring progressed into summer, gardens were planted around the neighborhood and with the ripening of each crop, we began sharing surpluses with one another, including fruit from long-established trees. We also shared flowers and other plants as they seeded or were divided, and helped one another with tips on and materials for growing this or that, each based on our wonderful successes and horrendous flops. Nevertheless, each person's experiences were valued—no matter the various outcomes.

Gradually, we began taking care of one another's homes, yards, and pets as vacations came and went, and we put out and put away one another's garbage cans on collection day. In addition, I had learned so much from building my garden pond, watching it mature, and protect-ing it from predators that I could help a neighbor rehabilitate hers after it was repeatedly devastated by a family of raccoons. This included sharing the thriving plants in my pond and the fish, which in two years had reproduced a small armada of sparkling orange, orange and white, and charcoal-colored babies. And finally, there was the business of helping to raccoon-proof her pond.

Beyond this, we visit with one another whenever occasion permits. With each kind deed, each bit of fun, the sense of community grows, and that is as it is meant to be. There are other times, however, when I yearn for the solitude and spiritual fulfillment I find within the boundaries of my garden.

Exercise In Conscious Awareness

How do you feel sitting in your garden listening to the noises of the neighbors around you as they go about their daily business? Do you know from the sounds who is doing what and where? Do you know your neighbors by appearance and name? Do you know what they do for a living? Do they have any children and/or pets? If so, how many and what are their names? Do you know the children by face and which pet belongs to whom? If your existence has been largely in isolation of your neighbors, and you recognize this, what are some of the things you can do to begin interacting with them?

The best way I know to get acquainted with a neighborhood and begin consciously to build a sense of community is to raise more vegetables and/or flowers than you need for yourself and take the excess as an unconditional gift to this person or that throughout the neighborhood, however you choose to delineate it. This simple act of kindness opens almost any door almost any time and asks nothing in return. And in opening the doors, it helps you to relate names, faces, yards, gardens, children, and pets to their respective houses.

When Zane and I planted a rose garden in our front yard, amazing interactions began to occur. While we were out tending our roses—and roses take a great deal of tending, as you may know—people out walking their dogs would compliment us on the beauty and often pause to chat. Others, who were walking or jogging, stopped as well. Suddenly, just by creating a small patch of color and beauty with our roses, we began to meet some of the neighbors within a several-block vicinity of our house. A small community atmosphere began to spring up through this serendipity.

To keep the serendipity alive, you can purposefully call on your neighbors, have an annual neighborhood block party as we do; and, should you find out that they are going on vacation, you can offer to put their garbage out, watch their house, or rake up their leaves. For this small investment of your time and care, you are giving the greatest gift of all in the sense of community—yourself and your time. When you do this repeatedly over a period of months and years, you will find a quiet sense of community beginning to surround you. And it all began with treasures of love from within the boundaries of your garden.

Boundaries are the Language of Sacred Spaces

*Life is a continual balancing act within and among
ever-shifting boundaries.*

In the beginning , when I planted cuttings in my garden, the flowers and shrubs were so small that the notion of their meeting in a competitive sense was nonexistent in my mind. I visualized perfect harmony, not cramped plants and overcrowded spaces. But the time came when the plants, such as creeping phlox and thyme, filled all the vacant areas among themselves and began to infringe on one another's space, not to mention that of other plants.

To the indigenous Americans, every individual had a sacred space, from the stone people, to the cloud beings, to the four-legged creatures, and the two-legged ones. The idea of an individual's sacred space has long been a part of every interrelationship of the traditional indigenous Americans. It is the sacredness and respect of individual space that allows the world to exist in harmony.

For contemporary Americans like ourselves, sacred space is equivalent to defining our own personal boundaries. Boundaries are those lines of silent language that allow a person to communicate with others while simultaneously protecting the integrity of one's own personal space as well as the personal spaces of those with whom one interacts.

The language of boundaries transcends individual space to include familial space, cultural space, and even national space. Understanding personal boundaries among individuals of the same culture is difficult enough, but expanding that concept into a fluid working ability among different cultures is a most difficult task. This is especially true in a country where one can neither understand nor speak the language.

A simple way of looking at boundaries is the adage "good fences make good neighbors." In this sense, novelist Margaret Atwood created a beautiful image of boundaries when she wrote of a bird as "a winged creature that lives in a territory bounded by song." In fact, the behavioral function of a bird's song is not only to attract a mate but also to protect its sacred space, its nesting territory, which is indeed "bounded by song."

Another example of boundaries is offered by cliff swallows, which attach their mud nests to such surfaces as the faces of cliffs, the sides of buildings, and the undersides of bridges. These enclosed, globular nests share common walls, which not only strengthen the nests but also keep the peace by preventing the inhabitants from peeking into and vying for each other's abodes. If, however, a hole is made in the common wall and the swallows can see each other, they bicker and squabble until the hole is repaired, which immediately restores tranquility.

A more complicated way of dealing with physical boundaries is to compare them to the home ranges and territories of animals. A home range is that area of an animal's habitat in which it moves freely throughout the course of its normal activity and in which it is free to mingle with others of its own kind. A territory, in contrast, is that part of an animal's home range that it defends, for whatever reason, against those of its own kind. This defensive behavior is most exaggerated and noticeable during an animal's breeding season.

How does this concept apply to us? Suppose it is Saturday morning and you leave your home to take care of a few errands. You simply go about your business without paying much attention to what is going on around you or to the people you pass, unless you happen to meet someone you know. In general, you are simply engrossed in what you are doing. When you have finished your errands, you start home.

The closer you get to your neighborhood, the more alert you unconsciously become to changes around you, such as the new people moving in two blocks away. This "protective feeling" becomes even more acute as you approach the area of your own home and notice a car with an out-of-state license plate parked in your neighbor's driveway. You get to your house and immediately notice, perhaps with some irritation, that a dog has visited your lawn again. If the dog had anointed someone else's yard with its leavings, you probably would not have noticed.

Thus, in general principle, the closer you get to your home, the more you notice what is going on, and the more observant and protective you become. The same pattern extends into your home.

How well you know someone and how comfortable you feel around them determines the freedom with which they may interact with you and your family and use your house. The closer someone gets to your own room, and beyond that to your physical person, which represents your ultimate territory, the more clearly and carefully you define your boundaries. The reverse is in effect, however, as you leave your room and go into the rest of your house or your neighborhood, which represents your home range.

To illustrate how freely someone may move about within your home, consider that an unwanted salesperson may not be allowed inside your home. A casual acquaintance, on the other hand, may be allowed in the living room and given the use of the guest bathroom, but he or she is not allowed to wander about the house without permission. If one of your daughter's friends comes over, she may be allowed into the living room, kitchen, family room, guest bathroom, and your child's room, but only with both your and her permission. The visiting child is not allowed into your own room or your private bathroom. At times, even your children may not be allowed in your room without your permission, or perhaps you in theirs.

Although the above dynamic may function in a "normal" manner for strangers, it often becomes so blurred among the members of a dysfunctional family that personal boundaries, including the physical body itself, are violated. In some families, appropriate personal boundaries are all but absent. Once this becomes apparent—and it is painful, it may take an individual most or all of his or her adult life to understand and establish the boundaries of his or her sacred, personal space.

Establishing our personal boundaries really tests our courage and sensitivity to others. But few endeavors are so important or worthwhile to our sense of well-being, because understanding and respecting boundaries is a critical part of the infrastructure of a behaviorally functional society in which appropriate social boundaries are a cornerstone in building and maintaining respect and trust. Respect and trust, in turn, make open communication possible.

Interpersonal boundaries are an absolute social necessity of communication, which means I must be exceeding careful when cracking a joke that it is not at someone's expense and thus automatically crosses the boundary of their sacred space. Another critical boundary that must be respected is listening to one another without interrupting. This is imperative because waiting one's turn is part and parcel of civility and equality, both of which are prerequisites for a safe environment.

Although we can by choice establish and maintain our own personal boundaries and respect those of others, I find that if I want the plants in my garden to be in proportion to my vision of harmony, I must often establish the boundaries for them. I maintain these boundaries in one of several ways. I may cut the plants back when they grow too profusely and then compost the clippings if appropriate. I may divide a plant, thin seedlings, or transplant one or more individuals to less crowded areas. I may give some away to other gardeners—and resist the temptation to take plants in return. I can sell some back to a nursery, or at times recycle the excess as organic material for the soil of my garden.

Some people might argue that I am infringing on the "rights" of my plants to grow as they will, and in some moral/spiritual sense, they may well be correct, because I am indeed imposing my sensibilities on their sacred space as individuals. This is a fine line of interpretation for which I have no good answer, because greater minds than mine have long struggled with the whole notion of "rights" in the sense of social morality. The dilemma posed by the notion of "rights" is one of just and ethical boundaries or limits with respect to how we humans treat not only one another but also our fellow travelers on this tiny planet—including how I treat the plants in my garden when I unilaterally control their growth.

L. E DC INGTON

Exercise In Conscious Awareness

Interpersonal boundaries, those sacred spaces between and among individuals, are at times difficult to define. This difficulty is due in part to shifting social values, such as the ongoing struggle toward gender equality in our society. If, however, you go into your garden, you may find the boundaries between two plants to be much easier to discern.

In fact, the instructions on each package of seed tell you how far apart to plant the seeds—the sacred growing space required by each individual—for the best results in growing adult plants. As you work among your flowers and/or vegetables, note how high they get, how wide they become, how fast they grow, how they vie for the sunlight, and so on. In this way, you will become aware of the space each plant requires to give you its best performance.

By way of illustration, consider daffodils. Their bulbs are hidden in the soil, yet each year they multiply by producing more bulbs. If, however, the bulbs become too numerous in too small an area, the blossoms above ground become progressively fewer and smaller owing to the overcrowding of their bulbs. The bulbs tell you exactly what they require below ground by what they are doing above ground. It is therefore necessary to dig up the bulbs and thin them out if you want nice big blossoms and healthy bulbs.

It is now November in my garden, and time to thin the gathering profusion of gladiola bulbs that bloomed last summer and cut back the ever-expanding clumps of asters lest they crowd neighboring plants with their runners. Here, in my garden, the invasion of available growing space between plants is easily seen. Although some plants maintain their own sacred growing space through the employment of toxins that permeate the soil around them as their fallen leaves decompose or through the production of toxins in their roots, other plants lack such an aggressive mechanism in the protection of their sacred spaces. It is thus my task and yours as gardeners to ensure that each plant has its sacred space held sacred.

Come spring, I will have to cut out the weak and crowding stems of the roses in order to allow the breezes to circulate through the center of each bush and keep it healthy. I did not at first know that each rose stem needs its own space of a certain width to allow the circulation of air that in turn prevents the concentration of humidity within the bush and thus helps to control such diseases as blackspot.

In the case of individual plants, the sacred spaces are between and among individual plants of different kinds, like the sacred spaces among unrelated people or between people and their pets. In the case of the roses, the sacred spaces can be likened to those among the members of a single family.

Because the analogies seem endless, it can be instructive for you to venture into your garden and consciously observe the sacred spaces contained therein. As you observe the various kinds of spacing and crowding among the plants and animals of your garden, consider, by way of analogy, the different kinds of sacred spaces that you can find in your own community. As you become aware of such spaces, your own included, you will begin to understand the silent language of sacred spaces, which in modern society are called "boundaries," and are attached to the notion of personal "rights."

Rights, although of Noble Intent, have become the Fodder of Injustice

*"Rights" were invented by humans and are granted by humans to humans,
but not equally. An animal, on the other hand, or a plant, for that matter,
does not have "rights" but rather "ecological integrity," which,
being of God, lies beyond the power of humans to grant.*

We assign to animals such things as hunting seasons for sport and control of populations, bounties to be paid on the death of unwanted individuals and species, and extermination in a garden as destructive pests (or weeds in the case of plants), but these are not "rights;" they are economically motivated conditions. I suggest, therefore, that animals (and plants) are not given and so do not have rights; they have "ecological integrity," which is unimpaired Universal wholeness and unity.

In contrast, the question of human "rights" has a long and complex history, because a human "right" is a legalistic construct based on some moral sense of privilege. A "right," for example, is defined by humans and assigned by humans to humans and therefore does not apply to animals or plants unless we purposely give specifically recognized rights to animals and/or plants. Although "rights" may have been originally designed to acknowledge equality among humans, they are predominantly selective in practice, despite the "Universal Declaration of Human Rights" drafted under the auspices of the United Nations. This selectively is based on some notion that one species, race, color, creed, sex, or age is superior to another, which means that differences and similarities of anything are based on our subjective judgments about whatever those categories are.

These differences in perceived outer, superficial, values became social judgments about the inherent, real, values of individual human beings, as well as other forms of life. Superficial characteristics are therefore translated into special rights or privileges simply because the individuals are different in some aspects and either perform certain actions differently or perform different actions. The more different a form of life is from ourselves the more likely we are to make black-and-white judgments about its perceived real value as expressed through our notion of its rights. (In an ideal world, however, if I were to sense a difference between myself and another, that would be my cue to be all the more careful to treat them equally.)

Such judgments are made against the personal standards we use to measure how everything around us fits into our comfort zone. We thus judge this person good or acceptable and that one bad or unacceptable, this animal good and that one bad, or this plant good or that bad, depending on how they conform to our standard of acceptability. Such judgments are erroneous, however, because all one can ever judge is an outer appearance. In addition, each person's standard is correct only for that person; it is not valid for anyone else.

For example, I consider killing another human being to be murder, but a headhunter would consider it a religious act, and a soldier would consider it a duty. Who is correct? We all are from our respective points of view.

There may be a number of judgmental reasons for these discrepancies in social stature, but none of them can be applied in the context of the real value of each person because everybody has a gift to give and each gift is unique and critical to the whole. The gifts are equal *and* different. What is true for human beings is true for every living thing on Earth, because every living thing is equal in its service to the Earth. Each species, each life, each function is equally important to the evolutionary success of our home planet—whether we understand it or not. Each species has its own excellence and cannot be compared to any other. All differences among all living things are just that—differences.

The hierarchies or judgmental levels of value are human constructs that have nothing whatsoever to do with reality. Every life is a practice in evolution and conservation, and every living thing is equal before God, however "God" is perceived. If, however, "God" does not figure into your scheme of things, then think instead of every living thing being equal before the impartiality of Nature's biophysical principles as they govern the Universe.

Thus, we must discard our view of the Earth as a battlefield of subjective competition where human "superiority" reigns not only over plants and animals but also over human beings of a stripe different from our own. We will be better off if we consider the Earth in terms of complementary efforts in which every living thing is equal in its service—not where one is better or worse, or more or less necessary than any other. Each is only different and in its own way is equally vital to the health and well-being of the whole living system because life demands struggle, tenacity, and refinement, which continually fits and refits each living thing to its function. If such equality is indeed a manifestation of the "Truth," as it is meant to be, how do we account for our Western industrialized society's notion about the unilateral, inalienable "rights" attached with ecological and moral impunity to our sense of private property?

Exercise In Conscious Awareness

The notion of human "rights," or "rights" of any kind for that matter, is an abstraction to the vast majority of people in the world unless, of course, they are in the monied "ruling class." The purpose of this exercise is to help you understand the difference between the abstraction and the reality—that a "right" is a privilege of birth or is acquired through financial/political power, but in reality is seldom connected to equality of treatment.

"Rights," as an invention of the human psyche and legal system, are a curious thing in that, while they ostensibly are designed to protect people from oppression, they can simultaneously foster oppression when people focus on their differences, such as the Israelis and the Palestinians, rather than their similarities and commonalties. Consider the living organisms in your garden and assume they all have the same right under the law. How would you control the slugs, pillbugs, aphids, or root weevils? If they all had "rights" equal to yours, you could not legally control them. So don't try to control them; try reasoning with them instead. Try actually treating them as though they had as much legal right to your lettuce or flowers as you do. But they do not have legally constituted rights, so you have the "right" to control them as you wish—and they have no recourse.

With respect to nonhuman organisms wanting what you are raising in your garden, there are times when they must be controlled if you are to have any vegetable fit to eat or flower fit to cut. But with humans, it is different, unless, of course, you want what other people have but cannot legally acquire it if they are seen as having "rights" equal to yours under the law.

We in the United States righteously condemn what Hitler did to those people whom he did not want in any land under German control during World War II, which was heinous by any definition. But—except for the scale or degree of magnitude of his reprehensible actions—how is it any different in principle when in the United States two white men drag a black man to death behind an automobile just because he is black and they hate him for it? If a person is murdered because of hate, is that not the behavior of a Hitler coming to the fore? What dark side of each one of us makes such inhumane decisions?

Now consider how equality under equal "rights" would affect the world if men and women had equal rights granted them, which they do not. How would the world be if men, women, and children all had equal rights? What a vastly different world our children would inherit if rights were in fact equal for all peoples under the law—regardless of gender, age, religious belief, sexual preference, race, or color—and the law was in fact upheld.

We, the wealthy industrialized nations, would have to share with those less wealthy, those less materially inclined, those less industrialized. We would have to give up our insatiable greed, our material edge, lower our standard of living, and the luxury of wantonly wasting resources—mostly the resources we draw from other countries. How would you feel about that? Regardless of how you might feel, the price of *true* equality is equal access.

L. Edgington

THE MISUNDERSTOOD PRIVILEGE OF TRUSTEESHIP

While I may in a legal sense "own" the land in which my garden resides, I can only borrow it in a moral sense. I am, therefore, both a temporary custodian and a trustee of my garden for those who must someday live where I now dwell.

I once had a neighbor whose garden abutted mine. One day, without any warning, he came to me and said that he thought my garden was encroaching about a foot onto his property, which lessened the rightful size of his garden. Although I doubted it, I agreed to a measurement, which ultimately proved his claim to be invalid. Nevertheless, this exercise stimulated my wondering about the whole concept of private property and the responsibilities such a notion might carry with it.

Private ownership of land is a very recent concept when one considers the length of time human beings have been on Earth. For instance, the pygmies of central Africa—the most ancient of all forest dwellers—hold no enforceable claims to the forests they have inhabited for at least forty thousand years.[10] Indigenous peoples on every continent find the notion of private ownership of land to be both ludicrous and impossible. So did the Europeans when they were still tribal, but that was long ago when they knew the sky belonged to the sun and wind, to the rain and snow; when the great azure vault of the heavens was graced by the wings of birds, not the roar of jet engines.

How can an individual human being own something that he or she has not created and therefore cannot control? How can a person own something that has been around for millennia before he or she was born and will continue for millennia after he or she is dead? How can an individual own something that is so obviously part of the global commons in both time and space that it belongs to every living creature in its turn and so to no one individual in particular at any given time? How is it that we in the predominantly Christian United States *cannot* legally steal from our neighbors in the present—meaning other adults in space . . . as the British and early Americans stole in the past from the indigenous inhabitants—but we *can* legally steal from our children and our children's children, which is stealing from our neighbors in time through nonsustainable overexploitation of resources?

Although fervently divided on this issue, society must somehow come to terms with it. Either this peculiarly human notion of land ownership and the rights of private property will continue as an illusion, or people must accept an alternative, that of trusteeship of the piece of Earth that one inhabits or otherwise has deed and title to as a living trust for the beneficiaries of the future. It is a question of "self-centeredness" versus "other-centeredness," which means that the morality of the idea of land ownership and unlimited rights of private property must be opened to rigorous debate. And make no mistake, the question of land ownership and the rights of private property is, at its very root, a moral one.

In such a debate, the questions must be: Does the holder of a deed to land of any kind "own" the land in an absolute sense, or is he or she only a trustee thereof? Does such a holder of a deed have the moral right to degrade the productive capacity of the land before passing it on to the next person who *must* use it? Put a little differently: Does any person have the moral right to *steal options* from the future for immediate personal gain by irreparably degrading the productive capacity of the land? If not, how can one be granted the legal right to do so through the absolute "rights of private property?"

If the outcome of such debate is in favor of the *status quo*, then biological sustainability is at best an academic question—even at the level of a backyard garden—and so is every other kind of sustainability. Before sustainability can be tenable, the ownership of land and the unlimited rights of private property must be modified. Such modification must be in the tenor of a person's privilege to enjoy being the trustee of the piece of Earth he or she inhabits or otherwise has deed and title to as a living trust for the beneficiaries of the future. Only then is the biological, and thus social, sustainability of the Earth possible.

Should the *status quo* prevail, it will do so because of what professor David Orr calls "conservatives against conservation."[11] The following discussion is taken from his insightful article.

"The philosophy of conservatism has swept the political field virtually everywhere," says Orr, and virtually everywhere conservatives have forgotten what conservatism really means. For example, conservative philosopher Russell Kirk proposes six "first principles" of conservatism, based on his "love of order," for which true conservatives are accountable:

1. Believe in a transcendent moral order;
2. Prefer social continuity, i.e., the "the devil they know to the devil they don't;"
3. Believe in "the wisdom of our ancestors;"
4. Are guided by prudence;
5. "Feel affection for the proliferating intricacy of long-established social institutions;"
6. Believe that "human nature suffers irremediably from certain faults."

The eighteenth-century British philosopher and statesman Edmund Burke is considered to be the founding father of modern conservatism, and, according to Orr, is "as much admired as he is unread." To Burke, the goal of order is to harmonize the distant past with the distant future through the nexus of the present.

Like the Republicans from a recent session of Congress, Burke thought in terms of a contract. But unlike the 1996 Republican contract, which was self-centered for a minority in the present, Burke's contract is between "those who are living, those who are dead, and those who are yet to be born." Those "possessing any portion of power," says Burke, "ought to be strongly and awfully impressed with an idea that they are in trust." In Burke's contract, freedom is "that state of things in which liberty is secured by the equality of restraint," not in which "every man was to regulate the whole of his conduct by his own will."

As the ecological-social shadow of the present stretches increasingly over the generations of the future, the wisdom of Burke's concern for the justice and welfare of the generations yet unborn becomes more evident. If conservatism means anything at all, says Orr, it means the conservation of what Burke called "an entailed inheritance derived to us from our forefathers, and to be transmitted to our posterity; as an estate belonging to the people." It *did not* mean preserving those rules by which one class enriches itself at the expense of another.

"What is conservative," asks Orr, "about squandering for all time our biological heritage under the pretext of protecting temporary property rights?" Clearly, not all conservatives think and behave alike, but many present-day conservatives scorn efforts by the public to protect such things as endangered habitats like old-growth forests, endangered species (such as spotted owls, coho salmon, and red wolves), clean air, and clean water. Almost any restrictions placed on the rights of an individual to use land as private property is being viewed increasingly as an *unlawful* "taking"—even when such use would irreparably damage the land and its surrounding environment. How, I wonder, is it any more of a *lawful* "taking" when one degrades land in the present that must be used in an impoverished condition by someone in the next generation and beyond?

Even John Locke, from whom we have derived much of our land-use law and philosophy, said that "nothing was made by God for Man to spoil or destroy." "The point," says Orr, "is that John Locke did not regard property rights as absolute even in a world with a total population of less than one billion, and neither should we in a world of six billion."

What, asks Orr, is conservative about the informed denial surrounding the mounting scientific evidence of impending climatic change? Climate change will have rapid, self-reinforcing feedback loops that could change the nature of the Earth's hospitality to human life for all time. What right do we have to run such a risk, when the consequences belong to the generations of the future and they are not here to participate in the choice?

What, asks Orr, is conservative about perpetual economic expansion when it not only has changed the Earth more radically than any other force in modern times but also is rapidly destroying communities, traditions, cultural diversity, and whole ecosystems throughout the world? What is conservative about passing forward a despoiled legacy to the future?

Social-environmental sustainability requires no less than the first of Russell Kirk's "first principles"—that humanity must be grounded in the belief in a transcendent moral order in which we humans, as trustees for future generations, are accountable to a Higher Authority. Anything less is not sustainable!

Edmund Burke put the capstone on land ownership and the unlimited rights of private property as a sustainable proposition when he wrote:

> Men are qualified for civil liberty in exact proportion to their disposition to put moral chains upon their own appetites... Society cannot exist unless a controlling power upon will and appetite be placed somewhere, and the less of it there is within, the more there must be without. It is ordained in the eternal constitution of things that men of intemperate minds cannot be free. Their passions forge their fetters.[11]

With Burke's statement in mind, I must ask myself what "right" I have to degrade or otherwise misuse the soil of my garden in any way, even though I legally "own" the soil in fee simple, which encompasses the most extensive bundle of rights available to a "land owner." And I have the Warranty Deed to prove it, which in some ways is not unlike a patent.

If I were the only person on Earth, or even the last person, that would be one thing—but I am not. Furthermore, when I am gone, someone else must live where I now live because there is a scarcity of available, livable space in my hometown, which means that leaving my house empty and the soil fallow is not a viable option. What, therefore, is my responsibility as a land owner?

My responsibility is the quality of the legacy I leave to the next person, which is the quality of my house and the care of its grounds, particularly the health of my garden's soil in which is stored the future's opportunities, much like a savings account. It is this legacy that I will one day pass forward to the next tenant, whom I shall probably not know. Although Zane and I have labored hard to remodel our house, care for its grounds, and rebuild the soil's fertility, I do not and cannot own my garden's soil despite the Warranty Deed in my hand.

With the thought of this Deed, there comes from across the years a refrain I have so often heard from people who think their possession of a Warranty Deed to a piece of ground gives them the unilateral right to do whatever they want, despite the impoverished circumstances they leave for the future: "Why should I worry about the future when I have no guarantee that the next generation will take care of what I leave in the way I want them to? This being so, if anyone is going to benefit from my land, it's going to be me! The future can take care of itself, just as I had to!"

True, there are no guarantees that the next person will care for his or her garden as I did when it was mine. But that is not the point. It is my responsibility to pass forward an unconditional gift of love embodied as available choices to be made in each and every option secreted in the soil of my garden for the next person to find. Unless I am competing with the future, how that person spends the options he or she discovers is not my concern because a gift is free of all liens and encumbrances, and the health of the soil in my garden is my unconditional gift to the next person, which, in the end, determines how I must participate with Nature.

L. EDGINGTON

Exercise In Conscious Awareness

Go to the courthouse or wherever the records are kept that will give you the history of the land on which you now live and have your garden. Reach as far back in the records as you can and study the history of your property. If you do not own it because you are renting, imagine that you do. Assume that you *have to live* there because habitable space is limited—a very real condition of human life in many countries.

Looking at the records, how would you feel if you knew that each person who once lived where you now reside had taken the best possible care of the land that you now own and thus passed forward to you the priceless legacy of healthy soil and the myriad opportunities for gardening that legacy holds? How would you feel if you knew that each person who once lived where you now reside had progressively trashed the land and thus impoverished the soil, perhaps irreparably, where you want your garden to be? How would you feel if you knew that the person who owned the land immediately prior to you had taken excellent care of it? How would you feel if you knew that the person who owned the land immediately prior to you had trashed it just before you purchased it?

Examine carefully your feelings as you ponder these questions. Did each of these people really own the land, where you must now live? Do you really own it? What kind of care are you going to afford the land during your tenure? In what kind of condition are you going to pass it to the next person who *must* live there? Do you really own the land if you cannot take it with you? What does it mean to "own" land? Is land ownership even possible? Or are we only renting or borrowing it temporarily? What advantage does having a legal title to a piece of land, as custodian and trustee, give me in being able to "develop" its potential (such as the pond I added to my garden) that are not available to someone who lives on a piece of land without a legal title to it? Whatever your answers, the question you must decide in your own conscience is: *Do I owe anything* to the land and/or to the next person who must live here? Finally, would I want to be the recipient of what I intend through my actions to bequeath?

THE WAY WE PARTICIPATE WITH NATURE

*The things we tend to remember the clearest and the longest are those in which
we have been forced by circumstances to participate most fully with our
environment, when it seems Nature has chosen to participate with us.
Such times are usually when we are out of control and terribly uncomfortable,
such as being caught in an earthquake or intense windstorm.
These are the times of our greatest aliveness, when we are forced to deal
firsthand with the raw power of the Eternal that molds and sculpts the Universe.
One of the reasons for the clarity of this remembrance is the impartiality with
which Nature treats us—like one animal that is equal in rank to all the others.*

The way in which *we choose* to participate with Nature depends on how
we see ourselves in relation to other forms of life. If we think ourselves
superior to all life forms, we can do nothing but subjugate all life to feed
our egos. But if we see ourselves as equal to but different from other
species, then we can allow and encourage each to fulfill its function in
the evolution of our home planet. The problem is that *we see ourselves
as superior.*

Suppose I go to a nursery and purchase a tree. What personal responsibility did I buy with the tree? After all, it is a living being. Do I have
the right to let the tree die in its pot because, having bought it, I now
"own" it and can do as I please with it?

Now suppose my neighbor to the east comes over and, seeing the tree
is too big for its pot, says that I ought to plant it, whereupon I explain
that I have not yet decided what to do with it. A little later my neighbor
to the west comes over and, noticing the tree, says: "Don't plant that tree
too close to my garden because it will not only shade my garden as it
grows but also spread seeds all over as it matures, and I'll spend forever
pulling out the seedlings." What is my responsibility to the tree and my
neighbors?

Do I owe my neighbor to the east any consideration in alleviating
his or her feelings by planting the tree even if I am not sure where I
want it? Do I owe my neighbor to the west any consideration in where
I plant the tree so as to protect his or her garden from unwanted shade
and falling seeds? Do I owe the tree itself any consideration in whether
or not to plant it because I bought it in the first place? Just what is my
responsibility and how must I accept it?

Now let's consider my responsibility from a different point of view.
I have feral cats that occasionally come into my yard. Feral cats are

domestic cats gone wild, usually because people either do not neuter their cats to control their breeding and/or because people dump unwanted kittens alongside some road to fend for themselves.

If I allow the feral cats to remain in my yard, they will likely kill the birds that visit my garden and fruit trees or make attempts on the lives of my fish, so I chase them out. So far, it has not been necessary to live-trap and remove any, but if that time comes, what will I do with them? I will either have to kill them, take them to an animal shelter to be killed, or take them away from my house and turn them loose. Is my responsibility to care for the birds I want in my garden, the fish in my pond, the feral cats, or all three?

I ask this because it is the tip of a much larger social issue, one I have struggled with for many years. To me, there are two salient questions: How do we as individuals and a society deal with Nature's long-term, rational impartiality and our short-term, subjective emotional inclination when it comes to allowing each living being to fulfill its appointed role in the evolution of our planet? How do we know what that role is—or can we even make such a determination?

In dealing with these questions, I will once again range afield from my garden, but be assured, I shall return to it. Before I begin this section, I want something clearly understood in deference to Zane. The story I will relate about the feral cats we fed while living in Las Vegas, Nevada, is from my memory, my understanding of the circumstances, and her responses to them. Zane remembers it differently, but has graciously agreed to allow me to tell the story from my perspective as an illustration.

WHEN "HELPING" IS INTERFERING

We must honor the integrity of animals as part of the sacred evolution of Nature. But we must consciously decide when our notion of helping animals actually interferes with the integrity of their naturalness, when our attempts to rescue animals really interferes with the sacred evolution of Nature's processes.

Humans often rush to the aid of wildlife in such cases as a whale trapped in a pocket of open water as the ice begins to freeze the polar sea, deer and elk starving during severe winters, and feral horses dying of thirst during severe drought. Ironically, people will mobilize in a supreme, costly effort to rescue individual animals from imminent death wrought by Nature's impartial evolutionary processes, while doing nothing to prevent the extinction of *entire* species through purposeful exploitation, environmental degradation, or the sheer lack of consciousness with respect to the direct and indirect effects nonhuman species must bear due to our self-centered behavior.

How is it that people, or even a society, will mobilize to rescue an animal in distress yet turn their back on a whole species facing extinction? Is it because an individual animal is a concrete entity that tugs at our emotions, while a species is an intellectual abstraction? What is our "need" to rescue?

Although I have no succinct answer, I believe most efforts to rescue animals in distress are not the benevolent acts we would like to think they are, but rather a way to reduce our discomfort at participating in the impartial, often harsh ways of Nature, ways we do not understand in our emotional selves and therefore want to control at any cost. This is not to say that some efforts to rescue individual animals are not motivated by true compassion. On the other hand, I wonder how many efforts to rescue individual animals are carried out because of our unconscious guilt at the terrible devastation we have wrought on our environment and the habitats of these selfsame animals.

Deer and elk, for example, periodically starve in great numbers when they become overpopulated with respect to their food supply. To rescue them under these circumstances may relieve our immediate stress at being out of control but will only prolong their overpopulation, which we may have largely caused in the first place by eliminating their predators.

Our attempt to rescue is a form of participating only with the symptom, which likely will allow the cause to worsen. If, on the other hand, we do not interfere and allow Nature's cycles to treat the symptom in relationship with the cause, the entire herd will rebuild toward the next moment of vigor and balance, which will last only until the next correction becomes necessary. In short, we, as a species, are so out of tune with Nature's rhythms that we too often intervene at inappropriate moments to reduce our own angst, which, as I indicated earlier, is a notion I have long debated within myself.

Also, as I said earlier, there are two salient questions surrounding the issue of our human interference: How do we as individuals and a society deal with Nature's long-term, "rational" impartiality and our short-term, subjective emotional inclination when it comes to allowing each living being to fulfill its appointed role in the evolution of our planet? How do we know what that role is—or can we even make such a determination?

Addressing these questions brings us to the aforementioned story of the feral cats, a story I will tell from two points of view: mine and my interpretation of Zane's. My point of view in this story is one of rational logic and impartiality. I have achieved such a point of view slowly, painfully over thirty some years of living with animals and studying ecosystems in a variety of places. I have worked with literally thousands of animals and have seen death well over a thousand times, including death in humans. My view of life is one of immediate circumstance mediated by the long-term effect of my choices, decisions, and actions.

My interpretation of Zane's point of view in this story is one of purely emotional responses to an immediate circumstance in which the long-term is seldom, if ever, initially considered. In fairness, I point out that Zane has not had the experiences with animals, death, or ecosystems that I have had. Nor is that her interest. There is no right or wrong in either point of view; they are only different with different long-term outcomes, and each is a matter of personal conscience.

One day, a magnificent Siamese cat wandered into our walled backyard while Zane and I lived in Las Vegas, Nevada. Zane had seen this beautiful cat roaming the neighborhood and wondered if it had a home. Finally, concluding that it was indeed a stray, she wanted to feed it.

I suggested we not feed it because our house was then for sale, and we daily hoped to sell it and move. Looking ahead as best I could to the long-term consequence for the cat if we began feeding it, I asked Zane what the cat would do when we left, and its food was suddenly cut off? She did not know, but that was clearly irrelevant at the moment. To her, the cat was both a stray and hungry, and that was the immediate point. With that thought, Zane exercised her prerogative of independent action and fed it.

As it turned out, the original cat did have a home down the block, but before we learned that, three *bona fide* strays showed up. I objected to feeding them for the same reason as before. But I still found no way to articulate my concern, that it would not only be unfair to the cats when the food they had learned to depend on was suddenly cut off because we moved but would also put them in a life-threatening position as they tried to return to their extremely harsh and competitive way of life, but without their former hunting territories. Because I could not get this point across, I agreed to feed them until we left.

The three cats soon became five, then seven, ten, twelve, fifteen, and perhaps even more under the cloak of darkness. It was clear that we had a major problem because our charitable feline "eatery" began drawing customers from far and wide.

In time, three scrawny kittens showed up, and Zane, who loves baby animals, began trying to tame them. Thinking of Nature's impartiality, I again objected, but to no avail. Zane said that she simply couldn't resist them.

I argued that they were domestic cats gone wild and would have to remain wild if they were to survive after we moved, which could be any day. But, Zane would have none of it. To her, I was just being intellectual because she could neither see nor understand the long-term consequences of her immediate actions. I, on the other hand, could not only see but also appreciate her emotional response because I had often struggled with the same response myself over the years, too often to the long-term detriment of the animals I tried to rescue.

Zane, with time and patience, was able to tame the skittery black and white kitten that tugged most strongly at her heart. Although our two older cats were less than thrilled at the prospect of a new housemate, in compromise, we adopted the kitten. Then, as often happens, we went to the local pound to find our new kitten a little friend—and came back with two. We now had five cats!

Then something shifted in Zane's understanding of the plight of our "eatery cats," and she became concerned about their welfare once we were gone. She was now ready to reach beyond the emotional immediacy of the moment to see the integrity, the naturalness of the cats as they were—wild cats. Now she was able to understand that by feeding and taming them, we would hinder their future survival. Why? Because we had stolen some of their wildness, some of their integrity, some of their ability to fit into their highly competitive environment after we left.

In addition, we had caused them to concentrate in unusually dense numbers in a small space, which effectively shrank with the addition of each new stray. We had displaced most of the cats from their original hunting areas. These areas, once vacated, would be taken over by other feral cats, and the ones we had fed for so many months would have no place to go without a fight. They would now be the "outsiders," a position from which claiming or reclaiming an already-occupied area in which to hunt would be most difficult.

We therefore began cutting back on the cats' food to force them to hunt more. Zane remained somewhat uncertain about the short-term "cruelty" of starving the cats into hunting. But when she realized that the wildness of these cats was born of necessity and that the integrity of their wildness was their survival insurance in the naturalness of their environment, she saw the whole drama in a new and different light.

She now understood that we had altered the cats' abilities to participate with Nature by making such keenly honed participation unnecessary, and that, if we really cared about them, we had a moral obligation to restore that which we'd stolen—the integrity of their wildness and their naturalness. This meant we had to withhold food, to love them with a closed hand. Such love transcends the unruly emotions, such as guilt and sadness, and enters the realm of rational impartiality, which in Nature is often the greatest love of all because it accepts the intrinsic perfection of the evolutionary process.

Zane was as right from her original point of view as she is from her present point of view, albeit they differed by 180 degrees. She had originally seen what she considered to be unnecessary hardship, and she was right when you consider the origin of these cats—the personal irresponsibility of those people who did not neuter their cats and/or dumped their unwanted cats alongside some road. Be that as it may, the cats were here now, and she began to see the integrity of the cats' naturalness in the context of their participation with Nature, the excellence of their fit into their environment.

But where in all of this, she asked, is compassion? Compassion is not stealing an animal's integrity in the first place. Compassion is the commitment to adopt the wild kitten plus two other abandoned kittens from the animal shelter. Compassion is acting from the conscious awareness of the long-term consequences we cause as a result of our short-term decisions. But most important, compassion is the heart-centered understanding that motivates our behavior, such as the woman's decision down the street from us.

As we were cutting back on the cats' food, a woman who lived a few houses away, unbeknownst to us, began feeding these same cats. So as we cut down on their food, she increased it. The wonderful part of this story is that she planned to live there for many years and made a long-term commitment to the cats, part of which was to live-trap each cat and have it neutered. In that way, she could continue to feed and care for them, and they in their turn, began to show the friendly, loving sides of their nature, but without multiplying their numbers.

CONSCIOUS PARTICIPATION

When Zane and I first began feeding the cats, it was to accommodate her perceived sense of compassion, her sense of caring, but in reality it was to relieve the unconscious sense of stress at seeing the impartiality of Nature in the apparently starving, unwanted cats. Even now, with a newly found understanding, it is still difficult for Zane to close her hand and withhold food.

Although I have practiced participating with Nature ever since I can remember, I still have much to learn because I, too, am a product of a society held prisoner by its fear of death and loss, or for that matter discomfort of any kind, which makes it impossible to participate fully with the vicissitudes of life. When motivated either by fear of or discomfort with Nature's impartiality, however, our sense of participation more often than not interferes with a more harmonious evolution of life on Earth.

We must therefore ask ourselves how we can live in the fullest measure of the moment, unconditionally saying "YES" to life, particularly when that moment is decidedly uncomfortable or even hurts. For it is by living consciously in every moment that we can participate most fully in the mutually beneficial evolution of our home planet, honoring the ecological integrity of our fellow travelers—the nonhuman animals.

Does this mean that I must never kill a pillbug or slug in my garden? No, it does not mean that, which is not to say that pillbugs and slugs do not share in the bounty of my garden, because they do. It is only to say that at some point either I get the lettuce and pansy or they do, and when the time comes to choose, I usually—but not always—opt to have it myself. After all, I purposefully tilled the soil and planted the lettuce and pansy because I wanted them.

But how then do I honor the pillbug or slug that I kill as it eats the lettuce or pansy? I honor it by consciously understanding I am killing it, that I am stealing from it the Divine Spark so that I might eat the lettuce and enjoy the pansy. I honor it by apologizing to it for taking its life prior to killing it and by asking God to bless it as I kill it. Thus I make certain, to the best of my ability, that I kill not out of anger or a sense of human superiority but out of a conscious sense of perceived necessity.

But, you ask, would I feel any differently about killing a slug if I knew that it was an exotic one; would I still honor it as if it were a species native to my garden? Although I personally would feel the same about killing an exotic slug as I do an indigenous one, this is an excellent question, because it teases an assumption that society has already embraced. Namely, that a species from some other place, even though it is knowingly introduced by people, is not a part of the ecosystem into which it is brought and therefore has no legal, ethical, or moral standing—that is, of course, unless we find an economically beneficial use for it. The nutria (a large, aquatic rodent from South America) is a prime example of this sort of social dilemma and the often unintended consequences thereof.

Nutria were originally introduced into Oregon sometime in the early 1950s, if my memory serves me well. They were brought to "nutria farms" to be raised for their pelts and their meat. I remember a breeding pair selling for $1,200. But when the bottom fell out of the market for their pelts and their meat was not readily accepted in grocery stores, the hype over getting rich quickly by farming nutrias died and they were simply turned loose by disgruntled, irresponsible people—the same kind who dump kittens and puppies alongside roads.

Then, because the nutria is larger and more aggressive than the indigenous, fur-bearing muskrat—a long-time staple of the fur market, they out-competed the muskrat for space and food, which caused a severe decline in some populations of the economically important muskrat. Now, the nutria is branded a nuisance animal that is neither native nor natural in Oregon and is therefore often killed indiscriminately, despite their superb ecological fit into our environment. This raises yet another question with which society is currently having to struggle: How do we as a society deal with our currently schizophrenic notions of "natural" and "native"?

Exercise In Conscious Awareness

How we participate with Nature depends on how we view Nature—as an equal partner or as something to be ruthlessly conquered and subdued. It is not uncommon in gardening to feel both ways, in partnership when happily tending and growing vegetables and/or flowers and in conquership when weeding and/or controlling slugs amidst the vegetables and flowers.

The next time you are working in your garden, be mindfully aware moment by moment of how you are feeling as you perform the various tasks you set before yourself, and recognize, to the best of your ability, that all gardening is ultimately a reciprocal relationship in which you choose how you treat Nature and Nature responds accordingly. When, through practice, you reach the inner point at which you can see and feel gardening as a conscious, reciprocal relationship between you and Nature in all you do, you will find peace and harmony even in weeding and controlling slugs, for the sword will have been removed from your heart and your hand and in its place will be the accepting wand of love. Then truly will you experience what Albert Schweitzer called "the reverence for all life."

On the Meaning of "Natural" and "Native"

We not only belong here and have a right to be here in the context of our "nativeness," but also we as individuals and as a society have a duty to participate in the creation of our landscape in the context of our "naturalness."

I am an inseparable part of Nature; therefore, I am as much a natural part of my garden as is any indigenous plant that grows therein, be it a weed or otherwise. But what about introduced plants, be they flowers or vegetables that I purposefully select to grace my garden or weeds that find their own way in? Are they not a natural part of my garden?

Sitting here, looking out into my garden, I wonder what is really meant by "natural." I wonder, because I feel a deep oneness with the soil that forms the foundation of my garden and with the plants and animals that live in it and use it. True, I kill some things to control them, such as slugs, weevils, and chickweed, while I simultaneously nurture others, such as the violet-green swallows using the nest box and the dwarf white pine by the back door. I wonder, because the term "natural" holds for industrialized society connotations that are by and large divisive, connotations that in the human mind often set one living thing against another on the scale of favoritism.

There is a pervasive, widespread notion afoot in Western industrialized society that Nature is merely a commodity or an object to be economically exploited. We are here, according to most forms of Judeo-Christian religion, to master Nature, and as masters, selectively to improve Nature's ability to function, to produce goods and services strictly for our benefit as we perceive it.

There also is a view in which human beings are seen as totally separate from Nature and thus as an unnatural intrusion into the world of Nature, where our very presence is defiling. Ironically, the same individuals who feel humanity is a defiling influence on Nature are those who love a wilderness trek or an overnight backpack for themselves, but who often want the masses to stay clear of their special areas.

Regardless of what we have gleaned from our political sanctification by organized religions, we, as human animals, are still animals. We may not like being called animals or being thought of as animals, because we too often look down on nonhumans; in fact, we too often look down on one another. We are, nevertheless, animals.

What sets us apart from the rest of our fellow creatures is not some higher sense of spirituality or some nobler sense of purpose, but rather that we deem ourselves wise in our own eyes. And therein lies the fallacy of humanity. We are no better than or worse than other kinds of animals; we simply are a different kind of animal—one among the many—and thus, an inseparable part of Nature, but not a special case apart from Nature.

Consider that "natural," as defined in today's dictionaries, means to be present in or produced by Nature, such as animals, as opposed to being made by humans, which is seen as artificial. Consider further that we humans, by our very nature, are produced in a natural way, through sexual union, the joining of sperm and egg, and live birth; that human mothers produce milk in a natural way with which to nourish their offspring; that we grow in a natural way, through the division of our bodily cells; that we both eat and void our bodily wastes in a natural way; that we both awake and sleep in a natural way; that we die in a natural way; that our bodies, if left alone, decompose in a natural way; and, that our molecules and atoms cycle through other processes and organisms in a natural way.

This being so, I think it safe to say that we are natural by virtue of our creation, existence, and demise. And, to be natural is to be inseparable from Nature, from which we are created.

Thus, as a part of Nature, is not what we do natural? This is not to say that our actions are wise, or ethical, or moral, or desirable, or even socially acceptable and within the bounds of Nature's biophysical laws. This is only to say that our actions are natural, because we are natural, which includes converting the landscape from Nature's design to human society's cultural design. According to Ralph Waldo Emerson, "a true man belongs to no time or place, but is the center of things. Where he is, there is Nature."

Admittedly, Nature's "original" design of the landscape not only may be more pleasing to our senses than are many of our cultural alterations of the same landscape, but also may function in a more ecologically healthy way over time. One design, however, is as natural as the other—only different in context. Nevertheless, our cultural alterations are often fraught with a schism between spirituality and materialism, a schism that is knocking at the door of our collective consciousness. This growing schism can be thought of as a gigantic social gong that is reaching an ever-increasing din while we act deaf to its opportunities for collectively elevating our consciousness toward our treatment of our environment.

Although I detect a definite psychological shift on the part of many people who are trying to reach back into human history, back into a consciousness that freely accommodates Nature, to recapture some primordial sense of spiritual harmony with Nature, I still see most of us struggling with a sense of materialistic separateness, due to the prevailing economic social trance—the context of our existence. Put another way, because we humans are an inseparable part of Nature, an area held as wilderness is just as natural as an area of forest that has been clearcut. They differ only in motive, hence in context.

Yet, because we still see ourselves as somehow separate from Nature, the connotation of natural is of something apart from human society, a purity without contamination by human activity or artifact. But this connotation of "natural" is invalid not only because humanity and human society are inseparable from Nature and therefore from the natural world but also because the notion of "native" is enmeshed with that of natural, which raises the question: when is a "native," a native? This is an important question because it ultimately affects how we see Nature and our gardens as a cultural part of Nature, as well as how we see and treat one another.

As people visit with me while I work in my garden, as I go to this nursery or that in search of plants, as I listen to my once-upon-a-time scientific colleagues talk about "native" plants, the meaning of the term "native" becomes increasingly fuzzy. Just because a plant is considered to be indigenous to an area is it automatically a native? Must a plant be growing inside the boundaries of my garden to be considered indigenous? Must something be indigenous to an area to be considered a native?

"Indigenous" refers to the origin of a species in an area, whereas "native" more generally refers to a length of time a species has been in a given area. For example, the American Indian was in North America long before the Europeans invaded the continent. When compared with the Europeans, therefore, American Indians are considered to be indigenous to North America, but the Europeans were not. And while people of European extract have now been in North America for more than two hundred years, they are still not considered to be indigenous because they were latecomers. On the other hand, I, who am of European heritage, can be a native of North America because this is where I was born and raised, but I am still not considered indigenous to the continent because I am of European heritage.

I was born in a hospital in New York State, where I remained but a few days. Am I native to the hospital? I live in the town where I was raised since I was three years old, albeit with absences of residence at various times during the course of my life, besides which I no longer live in the house where I grew up. Am I native to the town, which to me is my hometown? Am I native to my garden, even though it is not the garden of my childhood? Native by whose standard?

"Native" is belonging to by nature; originating, growing, or produced in a certain place. Stated differently, a native is a natural part of the area; a native is an acceptable, accepted part of Nature in a given place in a given time.

Unlike the indigenous Americans who were here prior to the European invaders, most of us who are Americans of European descent still act as though we are alienated from Nature. We still don't have a clear sense of "native" and "natural" as concepts joining us with Nature, because we see them as concepts that somehow exclude us as participants in the creative process of designing the landscapes in which we live and work and play.

What we are really considering, however, is a relative degree of "nativeness," which is thought of in the context of time, just as a relative degree of "naturalness" is thought of in the context of human intrusion as expressed through alteration of landscapes. Therefore, the further into the past we can trace our ancestry in a given place the more native and so the more natural we are thought to be, even within our own psyche. And the more native we feel ourselves to be, the more natural and "rightful" we deem our alterations of the landscape to be.

In the sense that we humans are a natural part of the ecosystem in which we live, and that what we do in the way of converting Nature's landscape to our cultural landscape is also natural, I see "naturalness" not as a definition but rather as a descriptive continuum of human alterations, which ranges from the most pristine end of the ecological scale to the most humanized end of the ecological scale. By the same token, I see "nativeness" not as a definition but rather as a descriptive continuum in time, which ranges from the most ancient, continuous habitation in an area to the most recent immigration into the same area.

Bear in mind, however, that humanity's habitation in and alterations of the landscape are a natural part of Creation and that we are active participants in the redrafting of Nature's design simply because we cannot do anything else by the very fact that we exist. So, the question we must now ask is, as trustees, how do we care for the Earth and sculpt and texture Nature's landscapes in a conscious way that will not only benefit us but also the generations to come? If we do not ask this question and *act* positively on the answer, we shall continue to be prejudiced toward our socially-environmentally destructive way of thinking.

Exercise In Conscious Awareness

Think back to when you first saw your present house. What feelings did it evoke? Were you excited when you decided to buy it? Did it already have a garden or did you create the garden yourself? How long did it take for you to make it "yours" with a sense of your personal values and creativity? When did you begin to feel a sense of "home" and of "place?" Or do you still feel like an artifact, a transient with no roots, a foreigner, or an exotic in your own home, in your own garden? If you feel that you belong, are you not then both natural and native?

Prejudice is Ignorant Judgment

Prejudice is irrational logic conceived in fear and ignorance and expressed as an adverse judgment formed before the fact.

"The morning glory blooms for but an hour, and yet it differs not at heart from the pine that lives for a thousand years." So wrote the 16th century Japanese poet Teitoku Matsunaga. Thus, are the morning glory and the pine seen in their intrinsic equality. Yet to many in Western industrialized society, the pine, which at once is not only a much larger physical entity but also can be converted into lumber, and therefore money, is seen as having far greater value than the morning glory. Is not this prejudgment about the relative value of the morning glory versus the pine an example of prejudice? (Prejudice is an unfavorable opinion about someone or something that is formed without knowledge, thought, or reason concerning the object of negative bias.)

I have in my garden a nesting box built for swallows, but each year the house sparrows try to take it over. I want the violet-green swallows to use it, which they do. Because I want the swallows to use the box, I plug the entrance when the sparrows come around. So far, they have always taken the hint and left.

If the swallows did not nest in the box, would I accept the sparrows? Unquestionably not. Although I have nothing against the sparrows per se, I am not enamored with the idea of their nesting in the box and having them around all the time because they are aggressive toward other birds, loud, and messy around the nest. Am I not saying that I value the swallows more than I do the sparrows? When it comes to having them in my garden, the answer is yes. What, then, is my behavior if it is not prejudice?

What about honey bees and aphids? I value the honey bees in my garden because they pollinate the flowers to the benefit of both the plants and me and because they are pleasing to my sensibilities. Aphids, on the other hand, suck the plants' juices to the detriment of the plants and therefore of me. Here I make an *informed* judgment; is that also prejudice?

I can make this same distinction between different kinds of plants, say a snapdragon and a thistle. The snapdragon I cherish in my garden, but a thistle I pluck out as a weed. Yet, I have seen thistles that are incredibly beautiful and have a wonderful aroma, but still I do not want them in my garden, although I very much enjoy them outside of it.

And what about lilies? They come in different sizes, shapes, colors, and odors. Because some sizes, shapes, hues, and fragrances either appeal to me more than others or I think will best fit in a certain place in my garden, I select them to purchase with discernment, as I think of it, while simultaneously rejecting others, which I have also examined with similar discernment and eliminated as candidates. Am I not saying that I value some lilies more than others or that I value snapdragons over thistles, that thistles are fine in their place, but that place is not in my garden? Can it be said that I am prejudiced against thistles and those lilies I reject as unsuitable for my garden?

With respect to vegetables, there are not only personal differences and standards in preference but also national differences. Most people in the United States select vegetables based largely on how appealing and flawless they are visually, whereas I have the impression that Europeans select vegetables based on succulence and flavor while being much less choosy about their appearance.

If I am prejudiced toward a plant, can the plant feel it? After more than 25 years as a research scientist, I have had it drummed into my head by numerous colleagues that plants have no feelings as we think of them, and surely cannot feel prejudice. Are scientists so sure that plants don't feel because they are silent and stationary—nondemonstrative? Although I do not have an answer from a scientific perspective, as I sit in my garden surrounded by plants, I cannot help but intuit that they sense how I feel about them. How can it be otherwise, I wonder, when the plants—all of them, even weeds—and I are in a mutual relationship within the confines of my garden?

Even some principles of physics say that I alter a plant's or rock's relationship to its environment by observing it. Of course, observation is a transference of energy between me and what I observe. Obviously that energy alters the plant's or rock's relationship to its environment because that environment must now include me. So it is that the energy of my garden is different when I am in it than when I am not.

Although this may not seem like an important point to you, it calls forth a critical question for me: Just because I can neither see a plant in my garden move of its own volition nor hear it in a communicative sense, does that mean that it is unaware of my feelings toward it, feelings that are embodied in the energy of my attitude, which I send toward it with my thoughts? While there may seem to be no obvious answer when it comes to plants, is there a clearer answer to this question if I pose it about the animals in my garden?

Does a slug in my garden eating my lettuce plant feel the intensity of my stare as I aim a pair of sharp scissors at its head with the firm intent to kill it? Would the slug feel differently if it were eating someone else's lettuce when I looked at it because I would be indifferent to what it was doing? Although slugs move so slowly that it is often difficult to tell what they are about to do, there are definitely times when I see a pillbug beginning to move away from my approaching fingers, with which I intend to squash it, long before I actually touch it. Is that chance or is the pillbug feeling my intent to kill it? I do not know.

But what I am certain of is the often extreme prejudice that we humans feel toward animals: a farmer toward mice, rats, and gophers; a sheep rancher toward coyotes; and many people toward snakes. Our prejudice toward animals is often fostered by the black-and-white contrasts we place them in. We call the male lion the king of beasts and the domestic dog a noble companion. We may love and romanticize horses and see butterflies as metaphors of personal growth and spiritual unfoldment, but we castigate rats as vermin and mosquitoes as noxious pests because in them we find no redeeming value in human terms.

We respect domestic animals that we think will serve us well, such as a particular breed of cat, dog, horse, cow, pig, or chicken, but we simultaneously reject others that do not produce enough meat or lay enough eggs. I remember ranchers with this kind of attitude for whom I worked many years ago.

If they did not like this dog or that or thought there were too many cats, they summarily killed those to which they objected without visible emotion or remorse. If they had a particular horse that had served them well for twenty years but now was too old to do the work required of them, they simply sold the faithful old horse for a few dollars to a glue factory, again without visible emotion or remorse. Their wives and children got upset, but the men simply shot or sold big animals they thought of as useless and put baby animals into a gunnysack with a rock large enough to weigh it down, threw it into the river flowing through the ranches, and let them drown.

Can animals feel this kind of prejudice? If they can feel love and act out of a clear sense of loyalty toward a particular person, how can they not feel the negative energy of prejudice? I intuitively feel they can.

I say this because I used to hunt, and I learned early on that if I looked too intently at a deer or elk with killing on my mind, even though it was initially unaware of my presence, it would suddenly know something was wrong, become nervous, stare intently in my direction, and leave. I tested this transference of focused energy again and again, always with the same result. Years later, I found that Ralph Waldo Emerson had succinctly captured this same phenomenon when he wrote: "Your attitude thunders so loudly I can't hear what you say." Nevertheless, I find that some people seem more or less oblivious to the transference of potentially prejudicial energy.

A neighbor came into my garden the other day and remarked how peaceful it felt to be there. This comment took me aback because my garden had literally been a killing field that morning as I squashed pill-bugs and sowbugs, cut slugs in two, fed caterpillars to the goldfish, and pulled up weeds.

Although I could not conceive of my garden as "peaceful" that morning, it made me wonder if I had achieved, in some measure at least, the ability to garden without prejudice, despite the fact, as I will discuss later, that I have no choice but to kill if I am to live. If, however, I have not found a measure of equanimity in gardening, then the question becomes one of just how far we have separated ourselves not only from our own feelings but also those of the world of Nature outside of ourselves. Just how blatant, I wondered that morning, must prejudice be before we humans feel it?

Although, once again, I have no answer, according to Professor Knud S. Larsen of Oregon State University,[12] the strongest and most common attribute among people who are prejudiced toward others is "authoritarianism."

"These people," says Larsen, "are generally submissive to authority, preoccupied with status, preoccupied with conventional middle-class values, and they persistently denigrate minorities. They make their way through society by conforming, and they have a very jaundiced eye toward those who do not conform."

Racism and other forms of prejudice increase, says Larsen, during times of stress, such as economic strife in society. Although some social psychologists refer to this phenomenon as the frustration-aggression hypothesis, it is more commonly thought of as "scapegoating."

Scapegoating is an ancient and convenient way of venting anger without accepting personal responsibility for one's own behavior and without facing the real problem.

... and Aaron shall lay both his hands upon the head of a live goat, and confess over him all the iniquities of the people of Israel, and all their transgressions, and all their sins; and he shall put them upon the head of the goat, and send him away into the wilderness... The goat shall bear all their iniquities upon him to a solitary land...[13]

Rather than dealing with the trials and tribulations of our often-frustrating society with its complex and demanding participatory form of democratic government and our competitive capitalistic system of economics, some people target and blame minorities, which they perceive as being somehow dangerously different from themselves. But where does our prejudice come from?

Outwardly it comes from our parents, who got it from their parents, who got it from their parents, and so on. But where did our parents and our parents' parents get it? What caused the original fear, which became the prejudice passed forward initially from parent to child that became an ongoing cycle? I do not know, but I feel certain that fear, which has its foundation in ignorance, is the root of prejudice.

Fear is the expectation of a disaster. It is false evidence appearing real, which comes into being when people take a past event, which may have happened only seconds ago, or 20 years ago, or that even happened to someone else, and project it into their own future and then become afraid it will either happen to them, or, if it happened once, that it will happen again.

Fear is the reason why insurance companies make so much money. We play into their hands by attempting to make our lives "circumstance-proof." Each time we buy insurance of any kind, we are betting that something bad is going to happen to us in the future, and the insurance company is betting that it will not!

People who are afraid of the future, which is all we can be afraid of, create fear then feed it. When enough people join one person's fear, mass hysteria evolves. In fact, the United States is a web of fear, because the nation with the greatest fear is the one with the greatest military and the greatest "defense" budget—us! Yet, there neither is, nor can there ever be, such a thing as a defensive weapon. One can only attack with a physical weapon of any kind and rationalize it as defense.

There is only one defense against fear and that is fearlessness in the form of peaceful acceptance of the other person's fear. Such defenselessness demands great strength, not of the arms and the body but of the heart and the soul. When such strength is combined with gentleness, they become one and the same.

Mahatma Gandhi made two important points with respect to the cycle of fear and violence: he observed that we must humiliate one another to control one another, and in the process of trading violence for violence—an eye for an eye—we end up making the whole world blind.

Violence of any kind is psychological sabotage and psychic murder and can never be justified as a corrective for violence. Violence does not have to be overt or physical, as author Robert Lewis Stevens observed: "The cruelest lies are often told in silence." It is not only a lie that can be consciously aimed at a person in silence but also an attitude.

I have a friend, a research scientist from northern China, who worked in the same building with me some years ago. Being Chinese, he encountered a degree of prejudice not only from the people in my hometown but also from other scientists. Although we talked about it openly, it was not until we were on our way to a restaurant to eat that I really understood what he was going through.

Sitting alongside Wang, I looked at the face of a friend whom I love very much. As I gazed at him, thinking myself fortunate indeed to have such a friend, I experienced a sudden insight into what it was like to be in Wang's shoes. I had the distinct feeling of changing places with him and of trying to understand why people hated me because my skin was thought of as yellowish brown and my eyes were slanted, neither of which were my fault.

I felt sick and ashamed for being who I was without understanding why I should feel that way. I looked into the eyes of other people and saw and felt their loathing, their shrinking, as though I was lesser than they were. What had I done that I might be able to undo and thus be acceptable to them? How desperately I wanted to be accepted as okay, just okay in my own right. In that instant, I understood, and the whole of my heart went out to Wang. What a burden fear places on us and in us!

Violence in itself is perpetrated solely from a position of fear, and in the long run, can never win over the principle of nonviolence, something Great Britain had a difficult time learning in India. While India was under Gandhi's leadership, it was apparent that if the British were not violent they would lose, and if they were violent they would lose anyway.

Because Gandhi not only understood this about the British but also used it potently against them, his most important contribution to posterity may ultimately turn out to be the psychological truth he demonstrated. He helped us to understand our potential for personal growth by separating prejudice from principle and adhering to the latter while discarding the former. Above all, he gave us a new vision of humanity, a vision of peace as the law of our species. He lived his life to prove peace was possible and in so doing demonstrated our human capacity for fundamental change and our ability to overcome fear by living in the present moment, admonishing his followers that if they would take care of today, God would take care of tomorrow.

The irony of all the hatred, prejudice, and violence is that, whether we realize it or not, whether we admit it or not, we need one another to know that we exist and have value. We, like the large old trees of an ancient forest, are bound together by an invisible commonality, a basic need to share. Consider: each grandparent tree signifies primeval majesty, but only together do they represent an ancient forest. Yet we do not even see the forest for the trees.

If we could see below ground, we would find gossamer threads of a special kind of fungus stretching for billions of miles through the soil. These fungi grow as symbionts on and in the feeder roots of the ancient trees. They acquire both food in the form of plant sugars through the roots of the ancient trees and in turn provide nutrients, vitamins, and water from the soil to the trees and produce growth regulators that benefit the trees. These symbiotic fungus-root structures, called mycorrhizae, are the termini of the threads that form a complex fungal net under the entire ancient forest and, as evidence suggests, connect all trees one to another.

In this way, the ancient forest reflects what physicist David Bohm calls the "implicate state" as compared with the "explicate state." The trees of the forest that you see above ground as separate, albeit related beings, represent the explicate state. But if you could see below ground, you would see a network in which everything is connected. Now, instead of judging things above ground only according to their superficial appearance, you can see things from the "backstage of the universe," as Sufi teacher Pir Vilayat Inayat Khan puts it. The trees are all different expressions of the one network that David Bohm calls the "implicate order."

Bohm says that the world is unfolding as discrete entities, such as the trees of the ancient forest. This is the explicate perspective that we can understand because our perception of the Universe is fragmented into categories or concrete entities. If, on the other hand, you watch the waves in an ocean, you will find they have no boundaries and thus form what is called an interference pattern as they compose together and intersperse in their flow and ebb. This is the implicate perspective of infinite relationships that flow perfectly one into another and are endlessly changing; this is the perspective that we see inwardly with our intuition or insight but not outwardly in the material with our bodily eyes.

If you turn inward, says Pir Vilayat Inayat Khan, you will find everything flowing into everything else, and you will be able to see the context as well as the apparent fragmentation of the whole into discrete elements. Everything that we superficially discern as discrete entities is interfused with everything else. The consequence is that you can see the context of the whole in the pieces and the pieces in the whole. In this way, what we experience as discrete entities at the surface of life is interfused with everything else in the depths beyond our physical sight.

The depths beyond our physical sight constitute the implicate state of the Universe, which is the fundamental state from which the explicate state is derived. Because the implicate state is almost beyond our comprehension, we are more comfortable with the material perspective in which we see everything as discrete, concrete objects.

Like the ancient trees, we are separate individuals, and like the ancient forest united by its belowground fungi, we are united by our invisible humanity—our common need for love, trust, respect, and unconditional acceptance of one another. As I look around the world, I see many wondrous people in a great variety of sizes, shapes, and colors, each of whom seems somehow separate from the rest but is nevertheless simultaneously united through the invisible bonds of human spirituality, bonds often expressed in relationships as conscious sharing.

We must, I think, share our experiences and feelings with at least one other person to express our connections with one another and to find value in life. This need to share echoes for me the words of Johann W. von Goethe: "The world is so empty if one thinks only of mountains, rivers, and cities; but to know someone here and there who thinks and feels with us, and who, though distant, is close to us in spirit, this makes the earth for us an inhabited garden."

So it is, when all is said and done, we need one another because, growing out of the varied soils of culture, we are united by the hidden threads of our common human needs. If, therefore, through prejudice, we lose sight of and touch with one another as human beings, we will find a diminishing value in life, and our common bonds will progressively erode into ever-increasing fear and separateness, which is like taking part in a circular firing squad.

Speaking for myself, I do not want to take part in such a firing squad of prejudice, and I know there is an alternative to such behavior. It is tolerance. In a tolerant society, spirituality is possible; in a spiritual society, tolerance is possible.

Tolerance is a lesson I struggle with every day I work in my garden, where I must confront the slugs eating my lettuce and beans; the tiny green caterpillars working diligently to defoliate my pear tree; the larval leafhoppers sucking the juice from my flowers, making them curl into deformed shapes; and the weevils eating notches into my lilies, roses, rhododendrons, weeping cherry tree, and anything else that satisfies their voracious appetite.

But most of all, it is here, in the privacy of my garden, that I confront myself as I encounter the creatures and fungi that want my plants for their own purposes—all of which are the antithesis to my own desires. And it is in confronting myself—examining the mirror of my motives and attitudes—with each act of gardening that I am able consciously and purposefully to convert prejudice into discernment.

Discernment, in turn, is an attitude of differentiation and acceptance of the intrinsic value of this creature or that, this fungus or that, even as they in their collective living thwart the visual perfection I have chosen for my garden. Discernment and acceptance, when borne with emotional equanimity, are the foundations of tolerance, which, mastered bit by bit within the confines of my garden, I extend increasingly beyond it boundaries, where it is my hope that by thought and deed I can help to cast a brighter reflection in society's mirror, which today is darker than it need be.

Exercise In Conscious Awareness

I remember once when I was much younger making a statement to the effect that I hated starlings because they were so aggressive they "outcompeted" native birds for nesting sites, whereupon my mentor looked at me and asked: "Did you ever consider how wonderfully adaptable the starling is? After all, they did not ask to be brought to the United States, but once here, they made the best of it."

Now I pass my mentor's question on to you. Did you ever consider what ecological function a slug, a snail, pillbug, weevil, or weed fulfills in the cycling of nutrients that over time helps to create and maintain the health of the soil in your garden? Before you kill another animal "pest" or pull another "weed," study it. Find out what it does, what its ecological function is. Read about it; ask an expert about it; observe it in your garden as objectively as possible. This is not to say that control of some organisms is not necessary in your garden; it is only meant to take the prejudice out of the act of controlling them and to leave awareness and compassion in its place.

I suggest this because it has been my experience in ecological research that every organism I ever studied benefited the ecosystem in some way, although I did not understand how until I unraveled the mystery. Nevertheless, I have inevitably changed my mind about how I saw this organism or that in relationship to the whole as I began to understand its function, its necessary role in the scheme of interdependent relationships. And my turn of mind has always been toward a more favorable view, one that is less prejudiced by ignorant judgment.

THE ENVIRONMENT IS OUR SOCIAL MIRROR

It seems to be a trait of Western industrialized society that if two people perceive value in the same thing, which they also perceive to be in limited supply, they will compete to possess it even if such competition destroys the very thing they value and with it the environment for every other living thing, present and future. To heal our sickened, degraded environment, we must first consciously heal ourselves and our society. The health and peace of each person reflects into society, and society in like measure is made whole.

I was indoctrinated in science with the notion that competition is necessary in Nature if this individual or that, if this species or that, is to survive. Much later, when I began learning to garden, I also began to question and reevaluate the whole concept of competition.

I began to question and reevaluate the idea of competition because if I allow my garden to lie fallow, to follow its own dictates as it were, I would likely find a changing, but not as complicated, progression of plants over time, much as I do in a forest. This progression is called "autogenic succession," which means self-induced progression or change.

There is no direct competition in autogenic succession. Rather each group of plants changes its habitat enough that it actually eliminates itself. Consider a forest that has burned. The first plants to come in are grasses and herbs, which begin in some way to change the soil just by living there. Given time, they change the soil enough so that their offspring may germinate but do not survive, which leaves open spaces for the next group of plants to come in, the shrubs.

The shrubs do the same thing that the grasses and herbs did; namely, they gradually change the soil as they live in it. At some point, their offspring cannot survive either. Thus, while the parent shrubs continue to live, the failure of their offspring to survive leaves open spaces for trees to move in.

There is no competition—as I learned the concept—in this whole process. Instead, one group of plants lives out its time in a given area and changes its habitat in the process. It cannot do anything else. Nothing can live without somehow changing the habitat within which it lives. This is equally true in my garden and in human society.

The whole concept of autogenic succession is changed, however, when we introduce the human discipline of forestry, which is really no more than trying to manage timber as a commodity. As soon as the idea of a commodity is introduced into a forest, people who stand to gain financially perceive any plant or animal or group of plants or animals that appears to get in the way of producing pure cultures of the chosen commodity as fast as possible to be somehow in competition with them. This is not a real competition between thistles and trees but rather a perceived competition between thistles and people.

Thistles are there because it is their time to be there, and space is available. But thistles are thought of as weeds by the people who see value only in trees, and hence plant trees on a site before it is the time for trees. In other words, people plant trees when it is the thistle's time and then accuse the thistle of competing with the trees. In reality, however, the people are competing with the thistle, whereas the thistle is not competing with either the trees or the people.

The same scenario is true in my garden. It is I who compete with those plants I deem weeds, not the weeds that compete with me. I am competing with the weeds for the space they take up in their growing because it is the space in which I want to grow the vegetables, flowers, and fruits of my choice. Be that as it may, the weeds are just doing what plants do—living as best they can.

In this sense, a rodeo is not unlike my garden. The animals, which are forced to take part in a rodeo, are not in competition with either one another or the people. In fact, the animals would most likely prefer not even to be there. But they have no voice in the matter even though they suffer great abuse by unconscious humans. The people, on the other hand, are in competition with both the animals and one another.

Competition between and among people is different from that in either my garden or a forest. Athletic competition, such as a rodeo, has a purposefully limited prize for which to compete. Although there are elaborate rules of human conduct that must be agreed to for the protection and dignity of humans before one is allowed to compete in an athletic event, in the case of a rodeo, the rules of human conduct expressly direct and encourage the abuse of the animals, the reward for which is money.

Unlike athletics in which one knows the rules and must agree to them before the game is played, there appear to be few rules governing competition in life itself, and those that do exist are often ignored. In our Western industrialized society, for example, it is assumed that competition is not only good for everyone, but also necessary for personal achievement and economic health. The former is equated with being superior to someone else, and the latter is equated with continual linear economic growth in which the strong, the ruthless, and the wealthy have the best chance of survival. Entire societies are run by the same set of standards only on a larger scale, hence the drive behind empire building.

Because our sense of personal and social survival is linked to economic gain, competition in Western society is geared almost exclusively around the amount of money we can each garner unto ourselves. Competition between and among people is thus born out of a perceived threat to a person's "right of survival," however that is defined. In turn, the perceived security of our right to survive is weighed against the number of choices we think are available to us as individuals and our ability to control those choices—the more money we have, the more choices we have, the more control and social power we have.

Perceived choices are ultimately affected by the real supply and demand for natural resources, the source of energy required by all life in one form or another. The greater the supply of a particular resource, the greater the freedom of choice an individual has with respect to that resource. Conversely, the smaller the supply, the narrower the range of choices unless, of course, we steal choices from other people to augment our own. And scarcity, real or perceived, is the breeding ground for competition and environmental and social injustice, both of which come clearly into focus each time someone steals from another rather than taking responsibility for his or her own behavior by sharing equally.

Consider here an example from my garden. When I have an abundance of vegetables and/or flowers, I willingly share rather generously some of each with those wee creatures that like to consume them. As my lettuce, Swiss chard, and snapdragons wane, however, I become progressively less generous with those same creatures.

On the other hand, while I daily examine and remove the eggs and larvae of the cabbage butterfly from my broccoli in spring, summer, and autumn, I am more generous in sharing my kale late in the season with these same larvae because I know that frost will soon come and kill them before they can do too much damage. Of course, I could always choose to augment my supply of broccoli from somewhere else, and in the process become more lax in controlling the larvae of the cabbage butterfly on the broccoli, as well as the kale. Thus, even my generosity or competitiveness in my own garden is based on my sense of abundance and array of choices or on my sense of scarcity and loss of control.

The variety of available choices dictates the amount of control I feel I have. This consequently affects my sense of security about my survival. What happens when I perceive my array of choices as fading or when they have been suddenly ripped away? Have you ever been told that you can no longer do something you have always done and therefore have taken the doing of it for granted? How did you feel? Was it just?

How would you feel if you were suddenly plucked from whatever you are doing without warning and for no apparent reason, thrown into prison without explanation or recourse, and held indefinitely against your will? Are such innocent people behind bars now? The answer is yes!

How would you feel if you were jerked out of the only life you know, smuggled into an alien country, and sold into the bonds of slavery, never again to see anyone or anything you knew or to enjoy the rights you once had as a citizen the United States? This is not a far-fetched scenario; slavery in its various facets and guises is very much alive in the world today!

How would you feel, as an average citizen with no political desires, if civil war suddenly erupted all around you, and you had nowhere to go while your family, home, and town were being blown apart? I had a small but terrifying taste of this powerless, helpless feeling when held at gunpoint on more than one occasion in Egypt while the country was under the fist of Nasser's dictatorial reign.

I ask these questions in the hope that you can imagine how you would feel deep inside if you were to suddenly lose your sense of safety and well-being—your sense of choice. I ask because I am convinced that destructive competition arises from a deep, albeit usually unconscious, sense of potential loss. This sense of loss may either be a chronic or acute fear of the future based on a disaster mentality. "Fear," American singer Marian Anderson once said, "is a disease that eats away at logic and makes man inhuman." It is not surprising, therefore, that Fear of potential loss is also behind the notion: if I don't get my share of it now, whatever it is, someone else will.

A refrain from a song popular some years ago, "freedom's just another word for nothing left to lose," speaks in a peculiar way to the "I want my share now" mentality as an apparent human truth. When I am unconscious of a material value, I am free of its psychological grip. But the instant I perceive a material value and anticipate possible material gain, I also perceive the contrary psychological pain of potential loss.

There is in the course of life, however, at least for gardeners, a time when the psychological pain of potential loss, hence the perceived need to compete, diminishes or disappears altogether as they approach their journey into the Great Mystery. As I move beyond sixty years of age, for example, I can foresee a time when I may no longer want to, or even physically can, take care of my garden as I now do. With relinquishment of the desire or the possibility of gardening, my perceived need to compete with the creatures that eat my vegetables and/or flowers will progressively diminish until it no longer exists, for this will be my time of letting go as I prepare for my own journey into that which lies beyond.

But outside my garden, the story is different, particularly for those who are still young in years. Here, the larger and more immediate the prospects for material gain, the greater the political power used to ensure and expedite exploitation, because not to exploit is perceived as losing an opportunity to someone else. And it is this notion of loss that many people fight so hard to avoid. In this sense, it is more appropriate to think of resources as managing humans rather than the reverse.

Historically, any newly identified, potentially valuable resource is inevitably overexploited, often to the point of collapse or extinction. The mentality of overexploitation is based, first, on the perceived rights or entitlement of the discoverer-exploiter to get his or her share before someone else does; second, on the right or entitlement to protect his or her economic investment; and third, on the initial impression that the supply is vast, an impression people are loath to reevaluate or change.

There is more to it than this, however, because the concept of a healthy capitalistic system is one that is *ever-growing, ever-expanding*, but such a system is neither biologically nor socially sustainable. With renewable natural resources, such nonsustainable exploitation has a "ratchet effect," where ratchet means to constantly, albeit unevenly, increase the rate of exploitation of a resource.

The ratchet effect works as follows: During periods of relative economic stability, the rate of harvest of a given renewable resource, say timber, salmon, grass for livestock, or dollars from tourism, tends to stabilize at a level that economic theory predicts can be sustained through some scale of time. Such levels, however, are almost always excessive, because economists take existing unknown and unpredictable ecological variables and convert them, in theory at least, into known and predictable economic constants in order to better calculate the expected return on a given investment from a sustained harvest, and then either forget or ignore the real scale of time.

Then comes a sequence of good years in the market, or in the availability of the resource, or both, and additional capital investments are encouraged in harvesting and processing because competitive economic growth is not only the root of capitalism but also tantamount to our sense of social security. When conditions return to normal or even below normal, however, industry, having overinvested, appeals to the government for help because substantial economic capital, and ostensibly jobs, are often at stake. The government typically responds with direct or indirect subsidies, which only encourages continual overharvesting and the mentality that breeds it.

The ratchet effect is thus caused by unrestrained economic investment to increase short-term yields in good times and strong opposition to losing those yields in less favorable times. This opposition to losing yields means there is great resistance to using a resource in a biologically sustainable manner because there is no predictability in yields and no guarantee of yield increases in the foreseeable future. In addition, our linear economic models of ever-increasing yield are built on the assumption that we can, in fact, have an economically sustained yield. But, this contrived concept fails in the face of the *biological sustainability* of a yield.

Then, because there is no mechanism in our linear economic models of ever-increasing yield that allows for the uncertainties of ecological cycles and variability or for the inevitable decreases in yield during adverse times, the long-term outcome is a heavily subsidized industry. Such an industry continually over-harvests the resource on an artificially created, sustained-yield basis that is not biologically sustainable.

When the notion of sustainability arises in relationship to economic competition, the parties marshal all scientific data favorable to their respective sides as "good" science and discount all unfavorable data as "bad" science, despite whatever the truth might be. In this way, competition for economic gain is the stage on which science is politicized, largely obfuscating its service to society.

Because the availability of choices dictates the amount of control we feel we have with respect to our sense of security, a potential loss of money is the breeding ground for both destructive competition and environmental injustice of intergenerational proportions. This is the kind of environmental injustice in which the present generation steals from all future generations by overexploiting a resource rather than giving up potential income, even for the sake of sustainability.

There are crucial lessons in all of this for today's society. First, history undeniably suggests that a biologically sustainable use of any resource has never been achieved without first overexploiting it, despite historical warnings and contemporary data. If history is correct, resource problems are not environmental problems but human ones that over the centuries we have created many times, in many places, under a wide variety of social, political, and economic systems.

Second, I believe that the seed of destructive economic competition is a perceived loss of choice about our own individual destinies, which we interpret as a threat to our personal survival. In this sense, the landscapes wherein we compete for the resources that we convert into economic commodities are the fields of battle in which the competitive wars are fought.

If you doubt this, look closely at the rapidly decreasing biological sustainability of the world's forests and grasslands over which human-created deserts are rapidly marching. Take inventory of the world's species approaching extinction and understand that we not only are the cause of their declines and/or extinctions, but also may join them if we do not change our competitive thinking and behavior toward one another and Nature.

Third, the fundamental issues involving resources, the environment, and people are complex and process-driven. The integrated knowledge of multiple disciplines is required to understand them. These underlying complexities of the physical and biological systems preclude a simplistic approach to what we euphemistically call "management." In addition, the wide natural variability and the compounding cumulative influence of continual human activity mask the results of overexploitation until the effects are severe and often irreversible.

Fourth, as long as the uncertainty of continual change is considered a condition to be avoided, nothing will be resolved. But once the uncertainty of change is accepted as an inevitable, open-ended, creative life process, most decision-making is simply common sense. For example, common sense dictates that a person striving to be sustainable in any endeavor favors actions having the greatest potential for reversibility, as opposed to those with little or none. Such reversibility can be ascertained by monitoring results and modifying actions and policy accordingly, which is precisely what I do in my garden.

Because I have this capability, I can move toward a biologically sustainable garden and so can others. This gives me hope.

Just as my garden is the mirror of my personal inner harmony, so the greater environment is the mirror of our social harmony—or the lack thereof, which reflects how we treat ourselves and one another. If we continue our insatiable competition to control one another and the economics of exploiting the world's natural resources, we will surely destroy the biosphere that produces the resources and ourselves in the process.

Of this notion, Wendell Berry makes the following comment: "There is an uncanny resemblance between our behavior toward each other and our behavior toward the earth. By some connection we do not recognize, the willingness to exploit one becomes the willingness to destroy the other."

If, therefore, we can grow beyond our fear of one another as competitors, and we can learn to cooperate and coordinate with one another in sharing equally and prudently the world's resources, then our growing

113

sense of mutual love and trust shall heal our environment and cast a different reflection in the mirror—a reflection of harmony, peace, and sufficiency. I am firmly convinced that this *is* possible because I have an unbreakable faith in the basic goodness of people, and that makes all the difference. In addition, I believe the state of our emotional and spiritual health as individuals is mirrored in how we treat ourselves and one another, which translates directly into the care we take of our environment as the legacy we pass to our children, their children, and beyond.

Exercise In Conscious Awareness

What is the mirror saying? Observe your garden right now, just as it is. What is it saying about your care, or lack thereof? Is it lovingly tended? Do you give it quality time, keep it orderly and harmonious? Is it thriving and happy? Or is it overgrown, disheveled, anemic, sickly, chaotic, unloved, neglected? Take a good hard look at what this reflects about you and your values. As Gandhi remarked that his life was his message, so the quality of the care you take of your garden is your message.

To understand the notion that the environment is our social mirror, consider how you feel the next several times you enter your garden to work therein. If you are at peace with yourself, how does your work flow? If you are in any way agitated, how does your work progress? You can also carry this conscious self-examination into your workplace or any area of your life, and ask yourself the same questions.

You will find, I think, that to the extent you are in harmony with yourself, you are correspondingly patient and peaceful in how you treat your garden and your work, perhaps with a feeling of great joy. To the extent you are out of harmony with yourself, however, you are correspondingly impatient and easily frustrated and may treat your garden and your work as though it was an aggressor and to blame for your emotional state. Your garden will faithfully reflect whichever way you are for that is how you will treat it and how it will respond.

If you now add millions of people all acting out the variety of emotions you possess, can you see what would happen if they all took their feelings out simultaneously on one another and their environment, which is exactly what happens every day? True, some people are at peace with themselves and treat the world accordingly, but they are decidedly a minority.

Then consider the many people who were in some way, say physically, emotionally, or sexually abused as children. Of these, some may feel such rage over the abuse that they translate their hostility into misdirected vandalism of a historic building or a state park.

In the corporate world, it might be a man who was an abandoned orphan who now becomes owner of a timber company and feels so insecure that he can never make enough money to assuage the sense of impending doom due to personal loss. He thus overcuts the forest despite the fact that such a choice and action costs the jobs of faithful employees because the timber runs out prematurely.

Although the list of possible scenarios is endless, I believe the point is clear, which brings us to the gate of personal consciousness.

115

Chapter 4

THE GATE OF PERSONAL CONSCIOUSNESS

HAVING NOW BEEN INSIDE my garden through the gates of Ecological Consciousness and Social Consciousness, it is time to enter the third gate—Personal Consciousness, which is your awareness of yourself in relation to the world. Before you enter, let me reiterate that one gate is equal to another in value because they are complementary, in that each gate reflects a different part of ourselves. This means that, depending on our orientation in life, one gate may be more familiar than another but not better than another.

Because those who enter my garden through the gate of Personal Consciousness are often struggling with their fears and concomitantly their self-centeredness, it is imperative that they see as well the goodness and creative power sleeping within them as they strive to accept the other-centered responsibilities of psychological maturity and adulthood. Having said this, I am obligated to forewarn you of the three challenges you will face on entering the garden through the gate of Personal Consciousness.

The first challenge concerns the immaturity of self-centeredness and greed, which an aging boxer, cut and bruised from having just fought his last match, captures eloquently as he turns to the audience and says: "I came into this world a babe with my fists clenched wanting everything. I leave this world a man with my hands open wanting nothing." In this spirit, Dr. Tichenor, part of the Volunteers In Medicine, lives by the principle that a living is made by what one gets, and a life is made by what one gives.

The second challenge is the impatience of youth, exemplified by a teenaged boy in a hurry who bumps into and knocks down an old man, saying: "Get out of my way, old man."

The old man, upon rising from the ground, regards the youth (who has paused momentarily in emphasis of his words), and replies: "Son, as you now are, so I once was. As I now am, so you shall one day be."

The third challenge is the legacy we leave our children and our children's children through the decisions we make daily. "For these are all our children," says James Baldwin, and "we will all profit by, or pay for, whatever they become."

The challenge of our personal legacy is encompassed in a question that was once posed to the psychiatrist Carl Jung. When asked if there was any hope for the world, Jung replied that it depended on how many people were willing to do their inner work. In other words, to heal the world we must first heal ourselves. This is but saying that the world is healed in the collective sense to the degree that we each individually heal ourselves.

In the sense that we collectively are each an integral part of society, society is a multifaceted mirror-image of ourselves. To change the image, if it is unpleasant to us, we must change ourselves. As we do so, we will find the reflection cast in our direction to be whatever we have chosen to become because this is the gate of personal choice and future consequences—the gate that leads to self-knowledge.

As such, this chapter has been exceedingly difficult to write not only because the issues are both clearly personal in an emotional sense and simultaneously elusive in language, but also because I must be openly honest with myself if I am to come even close to saying what I mean in a language fraught with limitations to the expression of feelings. Because this chapter has been an unmitigated challenge for me to commit to paper, I realize that it may be equally hard for you to read. Should that be the case, I ask your forbearance.

SELF-KNOWLEDGE IS A LIFETIME OF DISCOVERY

Inner struggle is the key to self-knowledge. Self-knowledge is the key to self-mastery. Self-mastery is the key to self-truth. Self-truth is the key to freedom.

Even though I do my best to plant the flowers and shrubs of my garden in places suitable for them, I sometimes misread their requirements for the amount of necessary sunlight. When this happens, I witness their struggle to survive, despite the planting instructions from the nursery. In addition, the whole unseen dimension of the soil and its health comes into play as a vital determinant of the outcome.

At times, I understand what a plant is telling me, and I move it to a more appropriate place, where it ceases to struggle and thrives. At other times, it struggles valiantly, but dies no matter what I do. Gardening is thus an open-ended experiment of life in which it is my privilege to participate, for not only do I learn about my garden and its occupants but also about the inner labyrinth of myself.

Like the plants in my garden, we humans also experience situations that cause us to struggle, often on a seemingly interminable basis. For us, however, struggle can be thought of as resistance to that which is perceived as "reality." As such, struggle, be it with a severe illness, the death of a loved one, or the loss of our job serves to focus our attention, to rivet our concentration on the circumstance with which we wrestle until it is resolved or transcended by acceptance of what is.

Dr. Carl Jung has written in this connection that "the most important problems of life are all fundamentally insoluble." His premise is that they can only be outgrown or transcended, which happens by accepting the problem and opportunity it offers for personal growth and development through inner struggle.

Circumstance is the doorway to experience; inner struggle is the key with which the door to self-knowledge is unlocked. And the key, as noted by James Allen, is turned by thought: "Act is the blossom of thought, and joy and suffering are its fruits; thus does a man garner in the sweet and bitter fruitage of his own husbandry."

We grow and change the most when we are out of our comfort zone. The result of being out of our comfort zone, even a little, is to gain a measure of freedom by expanding our comfort zone, by learning that we can survive our discomfort and thereby make the unknown (the cause of our discomfort) a known with which we can cope.

When Zane and I were first married, for example, she would become frustrated with new endeavors much more easily than she does now. In those early days of our relationship, I would ease her struggles by saying, "Here, Babe, let me do that for you," which was counter to the Dalai Lama's admonishment that we each learn the most from difficulty. Because, it is through difficulty that a person is helped to come into the strength and inner power of his or her own personality.

At first I thought rescuing Zane was an act of love, because what was difficult for her was often easy for me. Then one day it occurred to me that, by pulling Zane out of her struggle prematurely under the guise of "love," I was actually stealing one of her most precious gifts from life—her experience. What I was doing wasn't love at all but self-centeredness. I was unaware of my self-centeredness, however, because, to quote Henry David Thoreau: "It is as difficult for a man to see himself as it is for him to look behind himself without turning around."

What was difficult for Zane was easy for me only because I had already succeeded in my struggle to learn; I had already earned the necessary experience, and hence the knowledge, of how to proceed and the freedom of doing so. I was, however, uncomfortable watching her struggle, and I was unconsciously uncomfortable with my own struggle over her discomfort, so by focusing on her struggle and "fixing" it, I didn't have to attend to my own. But to quell or alleviate my own discomfort, I stole from her the value of her struggle, her key to experience, her measure of the freedom, which I already enjoyed.

By stealing Zane's struggle, I was largely responsible for her remaining stuck, because I kept her a prisoner of her fear. This was not only a great disservice but also an unconscious act of violence, because I had put myself in control of her behavior and maintained her in a perpetual state of humiliation until I learned to dignify her struggle by not interfering with it.

To grow and change, we must begin to appreciate inner struggle as an ally of the heart, as part of a process to be embraced even as we embrace life itself. Struggle, after all, is but an aspect of life and the freedom to live it. Pain goes hand in hand with struggle, and pain offers a gift with its own high purpose. An anonymous author wrote that, "The person who risks nothing, does nothing, has nothing, is nothing, and becomes nothing. He may avoid suffering and sorrow, but he simply cannot learn and feel and change and grow and love and live. He's forfeited his freedom. Only the person who risks is truly free."

The greatest value of inner struggle is that it directly opens us to the experiences and the muck and mess of life, which, if we choose, translates into compassion and a true helping hand for those who struggle as we do along life's path. Einstein said that only by widening our circle of compassion will we find our way out of the violence, mistrust, and exploitation that today formulates the world's curriculum. In her autobiography, Elisabeth Kybler-Ross looks in retrospect over the strenuous terrain of her life and concludes that the greatest reward is always accompanied by helping others.

Struggle is a tool of transformation when it is embraced as a positive lesson. In this sense, we are like children climbing the endless stairs of self-mastery one step at a time. Our most intense struggles come when we are trying to climb up to the step immediately above; this is our immediate circumstance or crisis. When we finally arrive on the next step, we have a level area on which to rest awhile and to travel at an easier pace. This is our time to assimilate the experience of our struggle and to distill the newly found sense of achievement into wisdom. This is our time to gather our strength and our courage to climb up yet another step, which is identified by our next crisis or opportunity for growth, which, as Jung emphasized, cannot be achieved without pain.

All of our struggles are ultimately experience aimed at self-mastery, which is our only true freedom, as poignantly summarized again by James Allen:

> Tempest-tossed souls, wherever ye may be, under whatsoever conditions ye may live, know this—in the ocean of life the isles of Blessedness are smiling, and the sunny shore of your ideal awaits your coming. Keep your hand firmly upon the helm of thought. In the bark of your soul reclines the commanding Master; He does but sleep; wake Him. Self-control is strength; Right Thought is mastery; Calmness is power. Say unto your heart, "Peace, be still!"[14]

Self-mastery is a silent strife deep within our hearts. It is the battle in which we stand inwardly face to face with ourselves in one of the most severe tests we face along the path of self-knowledge, which leads to self-mastery and spiritual growth.

I call these inner struggles, devoid as they are of distraction and instant relief, the foxhole test because they remind me of a soldier sitting wet, hungry, cold, cramped, and terrified in a muddy hole on a moonless night. A steady rain is falling, which makes sleep impossible even if he could quell his fear of the unknown creeping about in the black night of his imagination. This man has all the time in the world to consider what might happen as he faces alone and afraid that unknown time when the enemy has no face.

There is no one to support him, no one to see his bravery as he constantly strains his eyes and his ears for some slight sign of danger, all the while choking back his terror. And there is no hero's welcome, no special recognition, no medal of honor when the war is over for this valiant soldier. There is only the private knowledge that he did his duty to the best of his ability in a strange place, under difficult circumstances, and that he alone faced his test—the terror of his imagination.

I often find working my garden to be my foxhole test, especially after returning from working overseas, where the problems I face seem so huge, so impossibly complicated and hopeless that I want to run away from them, but cannot. Thus I go into my garden and work, but find nothing in my garden to distract me from the problems I must somehow resolve. My garden becomes my foxhole, where every direction in which I turn I find myself spiritually naked and intellectually bewildered.

At such times, I ponder of the notion espoused by Italian dramatist Vittoro Alfieri: "Often the test of courage is not to die, but to live." This is the inner test no one sees, the test only I know about. This is the test of my courage to keep on keeping on when all about people are oblivious to my struggle. This is the hidden, silent test that we each experience in the solitude of our own hearts. Then, at about age fifty, I learned something Russian-French author Anne Sophie Swetchine learned over a century earlier, namely that "In youth we feel richer for every new illusion; in maturer years, for every one we lose."

At some point in those early years of gardening I began wondering, as I watched this plant or that struggling to survive amidst its neighbors, if they conversed with one another or if they were alone in their fight to survive. Even though I was trained in science and taught that plants could neither think nor feel, I cannot help but wonder what lies behind the silence of their inner strife. While I still do not know because there is no way for me to share a plant's experience of life, a troubled plant has nevertheless become for me a symbol of the foxhole test, a test of life that I know well.

Exercise In Conscious Awareness

To get a sense of what the potential possibilities of self-knowledge can be, let's turn for a moment to one of the inspired verses of the Katha Upanishad, which many centuries ago clearly defined who we really are:

When the wise realize the Self,
Formless in the midst of forms, changeless
In the midst of change, omnipresent
And supreme, they go beyond sorrow.

Throughout all time, the journey towards greater self-knowledge and spiritual unfoldment has been the quest most worthy of one's courage—to see the Self and life truly, for at journey's end is the treasure of true wealth: the inner light of self-understanding. Indeed, the first invocation the neophyte encountered as he or she passed through the curved archway into the Temples of old was, "Man [Woman] know thyself and you shall know God." In the words of Zohar, a Persian mystic, "The disciple of spiritual mysteries gazes with perfect fixedness of attention upon the face of the Real."

Self-knowledge is like self-value: the more you know as it emerges from within, the better you feel, and the better you feel, the more you know of the emergent being coming forth. Abraham Maslow once said that in our process towards self-realization we are "simultaneously worms and gods." Yet as this process unfolds, we discover dormant forces, faculties, and latent talents that are activated from within and spring to life.

As you begin to turn inwards and shift the center of gravity from outer, external measures, you discover your true being behind the masks or roles you typically enact in the dramas of your life. The Self was waiting there all the while. One of the central ideas of Sufism is that what we see in the mirror in the morning is one of the most misleading of all "feedback systems," because what we are generally observing is "secondary aspects of our being," rather than perceiving the subliminal reality of who we really are. Consequently, it is the false self we see in the mirror, which only serves to cover one's real Self. This real Self is the Cosmic face, what mystic Nicholas of Cusa called the "Face behind all faces."

Now take a few moments to relax, allowing yourself the opportunity to go as deep within as you are ready to go. Feel yourself relaxed yet poised in the sense of Greek philosopher Plotinus: "You must close the eyes and waken in yourself the other power of vision, which is the birthright of all but which few turn to use."

When you are able to awaken this "other" power of vision, you will see "the One," as Plotinus called it.

Imagination, the "other" vision, is the doorway to all creative power and that which is lovely and harmonious is an expression of your soul. From the quiet center you have created, become aware of the beautiful garden of your inner world. Move now toward the simple arched gateway as though your guide is taking your hand and leading you safely within. Feel the gentle breezes, the quiet sunlight, and observe the emerald grass all around you dotted with your favorite flowers. Within your garden are some of the loveliest shades of green you have ever beheld—healing and uplifting.

You are aware that everything growing herein is an expression of your creative imagination and the spirit of the Divine. The colors and fragrance of the flowers and trees, the music of the birds, and the play of water in the lotus pool, even the very design of your garden is a manifestation of the highest, purest, and most harmonious Divine thought.

You feel drawn now to the center of the garden, where a lake of pure, clear water reflects a cloudless blue sky and the myriad colors of the flowers and trees, a reflection that enhances the beauty of the garden. Look into the water and see the gentle movements of the shimmering fish. Hear the soft lapping of the water at your feet.

The surface of the lake is so still that even to contemplate it brings a profound peace to your soul. You have entered a place of peace, and when your soul is here, at the center of your inner garden, you lose all care and strain.

Still water of the spirit is clear as crystal. Your soul surrenders, and you are bathed in Divine peace. Take a few moments and let every cell of your being open to receive the deep peace of your soul, so that you may gain a true understanding of the meaning of peace.

Standing by the lake, a thought comes to the fore—as the garden is reflected in the still waters, so is pure truth reflected in your heart. But to reflect this truth, your heart must be tranquil and serene. As you gaze into the water, you realize you are seeing the reflection of your real Self, for the waters of the spirit never deceive. Notice how your face shines with the light of love and how your eyes see with tender compassion into the secrets of your heart. In finding out who you really are, you can begin to know the Divine and its reflection in all other faces and all life, for every living being is connected to you.

Rest quietly for awhile by the shore of your lake and contemplate your true nature as it has been shown to you. When you are ready, feel the cleansing touch of the water on your feet, hands, and face. Cup your hands and drink as much as you need and feel yourself completely refreshed and restored. You feel totally unburdened and luminescent. Be still . . . totally at peace . . . in the sunlight. All is so still. All is well.

When you are ready to leave the lake, walk back through your garden, inhaling the perfume of life, taking with you a sense of well-being. Walk through the gateway and out of your inner garden. Begin slowly and deliberately to return now from this deep internal awareness to the consciousness of your outer mind, of the chair and room about you, and your everyday world. Gently use your breath to help you "back to Earth," so to speak.

After having been in your inner garden and having experienced a state of supreme rest, peace, renewal, and boundless joy and love, at least for a few moments, you may relate easily to what a great teacher of meditation in ancient India confirmed: "Now you see yourself as you really are."

In the words of Dogen, the 13th-century founder of the Japanese Soto Zen tradition,

To study the Way is to study the self
To study the self is to forget the self.
To forget the self is to be enlightened by all things.
To be enlightened by all things is to remove the barriers
between one's self and others.

I RELATE TO LIFE THROUGH EXPERIENCES AND THEREFORE, I KNOW I EXIST

Life is experience, and experience is life, which is all the time changing.
For the discerning mind, experience is the
passport to self-knowledge.

The sun is just peeking over the eastern horizon as I walk out into my garden. The early morning warmth feels delicious as the fiery ball ascends the heavens, chasing forever eastward the retreating night. As the day warms, scents from flower and leaf play with the teasing breezes as their aromas mingle, perfuming the entire garden. Standing in my garden as the day grows around me, I am aware of the twittering of swallows as they dip and weave high above and of the buzzing of bees intently exploiting the flowers.

All these things are coming from the Universe into me, into my heart, mind, and soul. And as I experience them, so they—bird, flower, and bee, sun, fragrance, and breeze—are experiencing me. I am thus the center of the Universe for all experience comes into me and goes out of me. In this way, the world, the whole of the Cosmos, comes into my garden even as I go out of my garden into the world and the Cosmos. But what is true for me is equally true for you and for everything else, which means that the center of the Universe is everywhere and nowhere because the center of the Universe is individual experience.

Experience is the active participation in events or activities, which leads to the accumulation of knowledge. All we do in life is experience ourselves experiencing life, and each experience is our point of departure for our next experience. Life is the process of experiencing ourselves experiencing ourselves, one another, and things in the Universe around us, and things in the Universe within us. The outer Universe, the world, our nation, state, city, neighborhood, and our home are all repositories of perception, where we can experience ourselves experiencing ourselves in differing levels of inner comfort. How can it be otherwise? To cease to experience on the physical plane is to "die." Conversely, the consciousness with which we experience determines the degree to which we live.

Although the consciousness of experience as a determiner of aliveness was not new to me, when Zane and I moved back to Corvallis, Oregon, as our permanent home, I really did, as T. S. Eliot wrote, "know the place for the first time."

I grew up in Corvallis and never particularly liked it or the Willamette Valley, both of which are in western Oregon. I had always wanted to live east of the Cascade Mountains in central or eastern Oregon, in the high, dry, sunny climate. So, I finally got to northeastern Oregon and loved it. Then, after five and a half years, people in the U. S. Forest Service and the Bureau of Land Management asked me if I would move back to Corvallis and study the issue of the old-growth forest. After some agony at the thought of leaving northeastern Oregon, I agreed and moved.

That was in October 1980. On the first of June 1981, I moved my new bride, Zane, from her home in Reno, Nevada, to Corvallis, and she didn't like it very well at first. We lived in Corvallis for nine and a half years before we moved to Taos, New Mexico, and then to Las Vegas, Nevada. As my time with the U. S. Environmental Protection Agency drew to a close, I asked Zane where she would like to go, and she said, without hesitation, "back home to Corvallis."

So we moved. But this time both of us made unfettered choices to come back, and we have discovered that we are "seeing" Corvallis for the first time, not just looking at it. This time our experience of ourselves experiencing Corvallis is different from how it was before.

It is while working in my garden, however, that I now—finally—am beginning to realize just how much of the world I experience in any one place at any one moment. The other day, for example, I picked up a wooden pencil, just an ordinary wooden pencil that I had purchased in town so I could mark the lumber out of which I was going to make the last raised bed for vegetables. And as I held the pencil in my hand, sharpened it, and then drew a line on the wood I was about to cut, I saw, really saw, an ordinary wooden pencil for the first time, even though I had used them for years.

When I buy a wooden pencil, what am I getting? I am purchasing the "lead," which is really graphite formed over the eons, which someone mined somewhere in the world as a job to feed his or her family. I am purchasing the wood that grew over the centuries in a forest, which someone cut as a job to feed his or her family. I am purchasing the labor of the truck driver who transported the wood from the forest to the mill and of the mill worker who cut the wood for the pencil factory, both of whom performed their services as jobs to feed their families. I am purchasing the paint and all its ingredients and the labor, from that of the chemist in the laboratory who formulated the paint to that of the worker in the factory who applied it, both of whom performed their services as a job to feed their families. I am purchasing the metal that holds the eraser fast to the wood, which someone mined somewhere in the world as a job to feed his or her family, and I am purchasing the invention, design, machinery, packaging, labor, advertising, marketing, transportation, and my experience of the person who sold me the pencil. If my pencil cost twenty five cents, I am also experiencing the metal that was mined, the design, the labor, and the armored vehicle, which transported the money from the mint to the bank, and I am adding to the history accrued by the money before it came into my possession.

I am purchasing an item that embodies human experiences—birth, death, suffering, struggle, despair, hate, love, defeat, and victory—and stimulating commerce around the world while adding my own experience to their experiences. I have touched and in turn am touched by humanity, unbroken chains of ancestry and experiences from around the world, all stretching back into the dimly lit past, to the first human beings and before.

We can thus experience those who have gone before us by the physical evidence of what they did and how they cared for the land on which we must now live. We, in turn, leave our experience of ourselves embodied in our decisions of today, decisions that will become physical evidence for those who follow not only by what we did but also by how we cared for the land on which they must live. So, it is that I experienced the people from whom Zane and I purchased our house and yard by the care they took of the property, including the garden, and the people who will one day buy what is now our home and garden will experience us by the care we take of the property—including the garden.

"But what," you might ask, "can I as a gardener do that would positively affect how the next person will think of me when he or she borrows this property from time?" You and I and every other gardener can nurture the soil of our gardens to the greatest health possible and thereby pass forward to the next person, the next generation all we have to give: our love, our trust, our respect, and the benefit of our experience secreted in the soil. And as the soil is cleansed, so will the water passing through it be cleaned, and in like measure, so will the ditch it may enter, as well as the stream, river, estuary, and ocean.

Thus, the peoples of the past chose our experience of them, even as we are choosing the future's experience of us by the evidence we leave to mark the passage of our time. And because experience is blind in the future, we may well leave our descendants one or more crises with which to deal, even as our ancestors left us with crises, but they need not be crises in the health of the soils of our gardens, for the relative health of our garden soil is but our choice.

Exercise In Conscious Awareness

That you experience things in your garden and thus know you exist goes without saying. The way in which you experience things, however, is your choice.

For example, the more compulsively meticulous you are about the appearance of your garden, or anything else for that matter, the more you unconsciously tend to focus on and see only its flaws and imperfections and thus your own perceived shortcomings. But the more you consciously focus on the relationships of things one to another in your garden and the wonder of Nature's processes, such as seasonal changes, the more you see its wholeness and beauty through self-forgetfulness.

Test these ideas as you work in your garden. Then decide the way in which you want to experience your garden and your life. The choice is yours and yours alone, and one way or another, either consciously or unconsciously, you must and will choose.

CRISIS IS THE FACE OF A FOCUSED OPPORTUNITY

A crisis is a choice focused on perceived danger to which there is nevertheless a positive outcome if we dare to choose it. Obstacles, troubles, denial, and setbacks are our greatest teachers and guides, for it is through delays, inconveniences, and discomfort that personal growth and consciousness is promoted.

Zane had long wanted a pond in which we could have some fish. Although we had lengthy, heartfelt discussions about the location, shape, and size of the pond she envisioned, as the design of our garden began to crystallize in our imaginations it soon became apparent that her idea of a pond and mine were vastly different. Accordingly, we decided it was prudent to wait until we had the general design of our garden figured out before we again discussed the idea.

Accordingly, we examined this shape and size of flower bed and that shape and size. We placed it here, there, and yet again over yonder, only to revisit our original inspiration. We then examined different kinds of rocks, which we think of as "rock people," casting about for the size, shape, texture, and placement of those rocks that would harmonize with both our shared years of growing together in partnership and our solitary years journeying down the halls of age. When the template for the flower beds was cast in stone, the location, shape, and size of the intended pond seemed obvious to both of us and agreement was easily negotiated.

And so began my experience of constructing a pond, an experience that I thoroughly enjoyed. But as I was to learn, there is much more to creating a pond than simply digging a hole, installing a plastic liner, filling it with water, landscaping the pond and its surroundings with the appropriate plants, and adding fish—even while carefully following all of the instructions.

Within a day after the pond was filled, water boatmen and back-swimmers (both aquatic bugs) plummeted magically out of the heavens to grace the water's surface. We were thrilled!

After a couple of weeks, when the chlorine had evaporated from the water, we added condemned goldfish. I say condemned because we chose to get fish with insufficient breeding to be worthy of given names other than "feeder fish," which meant their only value was as food for fish of known pedigree and high monetary value.

We selected seven fish from a tank of about 150 in a pet shop. They were not just any fish, but rather those that "felt right," that we could imagine adding to the harmony of our "water garden." How we loved watching them cavort in freedom about the pond, swimming in and out of the rock cave and other hidden places I had created. Their lives had been spared and ours were immeasurably enriched by the joy of our shared future.

Summer passed with cattails gracing the pond as they swayed in the warm breezes. Autumn came and went, and the cattails died back to their roots, leaving the chilling winds to rattle their now-dead stalks. Then Winter arrived, and the pond froze to a depth of two or three inches. This we had not expected.

We were neither prepared emotionally for this eventuality nor for the discovery of how much we had grown to love the fish—our fish, our "fish children." What would happen to our fish? Would they survive? Then one day, to our great relief, we saw them swimming leisurely under the ice.

Spring finally came again, and the waters of the pond began to warm, and with the warmth came a tremendous bloom of algae. Although the fish had survived their first Winter, I was concerned that the rapidly growing algae, which by now had the water looking like pea soup, might make it difficult for them to breathe.

True, goldfish are carp and therefore hardy, but just how hardy I did not know. Without taking the time to ask someone who knew more than I, my ego kicked into high gear and conjured in my imagination the worst possible crisis—our fish gasping the last of their lives away as the burgeoning algae clogged their gills, causing them to suffocate. In a growing panic of a perceived crisis grown evermore real in my mind's eye, I purchased a substance that was supposed to coagulate the algae without causing any harm to aquatic plants, snails, *or fish.*

Well, the algae coagulated alright, but it was so dense that the bottom of the pond, as well as the fish, became engulfed in a greenish, gelatinous-looking mass, which frightened me. What I thought would be a simple operation turned into a real, life-threatening crisis, but a crisis of my own making.

I borrowed a pump from one of my neighbors and began pumping the water out of the pond as fast as I could even as I caught the fish and put them into buckets of clean water. While I continued in blind panic to pump the water out of the pond, Zane frantically tried to save our fish, who by now were thoroughly encased in green gelatinous gunk that clogged not only their gills but also their nostrils and mouths. But despite her most valiant efforts, four fish died outright and one struggled for an hour to live, only to lose the battle. Two survived, however, thanks entirely to Zane's persistent efforts.

With the pond all but empty and only two of our seven fish remaining alive, but for how long I knew not, I wondered: "Now what do I do? Just refill fill the pond with clean water and start all over?"

Being in doubt, I called a pond expert, told her the situation, and asked for suggestions, the first of which was to put at least six inches of pea gravel in the bottom of the pond to act as a biological filter to clean the water. Her second suggestion was to incorporate some aquatic plants that grow submerged in the depths to use the nutrients derived from the feces of the fish and thereby deprive the algae of this source of energy. And third, she said to be patient, that the pond would balance itself, even with a mild to heavy bloom of algae once or twice a year. The fish, she assured—and reassured—me, would be fine.

I say "reassured" because even she, whom I had never met, who heard me for the first time in her life only through a telephone, could instantly tell that I was badly out of myself. That green-eyed monster of fear had seized my mind and distorted it like trick mirrors in a house of horrors. I was totally out of control and knowing it, I fervently denied it. But now I had to admit it to myself because even the woman on the other end of the telephone knew it.

What had begun as a crisis in my disaster mentality, I converted, as if by a recipe, into a real crisis of life and death proportions. But now, with the knowledgeable reason of the pond expert, my fabricated crisis turned into a pond with a beautiful ecological balance. In fact, dragonflies and damselflies began visiting the pond and even laying eggs in it. To me, this is a compliment to be treasured for it meant the pond had a greater ecological balance as I had a greater inner balance because of what I had learned.

I learned, for example, that maintaining a sixty percent plant cover in the pond would help control the algae by cutting out the sun's light and keeping the water cool for the benefit of the fish and the containment of the algae. I learned about using pea gravel as a biological filter and that submerged plants use excess nutrients produced by the fish's excrement. And I learned that the small, aquatic fern—commonly called mosquito fern, *Azolla mexicana*—grows profusely in nutrient rich water. By continually harvesting the fern, I ensure its perpetual proliferation, which keeps the water clear throughout the algal season.

I also learned, once again, how easily the green-eyed monster of fear can invade my mind when I relax my vigilance and loose sight of patience and faith, which brings to mind a Russian proverb: Pray but keep rowing the boat. Had I remained calm and called the pond expert to begin with, the real crisis would never have manifested itself and all of our fish would have lived. Alas, some lessons, such as patience and faith, are learned the hard way; they are initiated into being through the sick, empty feeling of loss, such as the loss of our five fish.

Although every crisis has two options—positive and negative, we humans do not always see the crisis or understand it, let alone see that it has a positive side, because we often lack the consciousness of cause-and-effect relationships. The Chinese character for crisis means "dangerous opportunity," because it is the decisive moment when everything may seem to fall apart, even to regress. This apparent collapse and regression is a sign of positive disintegration, for out of darkness and chaos comes light.

When, therefore, a crisis is viewed as a positive disintegration, it clears the way for and results in a reintegration. Indeed, decay is necessary if growth is to persist.

I have learned much from the crises in my life. My most immediately rewarding lessons have always come when I have been able to maintain an inner equipoise of character and have been able to consciously ask myself: "What am I to learn from this situation?" or "How can I respond to this right now in such a way that I can grow from it?"

My question has always given my subsequent struggle both meaning and a context of value and has given me a purposeful search for a positive outcome. This does not mean, however, that I always know immediately what I am to learn from a situation, only that there is a lesson I will learn through the experience. But first, I have a choice—either resist the crisis, such as the one in my pond, or accept it. The rest will take care of itself because, whichever choice I make, change is set in motion.

Exercise In Conscious Awareness

Into every garden a crisis must come sooner or later because novelty and creation in Nature's sphere are accompanied by catastrophic change of some kind, be it on a micro-, mini-, or macrocosmic scale. As gardeners, we may not always recognize a crisis when it occurs within a rosebush, for example, as it teeters on the threshold between living and dying because the symptoms are either very subtle or, when they finally show up, it is too late. But the bush knows. In such a case, we recognize the crisis only when the bush has already crossed the threshold and the symptoms of its impending death begin to manifest unmistakably on its outer plane—but then it may already be too late to save the rose.

The next time such a crisis occurs in your garden, try accepting it as an opportunity to explore all the possible outcomes that you can think of, instead of simply reacting to the crisis by attempting to keep your garden from changing in composition. I do not mean to imply that you necessarily have to replace your favorite rose with something else, it is only to suggest that you discipline your mind to stop to examine all the options before you act. I say this because I have found that each crisis has at its core the same message—it is time for me to consider a new option, even if that option is just a different way of seeing, a new way of appreciating my favorite rose bush.

If you will write down the options as they occur to you, you may well be amazed at the novelty and creativity of your ideas as you reexamine the interactive relationships in your garden. You may find that the change you make, should you choose to make one, may shift the sense of your whole garden in a way that just "feels right."

I know such shifts have happened in my garden when, for example, I moved a rhododendron that was getting scalded by the summer sun to a place I had never considered planting a rhododendron. This new spot was created when a few badly diseased rose bushes had to be extracted, which left a perfect opening, where the afternoon sun is much less intense.

Now the rhododendron's blossoms no longer wither with the sudden heat of summer and the leaves no longer scald in the sun, in addition to which the bush adds its color of flower and leaf, thus beautifully balancing the foliage of the plants surrounding it. And each time I see it, there arises an "Ahhhh" inside myself—this feels right! I imagine that for the rhododendron there is also an "Ahhhh." But it took a crisis for the rhododendron, of scalding by the summer sun for three consecutive years, to help me see a new possibility, which ended up feeling much more "right" as I saw the bush firmly ensconced in its new home.

Change is a Universal Constant

Change is one of the few things in Nature that is constant—the continual flow of unknowable and unpredictable relationships, which lead to choices, which lead to actions, which become events laden with consequences. Thus everything is in a constant process of becoming something else.

A flower or condition seems perfect in my garden for an instant or a season, but then changes suddenly, dramatically, and perfection seems lost, unless, of course, I see the process of change itself as perfect, not just its momentary condition. Change is a condition along a continuum, which may reach a momentary pinnacle of harmony within my senses. Then the process that created the harmony, which in itself is perfect, takes that sense of harmony away and replaces it with something else— always with something else. For all things arise; all things pass away.

In this way is one of Nature's great lessons revealed if we observe closely and participate consciously in life: knowledge represents our notion of the historical surety of the past; change flows as the ongoing current of the active present, and uncertainty is the womb of future possibility, whether in my garden, a farmer's field, a forest, or the world at large.

To understand the relationship between knowledge, change, and uncertainty, one must first understand the relationship of past, present, and future. The past determines the present and the present determines the future. The spiritual teacher White Eagle once told a group of followers that, "your thoughts and actions are like seeds, the harvest of which is certain to be reaped at some time, in the soul as well as in the bodily life; and will . . . shape your whole future." This is the outworking of the law of cause and effect, which is inescapable.

Within this relationship are contained three important notions: (1) Nature deals with processes and trends over variable scales of time, despite the fact that we often want to deal with absolute, predictable quantities and values in rigid, predetermined scales of time; (2) Nature's processes are a cyclical continuum, regardless of our human desire for things to be linear in accord with our predominant thinking; and (3) Nature is always in a dynamic state of becoming something else, which means that although we have some scientific understanding of the principles governing this dynamic balancing act, we can only anticipate the outcome of our tinkering based on our meager knowledge of Nature's biophysical principles.

Think, for instance, of a vegetable. It marches along the continuum of change from unripe, to ripe, to overripe. My task is to pick and eat it at the precise moment of lusciousness, or it will go to seed and produce again a plant of its own kind in a never-ending cycle of change. But if things are ever-changing in my garden, is anything constant, except change itself? The answer is "No."

Consider the circle of flat, round, "skipping rocks" that ring the jade green bamboo in my garden. I built the ring of flat, round stones on a solid, level foundation to hide the rim of the large plastic pot dug into the ground to contain the vigorously spreading bamboo. I constructed the ring, which is about a foot wide and six to eight inches high, of many more than a hundred stones and a good deal of patience. Creating the ring in early summer, I thought it would be a relatively permanent, unchanging arrangement. Then came Winter with its rain, which seems to drip constantly from the bamboo, its ice, and its freezing and thawing. By spring every stone seemed to have shifted its position ever so slightly. A few stones angled upward, some gently downward; others shifted more dramatically.

It has now been three years, and every stone has moved. Even though I witnessed the gradual process and found it magnificent in its own right, it was a trip to Malaysia that really spoke to me about change and constancy.

I was in southern Malaysia in 1995 and was everlastingly impressed by the evenness of the climate. It was hot and hotter, wet and wetter, humid and more humid, but all within a narrow range. Even the annual length of day varied by only about fifteen minutes due to the proximity to the equator.

In Malaysia, unlike the Pacific Northwest of the United States where I live, there is no sudden burst of spring colors in anyone's garden as the profusion of flowers begin to bloom. There is no discrete season for decay, for the dying and falling of leaves, when deciduous plants all bare themselves for the coming of winter. The seasonal variation to which I am accustomed does not exist. Malaysia has such climatic sameness that flowers are always blooming and dying, as are leaves. But the Malaysians understand the subtleties of their seasons, which they identified to me by the ripening of certain fruits. So it is that even in Malaysia, where I cannot read the subtleties of change, the dynamics of change exist nonetheless.

Now, I realize that all things have within them the seeds of becoming something else. All dimensions of change are fluid and dynamic, flowing together as rivulets that flow together as streams that flow together as rivers that flow together into the sea, where all waters merge and become dimensionless only to form again in the great cycle of raindrops and ice crystals and snowflakes. Change, by its very nature is the creative process and a constant in the Universe. Change, therefore, is the Universe.

Change seems often to force us to balance between extremes of risk and no risk during the course of living. The turtle, for example, must accept risk every day just in order to live. It has but two choices, to withdraw its head from the outside world into the safety of its shell and starve to death or risk sticking its head into the world to find food.

The fear of risk is born of self-doubt—the thief of dreams. People who are afraid of risk lead a planned life. A planned life is a closed life, which can be endured perhaps, but cannot be lived.

We must each stick our necks out daily if we are to grow either in the worldly sense or in the spiritual sense, because appropriate risks appropriately taken are a necessary ingredient if life is to be lived fully and richly. This is simply saying that if we are to realize fully the worth of our spiritual anchors, we must feel fully the force of life's storms.

But how many times in life do we retreat in the face of our moderate to excruciating discomfort? How many times do we eschew the opportunity put before us to actually sit in our discomfort, pain, grief, or terror long enough to move through it to the other side, where growth and self-mastery await? St. Teresa of Avila summarized the potential gain in three words when everything inside of her wanted to flee: "Now stand firm."

Risk rides the crest of a wave of perceived crisis. In this sense, risk is a measure of our faith and trust. It is also a measure of our willingness to consciously grow as individuals.

Understanding change is a matter of consciousness of the effect caused by a thought and subsequent action; the more conscious we are, the more flexible is our thinking. Unconsciousness, in contrast, is the lack of understanding of the relationship between a cause and its effect and the lack of discipline to achieve that understanding. The less conscious we are, the more rigid and immutable is our thinking. In the Upanishads, we are told, for example, that "one comes to be of just such stuff as that on which the mind is set."

We cannot stop change. We can only respond to it, and by our response, we may, to some extent, be able to alter its trajectory, speed, and outcome, or at least accommodate it. Remember, however, that choice comes from change and that change comes from the ability to choose. The great irony is that most people want choice without change, responsibility, or accountability.

Be that as it may, the wave of uncertainty called the future is coming. We can accept it, flow with it, and seek its opportunities, or we can resist it and fight it and make ourselves sick, but we cannot stop it because the Universe is always in creation and never created. Notice that the word "created" is past tense, and whatever is past tense cannot exist because it is history, that which has already happened, not that which is now happening. So it is that we can only interact with the past, present, and future now, in the present, knowing full well that our every thought, word, and action of this moment either creates or destroys our future health, happiness, and peace.

It is through actively observing and consciously participating in life that we learn we cannot relive history or know in advance what is going to happen, because what happens depends on choices made in the present. "Our plans miscarry," wrote Roman pilosopher Lucius Annaeus Seneca, "because they have no aim. When a man does not know what harbor he is making for, no wind is the right wind."

All we have is the present, the here and now, with which we must interact. How we interact with the myriad stresses of continual change and why we behave as we do depends on whether we understand change as a fluid process to be embraced or as a terrifying condition to be avoided.

The idea that everything is constantly changing, that nothing is permanent, can be viewed another way: acceptance of what is. What is, is. It cannot be otherwise. We cannot, for example, control a circumstance, but we can control how we respond to it. If we simply accept the circumstance, we are in control of ourselves; if we fight the circumstance and try to control it, it controls us. Thus, as every great teacher throughout all time has taught: accept everything. Accept the way as it is shown to you. Let life come naturally like the unfolding of a flower.

I can only accept what is if I am present in the here and now. There is a beautiful Sanskrit world *santosa*, meaning "contentment," which is a true and gracious acceptance of where we are in life right now because it is exactly where we need to be for our spiritual development. Yet people in Western industrialized society spend an inordinate amount of time wanting circumstances to be different and being frustrated when they are not. Frustration results from refusing to accept what is, as it is, now. I cannot, for instance, control how the weather affects my garden in any given year, but I can accept the weather as it is, regardless of what it does to my garden, and thereby control how I respond to it.

Many a time I have seen Zane in great dismay watching her beloved roses being pummeled by an unexpected rain just when the blooms were at their most magnificent. She looks at me. I look at her. We realize that this is the circumstance we are being given in the moment to accept and work with. Though we sometimes do not appreciate some of the natural effects of the rain, it simply is.

Change is the creative process that keeps the world ever-novel, interesting, and evolving. It is also a messenger of uncertainty and a tester of faith, which caused Egyptian President Anwar el-Sadat to remark: "My contemplation of life and human nature . . . taught me that he who cannot change the very fabric of his thought will never be able to change reality, and will never, therefore, make any progress." Sadat's concept is carried a step further by French philosopher Henri Bergson: "To exist is to change; to change is to mature; to mature is to create oneself endlessly."

Spring, for example, is a time of drastic change, a time when the plants of my garden are young and soft and tender, their leaves a new bright green, or burgundy red, or gentle silver like the leaves of dusty miller. By summer, the plants are mature and their leaves are often coarse and dull, with simple holes and creative lacework eaten into them by myriad insects, pillbugs, and ever-hungry slugs. With the arrival of autumn, the leaves begin to wither in hot, drying winds. But, it is the cold north winds of approaching winter that causes them to break loose their bonds and joust and bounce their way to earth, where they disappear from whence they came, into the atomic interchange of soil, which they will enrich with their passing.

As a babe, I, too, was tender, my skin smooth and soft, filled with the elasticity and possibilities of life. In adolescence, my skin was taut and supple as my strong muscles worked beneath it. Then came midlife and my skin began to change. It lost some of its softness, pliability, and smoothness as years of working in the hot sun and freezing cold, in the humid forests and dry deserts began taking their toll. And now, as I grow beyond sixty, the skin on the back of my neck has become leathery from decades of exposure to the weather, that of my arms is no longer drawn so taut, and an amazing variety of little beings—from warts, to brown spots, to moles, like animals in a zoo—are taking up residence over my body as my skin ages.

And so the life in my garden is constantly changing, and with it, I, too, must change and am changing. I have learned that to appreciate change as the perfect process of evolution, I must give up trying to control the outcome of my efforts in gardening and simply enjoy the wonder thereof as the perfect union of my labor and the circumstances to which I must respond. And, I have learned that I must accept with grace the changes of my body and the novel kinds of choices with which I am now confronted as I approach the land of the elders, as increasingly I hear the voices of my ancestors stirring in the many little winds that play in my garden.

Exercise In Conscious Awareness

That change is a universal constant, is axiomatic, but nonetheless, it engenders a variety of feelings in each of us. Some feelings related to change are pleasurable, like the blooming of the first flowers in Spring, whereas others are uncomfortable, like the death of a favorite tree. Yet every change has both a positive and a negative side.

To understand change as a creative process in balance with itself, begin the new year by keeping a journal in which you record all the salient changes you observe in your garden and how you feel about them. Note all those that make you feel resistant and uncomfortable and explain why. Do the same with all those that you find acceptable and pleasant and explain why.

Having written them down, consciously look for all the potentially positive aspects of the apparently negative changes that in some way make you feel uncomfortable and all the potentially negative aspects of the apparently positive changes you find pleasant. Be aware, however, that potentially negative outcomes tend to present themselves immediately in our minds, whereas potentially positive consequences are sometimes longer-term in their unfoldment and thus take longer to recognize. Such longer-term outcomes may at times be seen only in hindsight. You may, therefore, have to be diligent in your search for the potentially positive outcomes of that which you initially perceive as a negative, unwanted change in your garden. Remember the example of the rhododendron in the preceding exercise?

If, however, you keep your journal current for a year or two, I think it safe to say that you not only will find change to have been largely positive over time, but also will see change differently than you probably do now, which in no way means that all change is comfortable or ever will be.

I ALWAYS HAVE A CHOICE, AND I MUST CHOOSE

Choice is an inescapable condition of life.

With the decision to create a garden came a sudden plethora of choices, such as the size and configuration of the garden; the materials out of which to construct it; its contents, whether flowers, or shrubs, or vegetables, or all three; in what composition and proportions; where to plant them; when to plant them; and so on. Each time a decision was made, others were forgone, and each decision created a kaleidoscope of additional choices.

Now, with the garden designed and in place, I go each year into my garden before it stirs with spring's awakening, and in my mind's eye reflect on which plants are sleeping where. How, I wonder, did this plant or that survive the deep freeze of winter?

As the days begin to lengthen and the sun to climb progressively higher in the southern sky, I look for signs of life as each plant in its turn, following the nature of its kind, pokes its head out of the soil. Not all survive, however, and I must decide what to do with the empty spot, and so each year, I am faced with a physical and emotional loss and different array of choices.

Choice. A simple world with a powerful meaning. People have appropriated choice from the dawning of humanity because they value it and thus vie for it and often die for it.

I know the feeling of lightness that comes with being free to choose what to do in my garden, although Nature may at times thwart the outcome I want. But in the world outside of my garden, there are many people who have little or no concept of the indescribable feeling of joy that comes with being free to choose.

Thurgood Marshall and Mahatma Gandhi understood well the value of individual choice. They made no apologies for wanting it both for themselves and for all others who were denied it because of the color of their skin. They did much to make the world see that individual choice—implied by basic human rights—has no meaning unless it is universal. They made it clear that the ability to choose confers upon each individual a sense of value, self-confidence, and the dignity of being human.

They knew that all we have to give our children and our grandchildren—ever—are choices and some things of value from which to choose. Yet we are, in our daily exercise of liberty, wasting too much energy, consuming too many material goods, and investing too little in the health and welfare of the future. In choosing ever more for ourselves, we are simultaneously choosing a poorer life for all the children to come.

Yet if the outcome of a hard choice is good, then people will scarce remember the pain. Here one might hearken to Abba Eban: "History teaches us that men and nations behave wisely once they have exhausted all other alternatives." According to a bumper sticker even Noah had a choice, but may not have exhausted all other alternatives: "God is innocent. Noah built in a flood plain."

The question is: Are we ready for the hard choices? Ready or not, the choices are upon us!

Choice made with wisdom and foresight is the essence of the sustainability of our communities within the context of their landscapes. The need for collective choice that is both positive and other-centered has never been more urgent because the freedom and survival of democracy is based on accepting change as an ongoing process to be embraced, not as a condition to be avoided at any cost. To embrace change, however, does not mean blindly casting out the old as we unquestioningly clutch the new, especially when that which we are being forced to give up because of changing technology is finite in supply, intangible in value, and irreplaceable once lost. Furthermore, while the immediate choices belong to us, the adults of today, the consequences belong to the children of today and all the tomorrows to come.

Public debate is the only forum we have to help ourselves and one another consciously integrate proposed environmental changes into our lives and in the process grieve for the immediate and continuing loss of a safe and known past as we step into a progressively unknown and uncertain future. Open public debate must therefore be protected at any cost if we are to retain a free democracy that offers true participative, collective choice for future generations.

To me, eliminating legitimate emotions from land-use decisions, for example, is like being forced to plant flowers and vegetables in my garden that someone else chooses and tells me where, when, and how to plant, after which he or she simply walks away, leaving me to maintain my garden as they dictated it, even if I don't like anything about what they did. But emotions, the life and force behind relationships, are part and parcel of personal and collective values based on a local sense of place in the here and now. When these deeply held values are forcibly replaced with a developer's short-term economic agenda, especially the agenda of an absentee developer, all the local people can do is grieve. At some point, however, the inevitability of development must be seen as a circumstance over which you may have no external control, except in how you chose to respond to it, through acceptance or resistance. Otherwise you can become so stuck that all you can do is exist indefinitely in being stuck while true living seems forever elusive.

Exercise In Conscious Awareness

Choices always have effects or consequences, which become the causes of still other effects or consequences, and so on. Some of the consequences of our choices we may not like, but we must nevertheless choose because not to choose is still a defacto choice. To examine a few of the myriad options we face every day as we work in our gardens, let's consider a tomato plant.

Plant a tomato. When a flower appears, what choices do you have with respect to the flower? You can leave the flower alone and get a tomato. You can pick the flower and forego the tomato. If you pick the flower, what can you do with it? Write down all the things you can and cannot do with tomato flowers.

Now consider a green tomato. If you leave a green tomato on the plant, the chances are that it will ripen, but then you no longer have a green tomato. If, however, you decide to pick the green tomato, what can you do with it? You can make green tomato relish, green tomato pie, fry it, try eating it raw, or let it ripen on the kitchen counter. Consult a cookbook; is there anything else you can do with green tomatoes? Write down all the things that you can do with green tomatoes.

If you let the tomato ripen on the plant before you pick it, what can you do with it? You cannot make green tomato relish, or green tomato pie, or fry it green. Again, write down all the things you can do with ripe tomatoes, but now make a second list of all the things you cannot do with ripe tomatoes. What other possibilities do you pass up by choosing to let the tomato ripen?

What would happen if you left a tomato on the plant to fall to the ground and rot? What possibilities do you forego by letting the tomato fall and rot? What circumstances do you set in motion when the seeds germinate and grow into "volunteer" plants next year? What could you do with them? You could pull them out as weeds, share a few with neighbors, thin them and let some grow, let all of them grow, and so on. Write down all the things that you could do with the tomato plants and all the options you would foreclose in your garden for that year if you decided to keep all the seedlings (let's say, conservatively, fifty of them).

What would happen next year to the vegetable bed in which your tomato plant is currently growing if you just let it grow without deciding what to do with the tomatoes, and so by default you do nothing? What would you gain; what would you lose? Either choice opens you to consequences, while simultaneously closing the door on others. So it is day in and day out.

The power to mold and create that lies asleep in each and every choice is eternally ours to awaken by how we choose and thereby direct our destiny. The wisdom or folly of the power we embrace is ours. We are not, therefore, victims of life, but rather the products of our choices—and *we must choose*. In that we have no choice.

TO BE IN CONTROL, I MUST GIVE UP TRYING TO CONTROL

While I cannot control a circumstance, I can control how I respond to it.
I can accept the circumstance, ask what lesson it has to teach me, learn the lesson,
and let the circumstance go its way. Otherwise, the lesson makes its appearance
once again in another guise but with the same underlying message.
The reward for learning the lessons is always a greater joy, freedom,
and peace in living life daily as if life were really worth living.

When first Zane and I conceived of and designed the flower beds, I could in my mind's eye see them in spring's first blooming, summer's colorful riot, and autumn's late bouquet. In this garden of the future, everything was perfect. Flowers were planted and grew into the perfect profusion of hue, shape, perfume, form, and spacing, there to return year after year. But that is not how a garden works in real life.

The perennials looked pretty skimpy the first year, so the vacant spots were filled with annuals. Most of the perennials occupied their allotted spaces by the second year, and the garden of my mind's eye was indeed coming into its own. By the third year, however, some of the plants were crowding one another while others were simply taking over or dying out.

At first I tried to control them, to keep the beds manicured in perfect form. But I soon discovered that not only was I *not* in control, but also I was creating an increasingly labor-intensive situation for myself in which control was slipping ever farther from my grasp.

This situation makes me think of a swimmer who is intent on crossing a river by swimming against its swift and powerful current. Although the river does not tire in its flowing, the swimmer tires from swimming. Just because the swimmer tires when challenging directly the power of the current does not mean the river is uncrossable. It merely means that the swimmer must choose to go with the current to some degree, letting the flow of the river buoy him or her as he or she swims towards the opposite shore. True, the swimmer will be carried downstream to some extent *and* will arrive at the river's far shore.

By giving up trying to control everything in my garden, for example, I have the time to see its overall beauty and proportion rather than focusing primarily on the minuscule imperfections, such as weeds I missed or notches eaten into leaf margins of my rhododendrons by hungry weevils. I can also accept that I will always have more slugs and weevils than I might wish, but therein lies a hidden freedom, which reminds me of a story.

As autumn arrives in a distant monastery, a Zen master tells his disciples to sweep the path because it is being covered with falling leaves. The disciples obey as disciples are wont to do and mindfully sweep clean the path of orange and golden leaves. The Zen master comes at eventide and, inspecting the leafless path, tells his disciples to sweep it again the next day because they have not done a perfect job. Again they carefully sweep the path, and again he tells them to do it over because they have failed a second time to do a perfect job.

Finally, after the third try, one of the disciples asks the Zen master what is wrong with their job of sweeping because, he points out, the path is clean of leaves, whereupon the Zen master reaches up and taps a branch. Five leaves float gently onto the path. "Now," he says, "the path is perfect."

There also is a lovely Persian story, which renders a similar lesson. Persian rug weavers of old, although capable of weaving a perfect rug, always inserted a single hidden flaw because to create the perfect rug would be blasphemous since "only Allah is perfect." In this way, they honored their Higher Power and kept their "right size," which is to say they confirmed their humanity and protected themselves against the neurosis of perfectionism.

Finally, there is the charming story by Shel Silverstein about a circle from which a large, triangular wedge has been cut. The circle, feeling incomplete because it is no longer a circle, goes looking for its missing piece. Being incomplete, however, it can only roll slowly, but it can admire the flowers along the way and chat with butterflies while enjoying the warmth of the sunshine.

The circle does find lots of pieces, but none fit, so it leaves them all alongside the road and keeps searching. Then, one day, it finds a piece that fits exactly. It is so happy to be whole again, but as a perfect circle, it rolls too fast to see the flowers, or visit with the butterflies, or even to feel the gentle warmth of the sun. When the circle realized just how different the world seemed in the dizzying pace of rolling smoothly, it stops, leaves its once-missing piece by the side of the road, and rolls slowly, bumpily along, once again appreciating life.

If I try to control everything in my garden, even the uncontrollable, in an attempt to have what I might think of as perfect order and therefore perfection, I am a prisoner of the need to control through perfection. By trying to control my garden and all things therein, I become increasingly out of control of myself, which means that my garden becomes more of a frustration and chore than a joy and blessing. I therefore purposefully build a little imperfection into the art of gardening by leaving this weed or that, which helps to maintain my spiritual balance and thus a sense of being in control of myself.

The paradox my garden poses is that to be in control of myself, I must give up trying to control what is outside of myself, the things I cannot control no matter how hard I try. "Everything that grows is flexible," said Lao Tzu. "All enduring strength is flexible." So I follow the wise counsel of an old gardener who, observing others carefully labeling their plants, vowed to let the plants identify him. In this way I find that when I give up trying to control the uncontrollable, I become more harmonious and balanced, both as a gardener and a participant in life.

Sometimes, however, harmony and balance are exceedingly difficult to keep. I was just outside sitting in the sunlight by the pond. The two oldest fish have now seen three winters, with intermittent ice sealing them in. They have spawned twice, and their offspring are sharing the approach of summer. Yes, some of the original fish have died, but then death too is part of the garden.

Acknowledging that death is an inseparable part of my garden, I face the dilemma not of death *per se* but of killing. The question I face as a gardener, who professes to love all life, is: should I kill the predator to protect the fish in my pond or the insect "pests" to protect the plants of my garden?

Exercise In Conscious Awareness

Select one flower bed or one vegetable bed and describe it in some detail in a journal—the condition of the soil, the distribution and condition of the plants, the types and behavior of the weeds, and the kinds and behaviors of the pests, such as slugs, pillbugs, leafhoppers, and so on. Next, sit with the bed for as long as it takes carefully, consciously to determine just how you would like the bed to look and the plants to grow *if* the bed were to meet your definition of "perfection." Describe the perfect bed in your journal.

Now, using your journal as a guide, perfect the bed in real life, make it the way you would like to see it, and keep it in that condition throughout most of the growing season. This means, of course, that the chosen bed *takes absolute priority* over the rest of your garden—all of it. Remember, perfection has no substitute.

As you work with the bed, keep written entries of what you do, the time it takes, the "rightness" of how it feels, and note specifically what happens to the rest of your garden. How do you feel about the perfection of the one bed in relation to the rest of the garden? How do you feel about the rest of the garden in relation to the one bed?

Now, consciously build a little imperfection into the chosen bed. How do you feel about the bed with its imperfection? Is this little bit of chaos discordant for you? Does this change your feeling about the perfection of the one bed in relation to the rest of the garden? Does the imperfection change the way you feel about the rest of the garden in relation to the one bed?

L. EDGINGTON

Killing is an Act of Living that I cannot Avoid

Killing is a necessity of human survival on this tiny planet called Earth.
That I must kill to live is therefore not the issue.
The important point is that I must consciously, willingly understand,
accept, and be accountable for the suffering I cause in the act of living.

In the United States, it is illegal, without special permission, to kill a deer that is eating its way through my garden, because deer are politically important animals with strict rules governing the taking of their lives. They are considered commercially valuable game animals and are to be killed for sport, provided one pays a monetary fee for the privilege of doing so.

If, on the other hand, aphids, mites, snails, slugs, pillbugs, weevils, leafhoppers, symphylids, gophers, or ground squirrels are eating my garden, they may be killed with impunity. Why? What is it about the perceived social value of an animal that allows the moral justification of killing one kind with impunity but not another?

It seems to me that it boils down to the perceived potential for economic gain. A carrot, for example, is thought to have a greater potential economic value than a gopher; conversely, a deer is perceived to have a greater potential economic value than a rose bush. But who decides and how?

Although we may express our beliefs in the value of all life, when push comes to shove, and we perceive our immediate survival to be in danger (spotted owls vs jobs, salmon vs water for electricity or agricultural irrigation), most of us will opt for our own narrow self-interest—our sense of survival at any cost. What motivates me in gardening is either I get the vegetables and flowers that I plant and nurture or the aphids, mites, snails, slugs, pillbugs, weevils, leafhoppers, and symphylids do. If I'm going to get them, or at least most of them, then I have to control the numbers of my competitors. And that means killing some of them.

Because my competitors are such wee creatures, there are no legal restrictions on killing them, however I choose to do it. But what about moral restrictions? This is my soul struggle. And now I have a garden in which there is a pond, and I am once again faced with this seemingly infernal dilemma about killing. Must I now give up my garden and/or pond?

Not long ago, a raccoon made a night visitation and wreaked havoc in the pond by turning over the potted aquatic plants in an attempt to make the goldfish swim in panic to the surface, where they could be caught for supper. After making an unholy mess in my pond, it proceeded down the street two houses to our neighbors and killed "Ducker," a tame mallard drake our neighbors had reared from an injured baby to a magnificent thirteen-year-old adult that both acted like and was accepted as a treasured member of their family. Hearing the commotion from the raccoon's attack, our neighbors ran from their house calling for Ducker, but could not find him. Look as they might, Ducker had simply vanished.

The next morning, Zane and I found our pond torn apart, and I found the remains of one of our large pond snails, which told me in a twinkling that a raccoon was the culprit. Although it had failed to catch any of our fish, we both knew the raccoon would be back, a thought that weighed heavily in our minds.

Later that morning, we went to our neighbors to get starts of some plants they had for us, and we told them about the raccoon's destructive visit. They in turn told us about Ducker. Putting two and two together, we figured out what had happened. But where the raccoon had taken Ducker once it had carried him across the high wooden fence between our neighbors and their immediate neighbors was still a mystery.

Around noon we found a feather trail from our neighbor's house to ours, and discovered that the raccoon had dragged Ducker into the large cedar hedgerow that separated our yard from that of our neighbors on the other side of our house, and there had partially eaten him. After finding Ducker's body, I realized there was an interesting lesson in our having followed the trail of Ducker's feathers.

When I had been out watering the flower beds in the front of our house early that morning, I had noticed some white, fluffy down on the walkway.

"That's odd," I thought. "Cottonwood seeds don't usually travel this far from the river, even in a strong wind."

It was not until we were following the trail of Ducker's feathers later in the day that I realized the white, fluffy material I had seen in the morning was not cottonwood seed, but rather down from Ducker's breast. I had looked without truly seeing and saw without truly understanding. How often do I do this in my garden—or in life?

Having pieced together what had happened, I borrowed a live trap, which I set that afternoon in the hedgerow, where the raccoon had eaten Ducker. Then, just as dusk was gathering toward night, the raccoon returned and walked boldly past our pond on its way to finish dining on Ducker. Although we heard the door of the trap snap shut just after the raccoon entered the hedgerow, experience had taught me not to disturb a trap until dawn because it would unnecessarily upset the trapped animal, so I waited.

The next morning, however, I discovered that a large male opossum had gotten into the trap just ahead of the raccoon, which had left for parts unknown.

What would I have done had it been the raccoon in the trap instead of the opossum? I would have killed it. Why? For two reasons. First, it would sooner or later return to again raid the pond, and perhaps next time succeed in killing the goldfish. Second, to displace the raccoon by relocating it somewhere else would be tantamount to killing it anyway.

I say this because our area is already well endowed with raccoons. Wherever I would have taken it, therefore, another raccoon already lived, and both would have had to fight to see which one was going to live there. One or the other would be displaced and at a great disadvantage in survival, which, in Nature, usually leads to a violent end.

If I catch the raccoon and kill it, only one raccoon pays the ultimate price. But if I relocate the raccoon, at least two raccoons are likely to pay dearly for my act—the one I relocated and the one made to defend its territory, for death is surely the only victor in such a transaction.

I did not catch the raccoon, however, and I had no wish to kill it when it returned, but I also love my pond as it is, not as the raccoon would rearrange it. Must I therefore get rid of the pond to avoid having to kill the raccoon, or must I kill the raccoon to protect my pond?

As a reasonable alternative to filling in the pond or killing the raccoon, I put a low, relatively unobtrusive electric fence around the pond, which, as it turns out, is effective against cats and opossum, as well as raccoons. It might even ward off the seemingly ever-present herons that scout our neighborhood to raid backyard ponds for a quick and easy meal. Although aesthetically I would prefer not to have the fence, I love the pond and the fish therein, and I do not want to kill the raccoon. For the moment at least, technology offers me a palatable compromise.

Though I always tread as softly on the Earth and with Her creatures as I can, I still leave a mark. I can do naught else but leave my imprint simply because I exist, and I use energy in order to live and alter my surroundings in my act of living. My alterations will be simultaneously positive for some things and deleterious for others.

I simply cannot be neutral because I live from the center of my own experience, which is necessarily a subjective act of living itself, an act in which I inadvertently and sometimes consciously choose to kill. Humanity has killed both inadvertently and purposefully since time immemorial. Can it be otherwise? I think not, because the world is not a machine with parts that can be isolated one from another. It is instead reality as a seamless whole, a dynamic living organism, rather than separable fragments.

Because reality is an indivisible whole, killing will occur either inadvertently or by choice. Because life and death are opposites of the same dynamic, the probability is that killing will exist when many beings live in proximity and all want the same thing, which is in limited supply. Killing, whether inadvertent or by choice, takes many forms: disease; parasitism; predation; cannibalism (amongst animals); starvation; dehydration; or human violence, such as murder, war, suicide, and euthanasia. Each is a participation in the shadowlands of life.

True, killing is killing and some ways are clearly more violent than others. But how is the act of cutting a sheep's throat for a religious purpose any different than that of severing a head of lettuce from its root? It isn't. The difference is that the sheep is a warm-blooded mammal with demonstrable feelings, which we deem to be closer in likeness to ourselves than a head of lettuce because lettuce is merely a vegetable, which science says has neither feelings nor consciousness, and from which most religions withhold the presence of a soul.

Then should I, who attempt to see all life as equal and complementary, retreat from eating meat on moral grounds and become a vegetarian? I could, but I would still be killing plants to feed myself. And I would still have to compete with those organisms in my garden that want to eat the same plants I do, which are limited in supply. Even if I plant more vegetables, my competitors will only increase and consequently eat more. At some point I must do something to control the numbers of my competitors, or I will get little to no food from my garden. But, how can I deal with them without killing?

When I consider and examine each competitor as an individual living being, without judging what I perceive to be its unwanted interaction with me, I discover that it has a marvelous form, function, and adaptability in its own right, which, upon reflection, becomes a creative part of my sense of reality. Even a malaria-carrying mosquito displays a dazzling beauty under a dissecting microscope.

This realization poses for me a moral question. Is there really such a thing as equality amongst all creatures? Equality in what sense? Intelligence? Evolutionary (or social) status? Who decides and how?

I'm not sure that living is a matter of equality. I say this because, with rare exceptions, life thrives on life. The only exception I can think of might be those bacteria living around hydrothermal vents in the deep ocean floor, which, as far as I know, require no organic material in the form of either living or dead beings to survive. Be that as it may, as long as life needs life to live, the organisms that must kill in one way or another to survive will do so, and those that require decomposing tissue for their survival will depend in large measure on the killers to supply it. And in killing, the killers, at least in strength and cleverness, outmatch their individual preys' ability to survive. In the sense of survival as individuals, therefore, moral equality is not equal in terms of physical attributes.

I must kill or have someone else kill for me to live, so whether I kill or cause a creature to be killed for me is not the issue. Though I wish there was a way in which I could live without killing or causing someone else to kill for me, I know of none. At issue, therefore, is not that I kill or cause someone else to kill for me but why and how I kill or cause someone else to kill for me—my motive, my conscious awareness, and my demeanor.

Some people kill plants to make fresh or dried decorative arrangements out of them. Others collect, kill, preserve, and sell such organisms as beautiful butterflies for people to purchase by way of decoration for their offices and homes. Still others hunt animals and have parts of them mounted for various reasons of memory or vanity to adorn walls in dens, restaurants, and shops that sell sporting goods.

Beyond the limitations of the law, which are meant to serve and protect the social conscience, why or how one kills nonhuman beings—whether as food or to protect a supply of food, for sport as in hunting, or for economic gain as in making a living—is a matter of personal conscience, wherein my conscience is my own affair and yours is your affair. Having said this, however, I recognize that a goodly number of people are apparently without a keen sense of conscience when it comes to harming other creatures or people. They must, therefore, have their behavior controlled through the collective conscience of society in the form of laws passed to control behavior society deems unacceptable.

If I consciously recognize all living things as being intrinsically of equal and complementary value to life itself (including those organisms competing with me in my garden for my flowers and vegetables), then I must deal with my feelings when I kill them, and it hurts. I feel compassion and sorrow at my perceived necessity of forfeiting their lives so that I might enjoy the flowers as food for my soul and the vegetables as food for my body. My competitors are, after all, created and propelled by the same Divine spark that I am.

As long as I must kill to survive, I, who feel myself to be an inseparable part of the flow and ebb in an ever-changing current of the Universe, must neither shun nor repress my feelings of depthless regret. I must instead take them most seriously and share consciously in and be accountable for the suffering I cause in the act of my living on Earth. Thus it is that I both apologize to and ask the Eternal Mystery to bless those beings that I kill, be it a weed, a carrot, a slug, or a pillbug.

I therefore consciously kill out of perceived competitive necessity in my garden, but as selectively as possible, and to nourish my body and my soul. In killing, I cause death, a horizon beyond which I cannot see, and in my blindness, I must submit in humility to Faith, and hope that I have in fact done the best I can.

Exercise In Conscious Awareness

"Killing is an act of living that I cannot avoid," seems like a harsh statement, but is it? You can test this idea in your own garden simply by working in it for one day without killing anything—not a worm, not a slug, aphid, plant, or living organism of any kind. You can also test it by eating from your garden without killing anything.

If you succeed, I will become your first student.

If you fail, ask yourself how it feels to kill something. If you are in doubt, focus consciously on how the animal you are killing behaves during the process of your killing it, whether by accident or intent. Does it show any sign of trying to escape, which you might interpret as fear? Does it show any sign that could be interpreted as distress as its life ebbs? Does it move in a way that you could interpret as pain? How would you feel if something larger than you were treating you the same way you are treating the animal you are killing? Would you be afraid? Would you be in distress? Would you feel pain, either psychologically or physically?

What happens when you pull a weed out of the ground? Can you imagine having your feet stuck in the soil and literally being pulled apart? Assume a lettuce plant has consciousness and feelings, although scientists declare it does not. But, then scientists have been wrong in the past and could be wrong now. Whether something besides us possesses consciousness and feelings is, after all, only our interpretation of the outer behavior of another being, albeit a nonhuman one. So what if scientists are wrong, and plants really do have consciousness and feelings? How do you think a lettuce plant would feel as you sever its head from its roots? Imagine having your throat cut. How is it any different?

If we cannot live without killing, how can we at least learn to kill with dignity, consciousness, and compassion? How can we make killing a sacred act? How do we psychologically live with the constant act of killing, even indirectly by having someone else commit the act for us, say a butcher or a farmer?

Death is a Horizon beyond which I cannot See

*Killing is the taking of a life, but death is merely a horizon beyond which
I cannot see. Whereas killing is violent, death may, depending on my point
of view, be the peaceful beginning of a new journey or the continuation of an
old one. "Death is the temporary end of a temporary phenomenon,"
says the Compassionate Buddha.*

In spring, plants seem to arise in orderly fashion, like the eagerly anticipated birth of a child for whom I have long prepared. But in autumn, plants die without my planning or consent, and there is nothing I can do about it. In autumn, my garden seems to be in a prolonged state of chaos as each plant dies in its turn within a short period. For a while my garden is filled with fading colors, falling leaves, storm-tossed vegetation, and a sense of loss, grief, and mourning all about. I can, I find, more easily plan for a birth than for a death.

I have also discovered in my garden that killing and death are not the same thing. Killing is an act of which death is the result. But, what exactly is death? Death is an unseen component lurking in all living things all of the time because it is the nature of life to decline and decay, which begs the question: When is a plant or animal in my garden dead? When its last cell ceases to function? It seems easier to tell when an animal is dead because it no longer moves or breathes or has the pulse of life, if I assume that a lack of movement, breath, and pulse means death. But how do I know when a rose bush is dead?

The concept of death in humans has an additional dimension these days (when is a person really dead) because of the increased practice of transplanting organs between a dead person and a live one. But how does one know when someone is dead? At what instant are they dead, at least dead enough to take their organs without killing them?

This is a relevant question because cases are known in which a person was pronounced dead by a physician and then, an hour later, the dead person woke up! Corpses in the morgue have even awakened to find themselves almost buried alive! The question, therefore, is one not only of when is a person dead but also of what is death.

I, too, wonder, as I work in my garden, what death is. I have heard people and animals called "brain dead" by doctors and veterinarians, but a plant does not have a brain as we think of it. How, then, does one define death in a plant? Must it be "stem dead," or "root dead," or what? I don't know.

Zane implores me with the same question each time I extract from the soil a favored rose bush that has fallen victim to a late freeze: "How do you know it is really dead?" Sometimes I say this and sometimes I say that, but in the end, I don't really know. I must go by my feelings, which in part are based on prior experience; they are all I have. And still, after having observed an apparently dead rose bush for one or two months for signs of life prior to pulling it out, I have occasionally found the roots from the rootstock below the hybrid's graft to be alive and a tiny shoot beginning to come forth as it seeks the light, which poses a new dilemma. The grafted hybrid is dead, but not the rootstock onto which it was grafted. Is the rose dead? Well, it depends what you want, the grafted hybrid or the rootstock.

Although I yearly expect some plants, such as annuals, to die, it is the unexpected death of a beloved perennial that frequently gives me pause to reflect on how my life and garden have changed with its passing. A perennial, after all, has a continuity that it shares with me as the years come and go. And like me, it grows and changes with age as it passes through its seasons of life. In this sense, we grow together into a relationship in which each gives something of value to the other. I take care of the plant's needs to the best of my ability, and it feeds my soul with the beauty and perfume of its presence.

It's not that I can't replace a perennial when it dies, but the replacement is different. It does not grow in the way to which I am accustomed. It does not fill the emptiness left by a lost friend, even after a time of grieving.

If I do replace the plant with another of its kind, I must be careful not to compare them, for the new one may not live up to the memory of the old. In short, a relationship had evolved between the perennial and me that I cannot easily dismiss just because the plant was only a plant and it died. Perhaps for the plant, as with a loved friend, human or otherwise, death may only be a change of environment, a different level of being wherein more beauty and radiance is present.

When a plant dies, I commit it to the composter, where it is reduced to the individual elements and separate compounds that once interacted in the chemistry of life to form its being. Now that chemistry reconfigures as the plant is undone and converted into fungi, earthworms, pillbugs, and slugs during the process of decomposition. Then they too will die and disintegrate into still smaller parcels of energy, a process that is repeated many times through many organisms until the resultant organic material is incorporated into the soil from whence it came. The atoms of life that were once my plant are not necessarily atoms of life in the soil. So it is with plants; so it is with people, as I learned when it came time to scatter my mother's ashes by a mountain lake, where I remembered having had fun camping as a family in the late 1940s.

A lone cottonwood stood at the water's edge, a bright green tree embraced on three sides by darker green boughs of pines and firs. A few feet upslope from the cottonwood was a warm, sunny place carpeted with huckleberry bushes—just the place for Kim's ashes I thought. She loved camping here, and she loved the sunshine and ripe huckleberries.

Gingerly, I opened the well-taped cardboard box and found a cheap plastic container held shut with "Scotch Tape." Inside the taped plastic box, which I opened with a curious feeling of finality, was a knotted plastic bag, attached to which was a metal tag with a number stamped on it. So this is what we are reduced to in modern society—a number, a statistic.

Unlike every indigenous culture with which I am familiar, we in modern American society have sterilized death with certificates of passing signed by doctors; embalmed bodies; sterile, metal caskets with spring mattresses and satin linings; plastic boxes and plastic bags with numbered metal tags attached to them for the ashes following cremation. How did we become such a death-denying society that we distance ourselves from the physical attributes of death and decay in every conceivable way we can think of? When did we corrupt the dignity of death and decay, the continuity of generations embodied in touching the silent, breathless face of death with realness, of holding death consciously, willingly in our arms as the few remaining unspoiled indigenous cultures still do? How can we touch the authenticity of life if we cannot touch the reality of death and decay?

The sack, as I took it out of the box, was much heavier than I thought it would be. Unknotting it, I was greeted by a sharp fragment of leg bone—and the charred remains of a snap from my mother's clothing. I touched her bone, and the face of death peered with unwavering gaze through all of time directly into my eyes. Death is real.

I have seen death literally thousands of times in my garden and in a number of countries on three continents, but this was a different matter. This was all that physically remained of my mother, who once brought me into the world. Then I was releasing her last physical remains back into the freedom of the Great Unknown from whence she had come.

A whimsical, teasing breeze blew a film of ashes over my hands and arms as the fine, gray powder sifted through the huckleberry bushes onto the soil. Once again I was touched by my mother as her physical remains became the individual elements and separate compounds, which she had borrowed for almost eighty years in life and then returned to the atomic interchange of the soil. And should I journey this way again in some future time and eat of the ripe huckleberries, the elements that were my mother can once again nourish my body even as they did when I was in her womb more than half a century ago.

There is yet another side of death this sense of finality impressed upon me, namely, that words of love withheld today may be forever lost should death come to one person or the other before the morrow. Conversely, cruel words spoken in the heat of anger may be everlasting should death come to one person or the other before the morrow.

The Egyptian Book of the Dead pictures a soul after death being weighed in a scale against the weight of a feather. Ideally, we are not to create pain and suffering in life. If perchance we do cause suffering and pain as we strive toward ever-greater consciousness, we must then also make conscious amends so that not even a feather's weight is out of balance.

Balance. How do we balance life and death in our gardens and our lives? How do we balance joy and pain? How do we balance a plant's, an animal's, or a person's being here in vibrant physical form one moment and gone the next? When loss is so acute, so apparently final for those of us left behind, how do we know what to do next? That is the realm of grief.

Exercise In Conscious Awareness

For one day in each of the four seasons, beginning when the first blossoms open, go into your garden, walk about your neighborhood, and go out into Nature and consciously experience the awakening of the earth. How does the flush of tender new life make you feel?

As spring dies and summer is born, be aware of spring's variety of flowers fading from your garden. At the same time, be mindful of the delicately opening buds of summer and the growing length of each day's light. What emotions are evoked as the fading petals fall from summer's flowers and those of autumn open, but in a lesser array of colors, or as autumn turns to winter, when all about are plants dying and the once-long days of summer are rapidly giving way to longer and colder nights?

As life swells again, what stirs in your heart on the Spring Equinox, when the length of day and that of night stand equally at twelve hours apiece, after which the days become longer than the nights. Walk around your garden and be consciously present in the moment.

On the Summer Solstice, the longest day of the year, after which the days begin to shorten, visit your garden and sit with it, for now the year begins to die. Do the same on the Autumn Equinox, when the length of day and of night again stand equally at twelve hours apiece, after which the nights become longer than the days.

Then comes the shortest day of the year, the Winter Solstice, followed by the birth of lengthening days. Again, visit your garden on this day in the "dead" of winter and take stock of what you see.

Finally, look around you as the year progresses and notice consciously how many plants are forced by wholesalers to grow out of harmony with Nature's allotted time. Notice, too, how many people use these plants in their attempt to forestall the passing of the seasons by taking dying plants out of their gardens and replacing them with vigorous new plants forced in nurseries to grow out of sync with their cycles. In this way, people seem to feel they are able to negate, or at least minimize, the passage of time, the process of aging and rankness, and the approach of death. This, of course, is but wishful thinking, for the Angel of Death can neither be hoodwinked nor bribed nor waylaid.

To put death in perspective, begin the new year at the Winter Solstice and celebrate the rebirth of the sun. Then celebrate the Spring Equinox, the Summer Solstice, and the Autumn Equinox each in its turn as the ancient peoples did in order to stay in touch with their spiritual life, death, and rebirth of the seasons. At the same time, allow your garden to go through the seasons in the way Nature dictates—with absolute acceptance of whatever happens, for it is by living in harmony with the seasons that life is tasted in its full richness.

There is yet another way death can be honored in your garden. If perchance you have a loved one die, be it a pet or a person, you can select in their memory a lily, rose, tree, or other plant that has significance to you, as we have done. When our two beloved cats died, each of whom had been with us for more than twelve years, we planted lilies on their graves. We also selected two special, small angel statues to grace and protect these sacred places. To honor the memory of Zane's father, we planted a special red, old-garden variety of rose bush, and we think of him each time we see it.

Had we more space, we might have planted a tree, instead of a rose bush. Why a tree? Because trees are the oldest and longest living beings on Earth. As such, trees represent safety, continuity, and eternity and draw us to them, although we are seldom conscious of it.

Their presence, particularly that of deciduous trees, demonstrate for us the seasons of the year even as they remind and instruct us about the inner seasons of our lives. Some trees support within their mighty branches the playhouses of the young, while others become the coffins within which rest those departed. And special trees, those we plant as memorials to deceased loved ones, become our hope that the shortness of their lives and ours may somehow be counter-balanced by the longevity of the trees we plant in loving memory.

GRIEF IS THE OTHER SIDE OF JOY

Grief is an inescapable, multilayered initiation into the depths of the human experience. Joy is its twin. We therefore experience grief when we lose something we value and love in the same measure that we experienced joy when first we found it and learned to value and love it. Loss and grief not only are the price we pay for love and commitment but also are inescapable. It has been said that loss is a part of life as involuntary as a heartbeat, as inevitable as nightfall.

"Grief," says Catherine Sanders in her book, *Grief, The Morning After*, "is so impossibly painful, so akin to panic, …there is a fear that if one ever gives in fully to grief, one would be swept under—as in a huge tidal wave—never to surface to ordinary emotional states again." Nevertheless, grief is vital to the emotional acceptance of a painful circumstance, such as one's favorite flower dying in the midst of winter. Grief is also a necessary process through which we can reshape ourselves in relationship to an outer world that reflects a new reality based on our loss. In this sense, I grieve with the joy of each spring because every winter inevitably results in the death of some fondly remembered plants in my garden.

Thus, as I wander with the seasons among the beds of flowers, I grieve for those whose radiant faces that will not again arise from under the soil, where in darkness they disappeared into the unknown for a reason I cannot fathom. Because it is both safe and private in my garden, I can honor my grief and allow it to come forth uninterrupted. Otherwise, suppressed emotions of anger, guilt, sadness, and grief shoot out like bullets when I can no longer contain them.

What is not said, however, is that grief is the other half of joy. The greater the joy, the greater the grief; each is balanced by the other. In addition, the pain of grief has the capacity to open us up, to soften us toward ourselves and one another more surely than all the joys of the world.

British biologist Charles Darwin wrote in 1872 that one "who remains passive when overwhelmed with grief loses [the] best chance of recovering elasticity of mind." And, American professor Aldo Leopold in 1949 wrote: "For one species to mourn the death of another is a new thing under the sun." Taken together, these two statements—both from people with scientific backgrounds—underscore that grief is both necessary and reaches beyond the loss of life in human terms. Thus, when the grief of the world comes close to the door of my house, I go into my garden and dream among the flowers of how the world could be if we only were truly one another's keepers.

In the I Ching system of divination, hexagram #61 says, "if a wise man abides in his room [garden] his thoughts are heard for more than a thousand miles." In the privacy of my interior life, I gain strength and renew my spiritual center. But I cannot stay forever bound within the physical limits of my garden. I must venture into the outer world and learn to draw inner boundaries around the interior garden of my soul so that I can retain my spiritual center amidst the many complex issues with which I am daily confronted, issues that demand the utmost of my focus and patience.

Exercise In Conscious Awareness

Birth cannot exist without death, and death cannot exist without birth, for one is but an entrance into or altered state of the other. And to experience fully the joy of living, we must experience fully the grief of death, for here, too, one is but an altered state of the other and thus each is an exact measure of the other.

The next time you have a favored plant die, sit with it and consciously reminisce about the enjoyment the plant gave you. Muse about when, where, and why you got it; when and why you chose to plant it where you did; when and how you planted it; and what you were thinking and feeling at the time you included the plant in your garden.

In so doing, be mindful of the relationship you developed with the plant as the seasons passed. How did you feel when it died back at the end of its first year? Remember your thoughts when it reappeared the following year? Did you sense anticipation as you waited for the plant to grow, bud, and bloom, remembering its past glory? What were you feeling when the plant began showing signs of old age? What was it like for you when you could no longer deny that it was dying? What emotions arise now that your beloved plant is dead before you? How does it feel to remove it from the soil, from "its personal place" and dispose of it?

Remember, the depth of the grief you now feel is simultaneously the depth of joy you once felt. If you can learn to love with freedom, completely and fully, the depth of your grief, when it comes, will be more than compensated by the memories of your joy.

Patience seems an Eternal Lesson

Patience is the capacity of calm endurance, or as a friend once told me, "of not putting a time limit on God." In this sense, patience is the willingness to wait and to watch, while being actively focused on the process of waiting and watching. It is gratefully accepting the flow of life as it is, knowing that all things work out as they are meant to through the choices we individually make, which lead to other choices, which lead to still other choices, and so on— choices that ultimately control our personal destiny.

Patience is like a certain bamboo, which I plant as a seed in the spring and water until the onset of winter. The next spring the bamboo must again be watered until the onset of winter, and a third year, and a fourth. All this time nothing seems to happen, for nothing is visible above ground; there is no outward manifestation of growth, only a great, invisible gathering within the seed. Then, during the late spring of the fifth year, the bamboo sprouts and grows to eighty feet before winter.

Patience is paramount in gardening. If you recall the emperor who lived in the House of the Singing Floors, you may also recall his head gardener, the one who contemplated for a year with the mind of his heart and the heart of his mind the gardens of the palace before he physically created them. During that year, he sat with patience, as though patience was an invisible companion who guided his insights as he created the gardens in his mind and heart before he disturbed a single blade of grass. Only when all was ready within, could all be ready without. To this the I Ching adds: "Waiting is not mere empty hoping. ...It is an inner certainty."

If I get impatient and try planting my vegetables too early in the year, the seeds may rot in the ground, or if they do germinate, a sudden freeze may kill the young plants. On the other hand, I may get impatient with the slowness of my vegetables in their growing and apply too much manure. If I do that with certain vegetables, I will stimulate them to put on vast amounts of growth, but in the roots, stems, and leaves, not in the fruits that I want to eat. What, therefore, have I gained by being impatient?

Patience is its own reward, for out of it are born love, acceptance, tolerance, humility, peace, and serenity, all of which are but facets of patience. The outward sign of a person whose hand is firmly on the helm of patience is an equipoise of character, as a young Persian man was to learn when he wandered up into the mountains, found a cave, and went within.[15]

In the cave, he discovered a pearl of great price, but it was in the claws of a dragon, which appeared so overwhelming, that he knew he had no chance of getting the pearl. He therefore went sadly away, reconciling himself to an ordinary life, which was uninspiring once he had seen the pearl.

With time, he married, worked, and raised his family. Then in old age, with his children grown and gone, he was again free, and he said to himself: "Before I die, I will go back and look again upon the pearl."

He found his way back to the cave and looked inside, and there was the pearl, as lovely as ever, but the dragon had shrunk to almost nothing. Picking up the pearl, he carried it away. The dragon of impatience and ignorance, which he had been fighting all of his young life in the very practicalities of his daily existence, disappeared before the eyes of a wise old man who was rich in life's experiences.

To me, the mountains represent higher consciousness or insight, which the youth was not yet prepared to handle. The pearl is wisdom, and the dragon is the youthful impatience of ignorance. The young man as yet lacked the life experiences needed to prepare him to be worthy of the pearl. But by working and struggling in the "everydayness" of life, he gradually changed himself within, represented by the cave that he must go into to find his inner pearl. Time and patience brought him the necessary experiences, which he distilled into the wisdom he sought. Finally, having grown in consciousness, he had unknowingly slain his dragon of worldly impulses and earned the pearl.

I have in my life searched diligently for the pearl of wisdom, misunderstanding for the most part where to look. Then I met Zane, my wife of more than nineteen years, who helped me to see that the pearl of wisdom, for which I had so long searched, lies secreted—and accessible—within the depths of my own being. We all have our own pearls of wisdom burning quietly like little oil lamps of old within the depths of our hearts and souls. We simply have to earn them by living and experiencing the "everydayness" of life with patience and humility.

Exercise In Conscious Awareness

Gardening is an excellent classroom for patience—of "waiting on God," however you perceive God. Work in your garden for one full day and be mindful of every time impatience finds its way into your mind or actions. The instant you become aware of even the slightest twinge of impatience, examine its cause, let it go, and remember that God seems to delight in showing us the Divine way when we have the good graces to give up insistence on our way. If you will do this every time you work in your garden, you will find that your patience compounds remarkably over time and your garden becomes ever-more restful to your soul. And, believe me, patience is necessary if you want to enter the garden through the fourth and final gate, the gate of Spiritual Consciousness.

CHAPTER 5

THE GATE OF SPIRITUAL CONSCIOUSNESS

HAVING ALREADY ENTERED my garden through each of the gates of Ecological, Social, and Personal Consciousness, it is now time for the fourth and final entry—the gate of Spiritual Consciousness. Because spirituality seems, in these harried days of ever-faster technology, such an intangible thing to many people, I have drawn more heavily than in the rest of this book on quotes from mystics, monks, and other people who have had spiritual experiences. It is my hope, by presenting myriad facets of the intangible, that it may become more real to those who doubt.

You, who are now entering my garden through the gate of Spiritual Consciousness, are embarking on possibly the most arduous path. I think it wise, therefore, to pause momentarily and study the life cycle of the salmon, for the journey of self-fulfillment, of self-realization is, as the *Katha Upanishad* warns, "sharp like the razor's edge." Swiss critic Henri Frederic Amiel put it in practical terms when he said "the man who has no inner life is the slave of his surroundings."

A flash of silver, a swirl of bright water, a female salmon flexes her tail against the swift current as she propels herself to a small gravely bar just under the surface in the headwaters of a Pacific Coast stream. Again a flash of silver, then another, and another as other salmon press against the rush of crystalline water, each seeking the exact spot to which their inner drive to spawn impels them.

Suddenly, from somewhere in the shadow of trees overhanging the tiny, clear stream, there comes a large, magnificent male salmon of metallic luster; he swims alongside the female with powerful undulations of his body. They touch, and the female immediately turns on her side and fans the gravel with strong beats of her tail.

She continues spraying gravel into the current until a shallow depression comes into definition, after which she begins depositing reddish orange eggs, hundreds of them, as the male squirts milky-white sperm into the water. The cloud of sperm, enveloping the eggs as the current carries it downstream, fertilizes them as they settle into the shallow "nest."

Having spent themselves to ensure the essence of their existence, their offspring, the female covers the nest just as she excavated it, with powerful strokes of her tail against the gravely bottom of the stream. Now she and her mate, having fulfilled the inner purpose of their lives, swim into deeper water and rest.

Only now, exhausted from their long and difficult journey up rivers and streams from the Pacific Ocean and from their final passionate act of spawning, are they quiet enough for an observer to see small patches of the white fungus that has already begun to invade their bruised and battered flesh. As the fungus grows into their bodies, the life force, which has for so long served them well, begins to wane. They grow weaker and weaker, until the last cells in their bodies die and their now-spent carcasses are washed against the shore, where they will recycle into the atomic interchange from whence they came.

But in the gravely stream bottom, an opaque egg is secreted as the salmon develops inside. In time, the baby salmon hatches and struggles out of the gravel into the open water of protected, hidden places in the stream. Here it grows until it is time to leave the stream of its origin and venture forth into life. It can go only one way—downstream to larger and larger streams and rivers until at last it reaches the ocean, all the way beset by increasing numbers of distractions to explore and dangers to overcome.

Salmon from all of the various streams and rivers mingle in the ocean, where external things affect them in common, such as ocean currents, in what might be called a pool of commonalty. It is therefore impossible to view salmon in the ocean as discrete populations because they behave as an aggregate individual with no visible affinity to a particular river and stream.

Only after some years at sea will the inner urge of individual salmon dictate that it is their time to spawn. This inner urge will drive the adult salmon along the Pacific Coast to find the precise river they had descended years earlier, and in so doing, the aggregate population will differentiate into identifiable populations, each with its own affinity to a particular river. Once in the river, they will again differentiate as discrete subpopulations, each with its own affinity to a particular stream within the river system.

A salmon can only return to the gravel in which it was deposited as a fertilized egg if it knows where it is going and when it has arrived. Its objective is to reach a particular place in a particular stream within a particular time to deposit either its eggs or sperm, after which it will die.

As each salmon approaches a river, it must make a critical decision. If it selects a river other than the one it descended, it will not reach its destination, regardless of all the other choices it makes. If, however, it swims into the same river it once descended, it is on the correct course—until it comes to the first fork and must again choose.

Regardless of its immediate choice in the lower reaches of the drainage basin, the water is deep, polluted, relatively warm, and its current placid. Here the salmon swims easily, comfortably in the wide river among all the other fishes and river life, where there is much to distract it from its appointed upstream journey.

With time, however, it begins to feel an inner restlessness to go against the current, to seek its home waters. Each time the salmon comes to a fork in its journey, it must make a choice and must accept what the chosen fork has to offer and forego the possibilities in the one not taken. In this sense, each choice is an inescapable consequence of the other choices already made. Each time it chooses the correct fork, the salmon finds that the water, confined within an ever-narrowing channel, is flowing progressively swifter, purer, and colder than the water from which it has just come.

As the streams' banks become more confining, the salmon finds its focus on its destination becoming sharper and more urgent and the channel less and less crowded as those lacking sufficient determination drop by the wayside. Now the distractions of youth and the obstacles in the streambed, such as large boulders and low, swift waterfalls, are as nothing, so focused has the salmon become, so clear is its determination, so urgent is its inner need to arrive at the particular spot within the designated time. When the salmon reaches this state, its focus is so concentrated that it finds the current's force diminished against the internal power of its life's spirit, its inner drive to reach its place of origin.

Thus in youth, the many traveled seaward to become in aggregate the one. Although most died either on that journey or at sea, the rest confronted the external commonalties that helped to shape their lives. Then came the time of maturity, when the compelling inner drive to spawn, to achieve their life's purpose, caused them to separate into smaller groups of like-minded individuals. Many more died on the upstream journey of individuation, which reached its climax with the act of spawning, after which each fish died, returning to the Great Mystery from whence it came. But some of their offspring will live to swim the same gauntlet of decisions when their time to spawn arrives.

Our lives have a thread in common with that of the salmon, because every decision we make determines where we are, where we are going, and where we will end up, which fits well a verse from the Upanishads:

A man is what his deep, driving desire is.
As his deep, driving desire is, so is his will.
As his will is, so is his deed.
As his deed is, so is his destiny.

Our stream in life is the collective thinking of parental, familial, peer, and social pressures—the external commonalties. Like the young salmon, which goes downstream with the current to the ocean, we often accept, with little conscious consideration, the route of least resistance embodied in the collective social thinking that dominates our time. Essayist Logan Pearsall Smith terms this "the Voice of the World" or "consensus reality." In contrast, Albert Einstein foresaw a different way and boldly grasped it. "I soon learned," he said, "to scent out the paths that led to the depths and to discard everything else, all the many things that fill up the mind and divert it from the essential."

In this thought, Einstein touched on the esoteric meaning of a symbol used by the Greek philosopher Pythagoras to instruct his pupils about choice. The symbol can be likened to the stem of a stream where it divides equally into two forks, one going to the right, called Divine Wisdom, and one to the left, called Earthly Wisdom.

Youth, personified by a pupil walking the path of life in tutelage under Pythagoras, symbolized by the central stem of the stream, reaches the point where the path divides. If the pupil chooses the left-hand fork and follows its dictates of the lower human nature, he or she enters a span of folly, dissipation, and thoughtlessness, which inevitably results in his or her undoing. If, on the other hand, the pupil chooses the right-hand fork and follows its dictates of the higher human nature, then he or she, walking hand in hand with integrity, industry, and sincerity, will reunite with the immortals of the celestial spheres.

Although most salmon die and become part of the sea, a few survive and begin swimming against the current to fulfill their life's purpose. As people mature, most will drown in the ocean of mass thinking or silt-laden, polluted waters of materialism, going always with the current, seeking their sense of value through the acceptance of others, who are themselves drowning in mass thinking. Today, for example, the lives of so many people are consumed in feverish activities and untold distractions that they are exhausted nearly all the time.

A few, however, like Einstein, will chart their course against the current, driven by an inner need to find the "still place" within, where spiritual fulfillment can emerge naturally. They will dare to risk the unknown of continual change and fight their way upstream against the current of fearful, self-centered thinking embodied in the present social paradigm. The Buddha's term for meditation, *patisotagami*, fits perfectly into this upstream journey of spirit because it means "going against the current"—the mass conditioning, which has resulted in the rampant materialism and global destruction of our times.

As the stream narrows, these few will find themselves increasingly at odds with the thinking of the general populace in our morally troubled society, for the narrower the stream becomes, the purer and loftier become the ideals, the fewer the people of like mind does one find. "It is not that we love to be alone," wrote Henry David Thoreau, "but that we love to soar, and when we do soar, the company grows thinner and thinner until there is none at all."

If you are courageous and true to the calling (the literal meaning of "vocation") of your spirit, the main obstacle you encounter will for a time be a growing sense of apparent isolation as you face the mounting criticism of those who do not understand and are frightened by the changes they see in you. But if you dare to reach the place where spirituality puts materialism in perspective, you will find your focus so concentrated, your faith so strong, that what to others seems like a Herculean effort becomes to you increasingly effortless as you are learning the difference between what is truly valuable and what is valueless. If you then take the time to look back, you will find, as author Carl Perkins did, that "if it weren't for the rocks in its bed, the stream would have no song."

Saint John of the Cross sees the journey of consciousness a little differently in his Ascent of Mount Carmel, on top of which is Earthly Paradise—not heaven, but rather the grace of life as it is meant to be lived. Below the summit, the mountain is crisscrossed with paths, while at the bottom are the beginnings of two routes. One is wide and inviting, a path of self-will that says "yes" to the ego and at first glance is the obvious one to take, whereas the other is partially hidden, narrow, and tortuous as it wends its way among rocky precipices.

Whoever chooses the wide path is opting for a life of least resistance, but soon finds it coiling back on itself as it shrinks progressively until it disappears altogether in the impenetrable vegetation of the mountain's slope. The narrow path, so difficult at the outset, becomes gradually wider, smoother, and easier as it ascends the mountain, for this is the path of spiritual discipline, which guides the traveler with increasing ease and delight to the pinnacle of life's essence and fullness.

"What is the path?" the Zen Master Nan-sen was asked.

"Every life is the path," he answered.

As you discard the valueless, including what others think of you, you will hold ever more lightly the valuable, for you will learn that true value lies in the gentle touch of sharing, not in the death-grip of ownership. Value lies in the freedom of detachment from the material, not in the shackles of its possession. Value lies in keeping your own score in the way you live your life, ignoring all those in the prison yard who cry foul as they rattle their chains while screaming they are the appointed umpires. As you want less and less, you will find you have more and more. To be "poor" out of choice is to consciously embrace your chosen level of material simplicity and, in accord with that simplicity, hold hands with freedom, leisure, and spirituality.

To hold fast to the spiritual journey requires the utmost courage, for the time will come when in your soul the purple darkness of night will temporarily snuff out your guiding light. It is during this time of spiritual blindness that you must allow yourself to be guided by the invisible eyes of faith.

FAITH IS BELIEF WITHOUT EVIDENCE

Life is a matter of faith—not of sight. For those who believe,
no explanation is necessary. For those who do not,
no explanation is possible.

Faith, which is belief without evidence, keeps the dreamers dreaming and the doers doing. "Faith," says Indian poet Rabindranath Tagore, "is the bird that knows dawn and sings while it is still dark." In contrast, someone once wrote that "worry is interest paid in advance for a debt you may never owe." And the Chinese philosopher Lao Tzu, in dealing with the paradox of faith, said: "When I let go of what I am, I become what I might be. When I let go of what I have, I receive what I need." It is not by accident that "with faith" is the actual meaning of the word "confidence."

Virtually all the greatest thinkers of Christianity adopted faith as a principle that first appeared in the writing of St. Augustine:

> ...Understanding follows faith. We do not believe what we are already able to understand, but attempt to understand that in which we have faith... The fact that knowledge, or understanding, does not come before faith means inevitably that faith entails risk. The risk entailed in faith is of a very special sort; it involves no calculation... The emphasis in faith is on the willingness to risk, not on the chances of losing your wager.[16]

I learned faith as a young child planting peas. I would plant my peas and then immediately begin wondering if they were growing, so I would dig some of them up to see. Sometimes I even dug them up more than once a day. Those that I dug up too often died, but those I left in peace long enough or those I failed to find, germinated and grew. I could then see them coming up through the soil. I didn't know what went on in the soil, because I couldn't see, but I learned that if I was patient, the seeds would grow and that each pea seed would grow only into a pea plant. So my wondering turned into bewonderment, and out of my bewonderment I finally understood what Lao Tzu meant by learning to trust what is happening, because allowing and accepting what is happening is more potent than pushing for that which I want to have happen.

In a similar vein, have you ever looked closely at a leaf bud on a tree in winter? I am still awed that inside a frozen bud are miniature leaves just waiting for spring to release them from bondage. I find the same miracle in the seeds of a flowering plant. Each seed has already present, encrypted in the genetic code and hidden within its coat, the roots, stem, leaves, and all the flower's radiant colors, like an artist's paints stored in tubes. I can, as I gaze at the seed, imagine what the flower will look like when it blooms. But if my lack of faith causes me to become impatient and break open either seed or bud to *see* what is inside, I destroy the miracle.

"Any choice made from faith [such as my accepting the existence of flower and leaf within seed and bud] has the full power of heaven behind it," writes author Caroline Myss, "which is why 'faith the size of

170

a mustard seed can move a mountain.' And any choice," she continues, "made from fear is a violation of the energy of faith."

If I have faith, I believe in the outcome. If I believe in the outcome, I can be patient because everything has its own time for germinating, growing, maturing, and reproducing, be it a flower or vegetable in my garden or a book I am writing. Certainly, as St. Augustine taught, the most precious reward of patience is patience itself.

Time is the current of life's flowing. I can either accept it, learning to navigate life with ease, fluidity, and grace, or I can wear myself out like a swimmer trying with brute strength to defy the river's power by imposing my own strength of will.

The latter, I have found, is always a waste of time and energy. If I plant seeds too early in my garden because of my impatience to see them growing, I inevitably have to replant because I have entirely missed their timing in relation to the length of day and warmth of soil. If I plant too late in the season, I again miss the proper timing and must wait throughout the winter for another chance to cooperate and coordinate with Nature. In this way, the germination of each seed and the sprouting of each bulb I have secreted within the soil rewards my faith when its tender shoot appears above ground. And in like measure, each life's cycle within the Universe that intersects my own, be it that of an earthworm, a flower, a storm, or a comet, counsels both faith and patience.

Most of us, without even thinking about it, place an extraordinary amount of faith in taxi drivers to get us where we are going in one piece. I have had many and varied experiences in taxis in such places as different as New York City; Washington, D.C.; Cairo, Egypt; New Delhi, India; Tokyo, Japan; and Paris, France. I have actually gone through Cairo and Tokyo with my eyes closed, and in Paris, Zane dug holes the shape of crescent moons in my hand with her fingernails as the driver wove in and out of howling, bumper-to-bumper traffic at kamikaze speed. Yet, I've never been in an accident in a taxi.

In all of the above instances, I had faith in the outcome. With the taxis and airplanes, I have risked and still risk my life based on faith in the outcome of my venture. I also have faith that the trees will continue to leaf out each spring, and that the flowers will continue to bloom each in its own time.

We live by faith in secular things all the time. We do a thousand things each day with no evidence that they will work—from cooking breakfast, to flushing the toilet, to using the telephone, to turning on the television, to driving our car, to planting seeds and bulbs in our gardens—and we steadfastly believe in the outcome. Why is it easier to have faith in the outcome of material things, which we know are transitory and can break down, than it is in the outcome of spiritual things? I do not know.

Franklin Delano Roosevelt was certainly infused with a strong sense of faith, which is evidenced by his statement: "The only limit to our realization of tomorrow will be our doubts of today." Spiritual wakefulness comes, then, not in a perception of dualistic thinking by compartmentalizing our lives into spiritual practice and everyday life but in an ever-present awareness that life is spirit and life is faith—the physical manifestation of which often comes in the eleventh hour.

When, I used to wonder over and over, would my faith be strong enough to know itself without some outward sign that I had not been forgotten by the Universe? How much "proof," I used to ask myself, did I need before I dared trust unequivocally in that which I could feel but could not see? Faith, I finally learned, is a test of itself and, as such, often fulfills itself in the eleventh hour.

By way of illustration, I remember an important trip I was taking some years ago, which entailed that I drive over a mountain pass some fifty odd miles to the airport. I arrived at the airport in plenty of time to catch the plane. I parked my car and reached to the back seat to get my briefcase, in which I had all the papers necessary to my trip. It was not there! In severe distress, I wondered what to do because, on the one hand, my trip was all but useless without the papers and, on the other, if I made the more than one hundred mile round trip back to the office to get my briefcase, I would miss the meeting. Finally, feeling total despair, I got out of the car only to find my briefcase perched safely on top of the car, where it had resided the entire trip at sixty or so miles per hour from my office to the airport—how I will never know.

In another instance, Zane and I moved to Las Vegas, Nevada, in 1990, where I had been asked to take a job with the Environmental Protection Agency. We found a house and needed a certain amount of money for a down payment. I had just had two books accepted for publication and the advanced royalty, we decided, would constitute the down payment. Although the money was promised to come early, it did not. As the day for closing on the house drew near, I began to worry that the money would not come; I wavered in my faith. The money not only arrived in the afternoon of the day before closing was to take place but also was almost the precise amount required, including all of the closing costs involved in the transaction. As usual, I had worried needlessly.

Someone once said that it's not the load that wears you down but the way you carry it. The way we each carry our load is dependent on our understanding of and acceptance of faith as the foundation and guiding principle of life. And to learn faith, we must each practice *stabilitas*.

Exercise In Conscious Awareness

Since most of the exercises in this chapter are guided visualizations, it might be wise to refresh yourself on the instructions for a guided visualization given in the Appendix.

Sit quietly now, adjust your body for its greatest comfort. Your breathing is becoming slower, slightly deeper, and more restful as you become aware of the gentle, natural flow of your breath. Let it be more and more peaceful as everyday concerns of the physical world drop away and disappear.

Resting quietly and comfortably, releasing all tension, gradually become aware of your inner garden. Gently withdraw from the senses of the outer world and move through the arched gate into your beautiful sunlit garden within. All is so quiet and peaceful here. The air you breath is sweet and pure and fills your lungs with its nourishing life. You feel the soft, golden sunlight bathing you with comfort. The temperature is perfect. You notice the clear, blue sky and see the giant wingspan of a golden eagle as it glides overhead, riding the gentle currents of the air.

The flowering shrubs are aglow with blossoms of your favorite colors. Inhale their fragrance and absorb the essence of the flowers. Your feet are massaged by the soft carpet of tender grass intermixed with tiny perfumed flowers. Your feet do not crush these delicate blooms as you walk in the quiet of your garden with a sense of exhilaration and anticipation in your heart.

You feel yourself being drawn to a special part of your garden—a bed of roses. Walk amongst the roses, which are in full bloom. You have never seen such gorgeous roses in your life and now know why the rose is called the queen of all flowers. Inhale the fragrance, a most special and transforming odor.

Enjoy the peace and quiet for a time by sitting on a comfortable bench amidst the roses, where you notice one in front of you covered with golden blossoms. One particular blossom draws your attention, and as you focus on it, it gradually opens as the warm sunlight encourages its unfoldment. Smell its lovely scent.

Rest for awhile, for the golden rose is a symbol of faith, confidence, and assurance in the love of the Divine. Its gold is the radiance of the world of spirit, where the treasure of faith helps you accept the way things are and allows you to embrace with confidence the love and wisdom that guides your life. Faith in your heart can be a fearless trust that all is well and that any crooked places in your life are being made straight. It is only a matter of faith, trust, and time.

Rest here for as long as you like and remember that gold represents the ultimate alchemical transformation of consciousness, which leads you from fear to unshakable faith, in which your heart of faith has become your faith of heart. When you feel ready, with the renewal of faith in your heart, walk back through the roses and the rest of the garden, absorbing as you go the beauty and harmony of this special place. Take its essence with you and realize you can return any time you desire to see the golden rose of faith, which blooms forever in your garden. Now walk back through the arched gate of your inner garden.

Gradually, gently bring yourself back to the consciousness of the world around you, of your physical body, feeling well and truly earthed. You have withdrawn your attention now from the inner garden and are now once again firmly functioning with your outer mind in your everyday world. Feeling absolutely at peace and refreshed, with your faith renewed, you are ready to return to your physical life.

Stabilitas in Gardening facilitates Inner Transformation

*By committing myself to become a gardener, I am,
above all, making a promise of stabilitas or steadfastness.
The commitment of stabilitas is not only a promise to persevere within
a particular physical space but also, and most important, a promise to
persevere in my commitment to live as best I can and thereby make every
place I touch by my presence a place of safety and peace for all.*

In speaking of a garden, I do not in this case mean just the physical location in which a particular plot of soil happens to rest, but also the human-spiritual component of gardening as expressed most clearly in the monastic concept of *stabilitas* or steadfastness.[16] Simply put, the monastic concept of *stabilitas* implies not only abiding in a particular place but also identifying oneself with the community in all its simplicity and austerity, its works, its ups and downs, its tensions, joys, and sorrows. *Stabilitas* means perseverance in and fidelity with one's self and a community of people (or the community of a garden) over the long-term.

In monasticism, the vow of *stabilitas* is administered to prevent a monk from deciding to follow a path from one monastic community to another under the appearance of seeking greater potential, a "greener pasture," and in so doing lose the good already at hand. The purpose of the vow is to make a monk realize that steadfastness in and of itself is an immense good and that in a vast majority of cases constitutes a much greater good than might be superficially gleaned by changing monasteries, changing scenery, and changing people.

If a monk or nun will retain *stabilitas* or steadfastness, he or she will be able to affect the greatest and most significant change—the inner transformation into a more conscious human being open to the balance between spirituality and materiality, to live on a different, deeper level, where one is able to attend to other voices than those of the outer world, as Thomas Merton puts it. This may be likened to a thought by Minnie Richard Smith: "Diamonds are only chunks of coal that stuck to their jobs." So it is that if we in secular life continually seek outer distractions by moving from place to place and job to job, which dissipates life's energy, we too lack the focus to achieve the inner transformation that could be ours here and now.

In monastic life, it is not sufficient to remain in the same place; it is also necessary to be under the direction of a spiritual teacher. In secular life, it is not sufficient to remain in the same place; it is also necessary to be committed to a high purpose mediated through a spiritual teacher, which one may find in organized religion. I, however, found such a teacher in my garden, but only after I took the vow of *stabilitas*.

Stabilitas in gardening is not primarily for the perfecting of a garden in the sense of making it more stable and orderly, although that is a natural consequence of steadfastness. Rather, *stabilitas* (holding one's center amidst change) is to root the gardener in a search for meaning in such things as love, faith, trust, mercy, compassion, sharing, justice, and peace, and fully to live one's commitment thereto.

I came to gardening late in life. As a young man I was too impatient for knowledge of the adventures of the world to work the soil quietly, simply, faithfully with spade and hoe, hand and heart. I was taught that I needed to make my impression on the world more than I needed to be a part of it. Thomas Moore, in his book *Meditations*, says "in modern life it may appear that real work is located in the heroics of surviving and succeeding in the world. For the monk [and the gardener] the challenge is in nonheroic intimacy with oneself, others, and the world [Nature]. The monk's [and gardener's] occupation is soul work."

I was trained as a scientist to search through the labyrinth of knowledge for the answers to society's questions about Nature and our place therein, but after many years I learned that science does not hold answers to the questions most dear to the human soul. I say this because in the innocence of childhood I had no knowledge of Nature and little knowledge of animals, but I learned to know both through some inner sense of intrinsic connectedness. It was an intangible feeling of an expanding Universe, a mirror of purity and innocence in which I saw reflected the undefinable wonder of Nature.

I had no burning, abstract, scientific questions to ask about how or why this happened or that. I had only the childlike curiosity to observe, experiment, and observe again through the tadpoles I raised and the little mud dams I built in a roadside ditch. I watched the parade of animal tracks come and go, usually without knowing who made which tracks. I had no grandiose expectations or economic desires. I simply participated as an equal with Nature in such a way that Nature changed me even as I changed Nature, and in the process of interacting, we became one.

In hindsight, what spoke to my heart and called to my soul was the Eternal Governance of Nature—the Unseen behind the apparent, the

Knowing behind the knowledge. Nature, the visible manifestation of divine invisible laws, is the Cosmic Reflection of what I am. And as I participate consciously with Nature, I become. Therefore, I, too, am a reflection of Eternal Governance, the Laws of which I am free to keep or to break, but the consequences of which I cannot escape.

I entered science to better understand the Laws of Eternal Governance that I might freely follow them and honor the harmony of my soul. But when I entered science, I unknowingly forfeited Nature—and endangered my soul.

As I began sleuthing Nature's mysteries through the accumulation and interpretation of knowledge, it became increasingly clear that everything had to be separated, named, and classified for the affixing of value as befits social economics, which in turn demands economic justification for such a thing as a species to merely exist. To determine the value of a thing, therefore, and to justify its economic existence, I had to ask questions about it, questions that could be framed into nonparticipatory, objective, abstract hypotheses.

Over the years, I found that if I wanted to be reputed as a scientist in good standing amongst my peers, I had to make "objective" judgments about Nature based on hard data and the appearance of what was. In other words, I had to objectify Nature. I had to look with my eyes and the left half of my brain, but was not allowed to see with my heart and the right half of my brain. Science, I found, is the study of Nature by abstraction and duality, which becomes the perceived abstraction and duality of Nature.

I was not allowed, for example, to participate with Nature in a mutual context of being. I was allowed only to intellectualize about Nature, but not to express any feelings. My feelings for and about the sacredness of Nature were not admissible in anything I did. This insistence on cold, abstract intellectualism is the root of what I believe to be a common misuse of science—namely the insistence that scientists are objective when as people they cannot be.

Now, looking back on my transition from the wonder of Nature to the scientific study of Nature, it is clear that objectifying Nature leads us, the human animal, to disconnect from our spiritual roots, even to deny such roots altogether, which too often breeds a haughtiness in attitude and a foolish contempt for the Laws of Eternal Governance. By this, I do not imply that science has no place in the scheme of things, because it does. But science must be practiced with a great deal of humility because it is not our ignorance that is the problem, but rather the certainty we ascribe to our knowledge. That is the wellspring of our intellectual arrogance and empty, misguided superiority.

Even the process and practice of science, which I willingly accepted in research for more than twenty-five years, I now find to be lacking in its ability to touch—for a single instant—the meaning, wonder, and sanctity of life, which lie beyond and defy human knowledge. Science, therefore, will never be able to give us the answers to the searching questions in our souls, because science cannot prove anything. It can only disprove something, so it cannot be looked to for "the answers," only for "unanswers," which, nevertheless, are de facto answers, but not those we seek. The "unanswers" of science are like the accessibility to "emptiness" of the monastic life, where a monk becomes ever more silent, transparent, and available to Truth.

We in Western industrialized society are too often floating aimlessly on a sea of shallow scientific abstraction that is often in complicity with linear economic theory and industrialized greed. And it is clear to me that the current notion of science, as it is often practiced, is in deadly grapple with the spiritual foundation of human existence on Earth. The outcome of this contest between the intellect of the mind and the intuition of the heart will likely be determined within this century, and I hope, for the sake of human society, that it will be a consciously derived compromise—a balance between the two, for only together are they whole and mutually supportive.

I say this because my professional years were a personal struggle to understand and balance the two within myself, to find a moral place within human society and a viable connection between that society and Nature. Although I was often castigated for the intuition embodied in my science and labeled a "heretic," I still feel that worthwhile science depends on intuition for the basic morality of its philosophical foundation and the enlightenment of its questions.

Today I no longer see the world through the abstract veil of science, or materialism, or fear, but rather, I see the Spirit of life, the Divine investiture, that which lies unseen behind that which is apparent. Unfortunately, both biological science and social economics are mostly blind to this spiritual underpinning of the Universe as computers, statistics, quantification, and specialization take the place of spirituality, intuition, faith, imagination, and humility.

That I must continue working toward resolution between human society and Nature is the theme central to my life. But now I must also take the next step, that of reaching beyond where I have been. Carl Jung said that, as a practicing psychoanalyst, he could not take any client beyond the internal terrain he had personally traversed in self-transcendence. And so it is with all of us. I thus let go of scientific research. I let go of seeking answers external to my being. As I enter the reflective years of my life, I must come to grips with putting the lessons I have learned into the greater context of the Universe.

And what have I learned through all my years of labor? I hope a greater clarity of vision, for I have grown to cherish the inner silence of spiritual solitude. Spiritual solitude means standing squarely in front of myself with no distractions so that I may see, as truly as I have the courage to accept, what I am in light of what I might become. And in the process, I am learning to be a gardener.

But what, you will ask, is a gardener, other than one who tends a garden?

A gardener, I shall answer, is one who sees the world most clearly through a conscious double vision, like peering out of a house through a pane of window glass. Through the window one can see objects that lie outside the house while simultaneously seeing reflections of things that lie within. And it is through the art of gardening that this double vision is expressed as that which my soul casts without while simultaneously seeing itself reflected within. The Qur'an expresses this as "all faces are His Face."

Gardening is the act by which spirituality and art merge into the context of Nature. It is where we use the function of universal biophysical laws to transpose in graphic form the cultural beauty and spiritual harmony of our inner soulscapes to the fluid medium of Nature's outer landscape. Gardening is the conscious marriage of cultural myth and Universal Laws of Being. To garden well even the tiniest piece of the Earth, one must begin by gardening one's mind, which demands *stabilitas*, as British philosopher James Allen affirms so beautifully:

> A man's mind may be likened to a garden, which may be intelligently cultivated or allowed to run wild; but whether cultivated or neglected, it must, and will, bring forth. If no useful seeds are put into it, then an abundance of useless weed seed will fall therein, and will continue to produce their kind.

> Just as a gardener cultivates his plot, keeping it free from weeds, and growing the flowers and fruits which he requires, so may a man tend the garden of his mind, weeding out all the wrong, useless, and impure thoughts, and cultivating toward perfection the flowers and fruits of right, useful, and pure thoughts. By pursuing this process, a man sooner or later discovers that he is the master gardener of his soul, the director of his life. He also reveals, within himself, the laws of thought, and understands, with ever-increasing accuracy, how the thought forces and mind elements operate in the shaping of his character, circumstances, and destiny.[14]

Only when one has the discipline to garden the landscape of one's mind, weeding out all inharmonious thoughts, will the harmony of one's soul be consummated in Nature's landscape. In this sense, gardening means to negotiate a new reality with Nature, one based on Universal Laws as reflected in the level of one's spiritual development. This is simply saying that the patterns created in a backyard garden by an individual or on a landscape by a society are but a pictorial image of that person's or that society's spiritual attainment and ecological understanding—the greater the spiritual attainment, the truer the ecological understanding.

I say "spiritual attainment," because gardening is an act born out of love for the Earth and all living things. Love creates an openness or permeability to experience, an unfolding without judgment. It expands awareness of and compassion for oneself and others in relationship, and its intimacy permits connectivity of distance—even into the generations of the future. Love personalizes the Universe while keeping it intrinsically free to be itself. In this sweep of human thought are sown the seeds of all one has to give.

Gardening is giving to the Earth and all its inhabitants, including ourselves, the only things of value that we each have to offer: our love, our trust, our respect, and the benefit of our experience. The very process of gardening is thus the process through which we become intimately attuned with Nature and, through Nature, with ourselves.

To engage in the act of gardening is to know and to commune with the heart and the mind of the Eternal Mystery in ourselves, in one another, and in all of Nature. To treat the soil in the sacred manner of gardening, as a vehicle to approach the Eternal Mystery, is to enter into continual prayer in which one touches all the wonders of the Universe and finds enfolded all the problems of human existence on this tiny planet suspended in infinite space.

Exercise In Conscious Awareness

Before you get to this particular exercise in *stabilitas*, you need a little background on your shadow, that part of you that you would dearly love to disown but cannot. Dr. Carl Jung, the Swiss psychiatrist, defined the dark side of our psyche as the "shadow," which is a handy dumping ground for all the characteristics of our personality we choose to disown, that we fail to see or know because they have not adequately entered into our everyday waking consciousness.[17]

The shadow may be thought of as the despised quarter of our being, and is paired with being wrong, bad, or evil. But also held within the shadow of our psyche is the pure gold, the noble, creative aspects of our personality of which we are afraid.

The roots of this whole shadow-making process within us begin as we enter into culture and cultural ideals. We divide our lives and separate things into good and evil, acceptable and unacceptable, because culture insists—literally demands—that we behave in a particular manner.

These refused, unaccepted, buried-in-the-deep-dark basement parts of ourselves don't go away, for all our characteristics must appear somewhere in our personal inventories. Nothing may be left out. What we try to omit simply collects in the corners of our personalities and, when hidden long enough, takes on a life of its own, often with an energy potential nearly as great as that of our egos, which are those parts of ourselves we consciously know and accept.

When the energy of the shadow builds up too much, it can erupt as a black mood, anger, rage, harsh words spewed out of our mouths, some indiscretion slipping past us, as depression or even accidents and psychosomatic illness. Ignoring the golden qualities with ourselves can also be every bit as damaging as hiding our dark sides. It may even be necessary to suffer a severe shock or illness before a person learns to let out the magnificent inner gold.

Our work is to own and integrate every aspect of ourselves, rather than to disown those parts we do not want and thus project them outward onto someone or something else. We all know the story of the scapegoat driven once a year from the community with all the people's shadow elements heaped firmly onto its back.

Instead of heaping all our unwanted psychological parts onto a scapegoat, our task is to restore ourselves to wholeness by putting these fractured, alienated parts together again. If each of us can learn truly to love our inner enemies, then we can also begin in like measure to redeem and love our so-called outer enemies.

Many personal and collective benefits will result if we each see ourselves in totality. For example, we would fall in and out of love a lot less frequently because we would not be initially projecting the golden parts of ourselves onto another and then, as love grows thin, reverse ourselves and project those parts that are annoying, distasteful, and even downright intolerable.

If we saw ourselves in totality, relationships in general would be truer and more enduring than they currently are. Hero-worship in its varying degrees would cease because we would each accept our finest qualities and be responsible for them. We would stop making others the bad guy and look first within to assess what about ourselves we are refusing to see, know, and accept.

The shadow is the cause of war on all levels, both within and without. In addition, the process of owning our inner heaven and hell is the highest form of creativity. A great deal of energy is released and begins to flow as we reach a place of inner wholeness. This place where light and dark touch is where miracles arise, where personal and collective peace are possible.

If you do not think you have a shadow, ask yourself how many times a day you employ compulsive substitutes for emotions, such as food, sodas, alcohol, cigarettes, television, and so on? How many times do you run away from facing your emotions through the use of distractions?

You cannot run away from something that is negative; it will only grow larger and stronger each time you try. You must exercise *stabilitas* and steadfastly confront your fears by moving through them toward something positive.

When you are at home and find yourself getting restless because some unconscious, unwanted emotion is making itself known, causing you to think about some kind of distraction, go into your garden and work, taking nothing in the form of distraction with you. While working, focus on becoming aware of the emotions you are trying to avoid through dissipative, addictive behaviors. Notice how many times you have recently distracted yourself from thinking about or confronting a particular emotion or issue you need to deal with. Notice, too, that over time the emotion is requiring ever-increasingly potent distractions.

If you have a thought that causes pain to rise to the surface, tell your story to a rose bush or a flower, and if needs be, give yourself permission to cry in the process. You will find that plants are excellent listeners who never interrupt, talk back, speak out of turn, tell secrets, or blab about confidential conversations. This is a form of shadow work—the very essence of *stabilitas*, and the plants in your garden are superb confidants.

Making Sacred that which is Material

Although I spend inordinate amounts of time attempting to materialize spirit, one of life's chief tasks is to make the material sacred through the spirituality of my thoughts, aspirations, motives, and actions.

Sitting in the cool shade of the Norway maple trees along the southern border of my garden on a warm afternoon, I drift gently into that world between waking and sleeping. It is here, in this in-between time, that I go through the veil of materialism into my garden within my garden, which some would call "meditation," which author Manly P. Hall calls the "doorway between the material world and the transcendental spheres of Nature."

Here, amidst the rosemary, sage, and thyme in the garden of my soul, is the active stillness of the Universe. Here, in absolute peace, I reflect on and am given a glimmer of the unifying principle between spirituality and materialism, a concept uniquely suited to gardening. Here, as Kakuzo Okakura wrote in *The Book of Tea*, is "recognition of the mundane as of equal importance with the spiritual. [Here] it [is] held that in the great relation of things there . . . [is] no distinction of small or great, an atom possessing equal possibilities with the universe."

Most people think of the spiritual path as being necessarily devoid of materialism. Yet, it is material life along the path that bestows upon us the opportunities for greater "wakefulness." Life itself is our opportunity for awakening and awareness. It is only through our dualistic thinking that we compartmentalize our lives into spiritual practice and everything else. Spiritual awareness is a product of a lifestyle rather then compartmentalized practice.

Hence, materialism and spirituality are each but a facet of the other, each a part of the same path. "All opposites coincide in God," wrote mystic Nicholas of Cusa. Without the one, how would we know the other? How would we be whole?

To have one without the other is but an illusion. The material is as much a part of the Universe as is the spiritual and vice versa. Part of the problem lies in our notion that the material is necessarily of the intellect and hence pragmatic, while the spiritual is necessarily of the heart and thus intangible, which is like saying that I must be logical and plant all vegetables in my garden or be emotional and plant all flowers—but not both.

There is, however, an alternative to this dualism, to heal the schism between our thinking and our feeling. We are taught to *think* with our minds and *love* with our hearts, but that is a house divided, like a garden of either vegetables *or* flowers, where the one feeds the body, the other the soul. But nowhere in such a garden can the totality of body and soul be integrated. We must therefore learn also to love with our minds and think with our hearts, which can be likened to a garden in which the balance and harmony of vegetables and flowers nourishes the whole human. Then we experience a whole-ness, a holiness.

Only when we see in the vegetables of our garden the same beauty we behold in the flowers will we see the material made spiritual in the heart. Only when we see in the flowers of our garden the same necessity for daily life that we discern in the vegetables will we see the spiritual

184

made manifest through the mind. This is merely saying that all things are indivisible because everything is defined by its relationship to everything else; nothing can exist out of relationship to the seed of its apparent opposite.

Nevertheless, to our Western industrialized minds there is a tendency to think of the spiritual and the material as representing a juxtaposition of mutually exclusive opposites. We thus think one who is materialistic cannot be spiritual and one who is seeking spirituality must give up the material, that to have one we must necessarily forsake the other, rather than of life as a gradual unfoldment of an inner awareness illuminating the divine in the mundane.

It is true, however, as Thomas Merton wrote in *Cistercian Life*, that when a person takes a vow to follow the monastic life "the things the monk seeks do not belong to the world of the market and he [or she] is not for sale."[18] One of the purposeful essentials of monastic life is its separation from the world in order for the monk to seek the true monastic silence and, in the process, to ignore all things irrelevant to the monastic calling.

Spirituality and materialism are no more than different views of the same world, for both are guided by thought, which is the greatest power in life. Spirituality is the interpretation of physical, biological, psychological, and social principles in terms of an order higher than oneself, which compels us to share with others, to be one another's keepers, present and future. Materialism, on the other hand, is the interpretation of those same principles solely in terms of one's own benefit, as though the individual is the sole proprietor and beneficiary of all things, hence the most important individual in the Universe.

This does not mean the twain shall never meet, for surely they must. Accepting one to the exclusion of the other is to walk the shadowy path of illusion. The materialistic and the spiritual are each a part of the other and we must learn to live equally well with both simultaneously, which means to live in the world softly, as an asset to others and to life itself, yet not to be entirely of the world. Was it not Jesus who wisely suggested that we render unto Caesar what is Caesar's and unto God what is God's, thus making it clear that life was a matter of personal choices along the path one must tread?

The path along which I daily tread stretches from horizon to horizon as my past gradually fades from view while my potential future gradually comes into view. It is the neverending path of choices, a path that is never clearer than when I am working in my garden.

Here, every choice I make bears fruit immediately, or within a week, a month, two months, or a year, all well within the vision of my memory, which allows me to trace each consequence to the causative choice of its beginning and see where my thoughts and actions are accountable for the results. Thus, while I can create unity in the beauty and utility of my garden by planting flowers amongst the vegetables and vegetables amongst the flowers, I must first risk change, by reaching beyond the supposedly mutually exclusive duality of materialism and spirituality that I was taught, and balance the one with the other.

Exercise In Conscious Awareness

Profound good can come if we quietly withdraw daily from the turmoil and conflict of physical life into the silent center within. Deep in this place of silence and tranquillity, a true perspective can be gained and wisdom may be found. Peace of mind resides here as well.

Thomas Moore calls this the building of the inner temple and the creation of *temenos*, which is space set aside for sacred use. By going within, we not only find the sacred foundation of all life but also bring it back with us, where we can apply it in our everyday physical life. We begin to discriminate with clarity between the things that matter, the eternal spiritual truths, the real things of life, and those that are transient, trivial, and evanescent, those with us for a moment or a day, but which pass tomorrow into the unknown. We also begin to know with our hearts that all creation is permeated with the presence of Divine Being. People of the Jewish faith call this the *Shekinah*—the beautiful light, which is the presence of God everywhere.

Before beginning your time of quiet, relaxing renewal, allow the words of Brother Lawrence, a Lay brother among the barefooted Carmelites of Paris in 1666, to gently permeate your thoughts and feelings:

> The time of business . . . does not with me differ from the time of prayer; and in the noise and clutter of my kitchen, while several persons are at the same time calling for different things, I possess God in as great tranquillity as if I were upon my knees at the Blessed Sacrament.

Heaven, which actually means a state of harmony, happiness, and holiness, existed every moment and in all activities for Brother Lawrence. Every aspect of his life was sacred and holy. His mind did not differentiate or categorize sacred acts from profane ones; all life blended into an indivisible whole permeated with the Divine essence.

Begin now to shift your awareness from any noise and turmoil of the outer world and your surroundings to your inner world of peace and quietness. Let your shoulders and arms feel heavy yet comfortably at ease. As your shoulders relax, feel all the cares and tension melting away. Let go now any and all mental and physical tightness or strain anywhere in your body, and be still and comfortable. A gentle relaxation is spreading through your entire body.

Notice that your breathing has become quiet and peaceful as you are gently led through the soft light bathing the gate of your inner garden. The feelings and sights in your garden are familiar by now, for this is the special place of your own imagination. Open all your senses to the delight and beauty of this sacred place. With each breath, you feel the healing power of Nature in your garden.

The very beautiful and spacious garden of lawns and colorful flowers interspersed with magnificent trees draws you to the still pool of azure water in the center of your garden. It is so peaceful here. The sights, sounds, and smells are themselves a healing balm. If you wish, sit beside the pool in quiet contemplation.

Notice that on the still water of the pool floats a pure-white water lily. As you gaze at the lily, the petals open gently to the sunlight. You sense as clearly as you ever have the sacred life, the Divine essence, in each glimmering petal and in its golden center. In the heart of the water lily is cradled a transparent jewel, like a sparkling, many-faceted diamond. Its brilliance and perfection transfix you.

As you sit quietly beside the pool, breathing in the purity and the fragrance of the white lily, you are aware that from the center of that shining jewel you may receive wisdom, strength, upliftment, and blessing. Be still as your mind and heart receive the teaching of the sacredness and perfection of all life.

Remain here, basking in the holiness of each aspect of life for as long as you wish.

When you are ready and feel it is time to return, gently move back through your garden, remembering each detail of form and color, especially the wonderful feeling they give you. Retrace your steps through the gate. Slowly and gently breathe your way back into consciousness of the room and world about you and your physical body. Notice the sense of well-being that fills you with peace and harmony. Within your heart, you have a true understanding of the sacred oneness of all aspects of life.

Whether you are washing a dish or kneeling in selfless prayer, all activities in life are sacred if you think they are, if you consciously live your life in a sacred manner as did Brother Lawrence. Now go into your outer garden and practice transferring the peace of your inner garden into such everyday activities as planting bulbs, weeding, raking leaves, and pruning a tree.

Balancing Activity with Inactivity

Evolution and personal growth follow a similar pattern.

In spring, when the first flowers poke their bright, colorful faces out of winter's dark soil, perhaps while snow is still in patches on the ground, my garden is simple in appearance and easily accepted as being in order, for all is blooming and nothing yet is dying with the seasons.

As summer arrives and the plants of spring begin to die, the simplicity gives way to increasing complexity as life and death commence to mingle in a state of accelerated activity. It thus becomes more and more difficult to keep order in my ever-changing, thirsty garden in which weeds seem bent on taking over. Now is the time I wander slowly through my garden, looking not at the work to be done, but rather allowing myself to marvel at the perfect order of Nature's processes as once more life cycles through itself in the eternal dance of becoming and disappearing.

Unlike spring, when all seemed in order, or summer, when the changing seasons still held the promise of life's vital bloom, autumn is the time when spent plants begin to rattle their desiccated skeletons in the scurrying breezes as a portent of coming winter. Although the colors of autumn still nourish my soul, it is a lesser bouquet of flowers and a diminishing array of colors that greets my eye.

With the onset of cold nights, leaves turn different hues and commence one by one to journey earthward. Then comes the first storm of the dying year in which everything is blown asunder and all about the desired order of my garden has vanished.

Once again, I stroll through my garden as dead leaves crunch underfoot or scuttle here and there in the cold breath of the North Wind. As I wander the pathways that still hold in memory the warming days of spring and summer's palette of color, I observe with quiet detachment how life departs *en masse* in autumn, leaving behind the unplanned chaos of dying.

Now is not the time to think of the mounting work at hand, but instead to notice how life is withdrawing as root, bulb, and seed into the soil from whence it came and from whence it will come again. Now is the time to contemplate and give thanks for the bounty of the growing season just past and to prepare my soul to let go the sunny days of butterflies and whispering breezes, of rose perfume and spicy mint. The time is at hand to turn my thoughts inward and accept the dying of my garden as winter's icy grip comes daily closer, for it is written in the Bible (Ecclesiastes 3:1-2) that "To every thing there is a season and a time to every purpose under the heaven."

Watching my garden come and go from season to season and year to year, I am aware that its developmental trend is similar to that of personal growth and evolution, from the simple to the complex and back to the simple. This trend is neither gradual nor smooth nor predictable in its happening, and there are many avenues it can take.

To illustrate, in a good seed year for maples, during which the wind distributes the seeds well, there is an instant potential that the following spring would see throughout my garden the beginnings of a grove of maple trees, were I not to intervene. On the winds of another year, there might come into my garden the seeds of thistle and fireweed, having been borne aloft from distant places on warm days in September. Again, I must intervene should I wish to have my garden—as nearly as possible—as I want it, otherwise it follows the path of evolution, a path we humans understand only in theory.

In evolutionary theory, the dynamics of the evolutionary process are applied to an entire ecosystem, which is comprised of living organisms as they interact within their environments. Evolution of species occurs when an established species is destabilized within its habitat. The cycle of dominance is broken when the old species is suddenly replaced by the emerging new species in a quantum leap of evolution rather than a slow transit.

When I first encountered this concept of long periods of evolutionary quiescence punctuated by bursts of evolutionary activity, I realized that my life follows a similar pattern, although not in the strict sense comparable to evolution. As a consultant, for example, I find that phone calls, engagements, and travel come in short flurries when I may be intensely busy for two to three days here or three to four days there, then all is quiet for two to three weeks, often more.

It is precisely this kind of unpredictable pattern that causes many would-be consultants to give up because our Western industrialized society is so devoted to acting, doing, and accomplishing that little credence is given to the domain of being, contemplation, receptivity, and inner stillness: the so-called down side or down time of the cycle. And, I am the first to admit that if I did not love writing books, hiking, and working in my garden, I would have an extremely difficult time solely as a consultant waiting for the next round of activity. As it is, however, I cherish my "quiet times" for writing because in these times of solitude are the deeper spheres of my psyche revealed.

These long periods of quiescence and waiting show up even in the Runes, an ancient Icelandic Oracle last used by Rune Masters in the seventeenth century. The Runes are a personal system of divination akin in function to the Tarot and the Chinese "Book of Changes." The Runes served as the *I Ching* of the Vikings.[19]

In the progression of the Runes through the evolutionary cycle of self-transformation, one can draw the Rune *Isa*, which is "Standstill, That Which Impedes, Ice." *Isa* represents the winter of spiritual life, where positive accomplishment is currently unlikely, and a chilly wind blows over the ice floes of conditions, behaviors, habits, and desires that must be shed, released, and cleansed away. Basically, it is a period of gestation that precedes a birth and only patience will suffice.

How many times do we actively resist these naturally inactive periods of our life's cycle only to court the danger Thomas Merton holds before us: "There is a pervasive form of contemporary violence to which the idealist . . . most easily succumbs: activism and over-work. . . . To allow oneself to be carried away by a multitude of conflicting concerns, to surrender to too many demands, to commit oneself to too many people, to want to help everyone in everything, is to succumb to violence. The frenzy of the activist neutralizes his [or her] work for peace. It destroys the fruitfulness of his [or her] own work, because it kills the root of inner wisdom which makes work fruitful."

However, by embracing the message of *Isa*, we gladly accept even those times when we are most inwardly engaged in self-transformation. And then, as if by magic, the Rune next to *Isa* is *Sowelu*, the final Rune of this cycle of self-realization. *Sowelu* stands for "Wholeness!"

From what I have seen, most people's lives follow a similar pattern. But it is the periods of inactivity that we notice most, because they are uncomfortably "empty" of outer action—like winter when my garden is sleeping and all appears still, withdrawn into the silence of the earth, where seeds are secreted, conserved, and protected in readiness for the time when new life will be called forth. These are the periods when we are inwardly alone with ourselves, an often excruciating experience from which most of us desperately flee. So, it is these quiet times that we compulsively fill with tightly scheduled activity, such as entertainment or various addictions, anything to keep us from having to confront our inner selves. During such times we too often dispense with the indispensable rather than with the superfluous.

The concept of long periods of evolutionary quiescence punctuated by bursts of evolutionary activity, almost like the opening of a new chapter as the old one ends, relates equally well to my spiritual evolution. Here I use the term evolution advisedly for I know naught where I am going—only that I am going, and each new chapter represents a quantum leap in my evolution because it calls forth ever-deeper consciousness.

As my dominant beliefs and patterns of thought are destabilized by a circumstance, a sudden awareness is triggered. The dynamic and hard-won equilibrium of my old beliefs and views is broken and suddenly replaced by the emergence of a new understanding, a new insight—a leap in spiritual evolution. As I look back over my life, I see the pattern of long periods of incubation and preparation when I felt alone inwardly, which for me brings to life crossing the desert of spiritual silence. Even Jesus spent forty days and forty nights wandering in this desert.

Esoterically, forty relates to periods of confinement, darkness, and powerlessness, such as the forty weeks a babe rests in the womb of its mother or the forty years that Moses and his people wandered in the wilderness. Medieval Christianity called this time the dark night of the soul, and Dante referred to it as the journey through hell and purgatory. It is the journey in the belly of a fish for many a hero.

Thankfully, these periods of aloneness are interrupted by short periods of intense insight, the oases of spiritual illumination. The Sufi Master Pir-o-Murshid Inayat Khan explained that higher consciousness is reached by finding conditions favorable to being peaceful, silent, aloof. Silence in this case in not just of the body but also of the mind, emotions, and consciousness.

I find as I grow older, that the spiritual silence is deeper, more profound, and often lonelier than in my youth when I "knew" more than I do now, when I was certain of the uncertainties, when I thought "knowledge" was knowing, and when I saw with warrior's eyes a world to conquer and my "mark" waiting to be made. But now, with the eyes of a gardener, I see the world simply as a classroom suspended in the great arc of the Universe, a classroom in which I am to learn both what I am and the consequences of my choices that I may better relate to all those who share with me this tiny, fragile planet.

And I find that I need to withdraw my attention from the clamoring of the outer world and focus instead on the spiritual seed growing within.

Thus, I find myself evolving as I change my sense of values and choices from the merely physical and psychological to the sacred and sublime.

I also find as I grow older that my spiritual illuminations are deeper, more profound, and give me a definite "knowing" that I am not alone in some great spiritual void. It is only now, when my pilgrimage on Earth surpasses sixty years, that I see these alternate periods of stillness and motion to occur simultaneously on the inner spiritual plane and the outer secular one, but not necessarily in sync. And as I stand today atop one of the inner foothills of maturity and look back down the path to the valley of my youth, I see that my entire life has been and is an inner journey of spiritual evolution, even when I didn't think it was, even when I was adamantly opposed to and staunchly rejected such an idea.

From my present vantage, I see behind me the "valley-of-what-was" and before me the great "peak-of-what-can-be," and I know it will not be easy to climb. For even with firm resolve in my heart, I am aware that, between where I now stand and where I must go, the path wanders through great spiritual deserts of barren silence dotted only here and there with oases of refreshment and illumination. Thus is defined the one path and the many paths of spiritual evolution as they converge at the summit. This is the spiritual desert I encounter even amidst the bloom of my garden.

During the "dark night of the soul," when the inner guidance of spiritual light seems to have vanished forever, and the soul is stripped of all external security. Jungian analyst and author Robert Johnson tells us that this moment of painful despair and unendurable suffering is also the moment of redemption and enlightenment. In the Bible it is referred to as the "wilderness," which is similar to the "forest" of fairy tales. To Joan of Arc it was the apparent abandonment and the unbearable silence of her "voices" while she was imprisoned prior to being burned at the stake as a heretic. In each case it represents the unknown labyrinth of the unconscious, where the mettle, faith, and trust of a soul is tested before being allowed to proceed farther with fuller awareness. It is also, I think, what St. Augustine meant when he admonished us that "God is inside. We are outside."

I use the desert of silence as my metaphor of those periods when my spiritual light seems to go out and I feel empty, stumbling, lost, and alone because, having worked in both the Sahara and the Nubian Deserts of North Africa, I know the seeming timelessness and eternal silence of those deserts, where forever hangs like a pall over barren vastness. Here, as far as the eye can see, reigns shifting sand, blowing wind, and the emptiness of limitless space. This vastness of space somehow caused me to feel "hemmed in" by its very limitlessness, where by day the white-hot sun scorches the body and simmering heat stifles the mind and by night come forth the scorpions, vipers, and cobras, and howling demons ride the midnight winds of the imagination.

Here, in the desert of suffocating spiritual silence, am I in ultimate confrontation with my fears. Here is the quintessential test of mortality, for there is nothing to quench the terrible thirst and hunger of my soul, and wherever I look, God, in whatever form God is perceived, is not to be found. Here I have the sense of being profoundly and truly alone. "Loneliness is a word to express [the] pain of being alone . . .," wrote American theologian Paul Tillich, "and solitude is a word to express [the] glory of being alone…"

It is while wandering blindly without a spiritual compass in this interminable desert that my faith is easily lost. Finally, however, after what seems like aimless wandering without end, I am brought to my knees in humility, to be born anew at some greater vantage along the path of spiritual evolution. That rebirth can take place only when the desert of spiritual silence has burned away the dross, that dead and useless part of the old, rigid self, to make way for the openness of heart necessary to receive spiritual illumination. What has been full, must empty. What has increased, must decrease. This is an abiding law of the Universe.

As inactivity, like my garden sleeping in winter, makes way for activity, like its counterpart of awakening in spring, so too the inactivity of spiritual incubation must take place prior to the activity of spiritual evolution. And like choosing which flowers and vegetables to plant in my garden and when, I must choose how to walk the path life has offered me; for in the end, choice and the necessity to choose are all I have. "Choices," observes author Edwin Markham, "are the hinges of destiny," hinges that include knowing when enough, is enough.

Exercise In Conscious Awareness

Just as life in our gardens begins in spring and builds to a crescendo in summer only to wane in autumn and sleep peacefully throughout winter, so too must we balance the activity in our lives with inactivity. The question is how well balanced between activity and inactivity is your life? This is an important question, because continual activity without time for reflection seldom culminates in a wise or healthy outcome.

Remember a time in the past when you were forced into inactivity, when control in the outer world was stripped from you through illness, temporary disability, or unemployment. What was it like for you? Did you accept it peacefully? Were you grateful for the quiet withdrawal of inner solitude, or did you resist and fight the loss of outer control and activity? Was your identity and self-confidence based on the treadmill of constant activity and production?

To find out how you react to inactivity, how well you accept it as a part of your life, go into your garden and just sit. Let go all clamoring thoughts and still your mind and body as much as you are able to. Let go all things that press in from without. Quiet yourself, and kindly invite your inner nature to come forward. Allow your day its true perspective. This is important because activity without inactivity and the time to reflect is missing the heart of wisdom.

Sit, therefore. Do nothing. Be patient with your garden—and yourself. Feel what arises within. Notice the vibrant colors of your flowers, the health and succulence of your vegetables. Little breezes may caress your face in their passing. Insects may hover near and serenade you. Butterflies may flit about and display their fragile beauty. In the clouds overhead, you might see the face of a person or of an animal-totem appearing as a messenger.

Wisdom, the fruit of life's experiences, ripens only when your mind is still, for only then can reflection move softly with discernment amidst the thoughts of your inner garden, weeding the impure out of the pure, the valueless out of the valuable, the unwise out of the wise. As your mind becomes silent, only then can you hear the still small voice within—the true bearer of wisdom and effortless effort. Only in the quiet stillness of inner solitude can you accompany the Master in caring for the garden of your soul.

MAKING ENOUGH, ENOUGH

There are two ways to wealth: work harder to satisfy insatiable material desires, or want less. With the former there is never enough to satisfy the fear of scarcity and hence a restlessness of the ego, which is manifested in an aggressive attachment to and recognition of that which is physical. With the latter there is a growing sufficiency and hence a contentment of the soul, which is manifested as a gentle, progressive detachment from the physical. It translates as a pervasive sense of well-being, as an economy of life and energy in the best sense of the words.

Our neighbors watched Zane and me make many trips to the mountains to collect lava and other rocks with which to construct the various shapes in which we planned to enclose flowers. They watched the progress as I built raised wooden beds for vegetables. They watched with curiosity as we selected plants with which to populate our garden.

Then, after three years of hard work, I said to one of my neighbors: "Well, I guess we're about done with the initial creative phase. From now on it will be maintenance."

He looked at me for a moment and said, "you'll never be done. You can't stop doing things, making things, adding things to your garden."

His absolute certainty gave me pause to consider. Even though what he said so matter-of-factly was a projection on his part, it wasn't something I could easily dismiss. At some deep level it called into question something I needed to examine within myself. I had never before lived in a place where I considered staying for more than a few years. I had always felt an inner sense of restlessness and knew that I would move again, so I had always held something of myself back—an unequivocal commitment to a place, a sense of *stabilitas*. But not this time, not now.

Still, I had to ask myself, what does it mean, really mean, to achieve a level of physical accomplishment beyond which there was nothing more to attain, nothing to prove to myself or others, nothing to want? This notion of sheer contentment did not compute with what I had been so assiduously taught; namely, there was always something bigger, better, and more stimulating and sensational to achieve, and my mission in life was to continually seek that next brighter encore. By way of example, consider the recent advertisement in my local newspaper by a local car dealer: "To hell with downsizing. Introducing the new Volkswagen Passat. Starting at $20,750, it's proof that bigger is not only better, it's also a lot more fun. Live large. The New Passat." With this in mind, the question gradually framed itself: When is enough of something, enough?

Thinking about the meaning of enoughness, I am reminded of one of our friends who is the Abbot of a Trappist Monastery. Some time ago, he told Zane and me that his familial brother had asked him the pointed question on the day he took his final vows to become a monk: "Well, what happens next?" Nothing external, our friend explained, but his brother simply could neither understand nor immediately accept that our friend was not withholding the news of something bigger and better in the future. In this, the Abbot's brother is like the rabbi in the Hasidic tale who walks back and forth over buried treasure every day without ever guessing what is beneath his feet.

This story highlights the point that the difference between the mystic's narrow path of renunciation and the broad super highway of the secular world seems to be an ever-widening chasm. Even Henry David Thoreau, though perhaps not a mystic, thought the essence of life could be expressed in three words: "Simplify, simplify, simplify." He therefore had three chairs in his cabin—one for solitude, two for friendship, and three for society. Be that as it may, the question of enoughness is becoming increasingly crucial as we move toward a millennium in which ecological scarcity will no longer allow itself to be ignored.

A marvelous example of enoughness occurs in the motion picture *Sabrina* with Harrison Ford and Julia Ormond. At one point in the movie, Sabrina, played by Julia Ormond, tells her father that what she likes best about him is that he chose to become a chauffeur because it would give him time to read, which he dearly loved to do. His love of reading made a chauffeur's job enough for him, and he was content.

When is enough, enough? seems like a simple question on the surface. When I have eaten my fill, for example, I quit eating because I know I have had enough, for the moment at least. But what about enoughness in the material sense, other than being immediately satiated with food? Spiritual teacher and writer Eknath Easwaran warns that the more "sense oriented" (materialistic) we become, the farther we stray from the roots of our being, the more separated and alienated we feel.

Our sense of material enoughness really has to do with our level of fear and our sense of survival. Unfortunately, for many people, the sense of survival is based on an escalating disaster mentality that constantly conjures the next more frightening calamity for which they don't think they have enough material things to feel secure. And, according to insurance companies, there is always some catastrophe on the horizon for which we don't have enough insurance, unless, of course, we are already heavily insured against it, whatever "it" is.

This sensation of never having enough relies on the notion that once our immediate needs are met and fears quelled, our desires must be aggrandized. The ever-increasing rates of acquisition of unnecessary products and their faster disposal feed the manufacturing industry first and garbage dumps, euphemistically called sanitary landfills, second.

The ever-expanding plethora of catalogs points out that our materialistic social appetite seems to have reached a compulsive, addictive state in which to want is to have to have! Ralph Waldo Emerson called this our "bloated nothingness."

What a stark contrast our society is to the simplicity that was everywhere visible at Gandhi's ashram in India. As individuals, the people living at the ashram took the vow of *maganvadi*, of nonpossession. We, on the other hand, have made synonyms of "desire, want, need, demand," and in so doing have lost sight not only of the land's ecological capability but also of the difference between necessity and material crutches—the illusions of happiness—and our inner sense of leisure.

The Chinese character for leisure is composed of two elements, which by themselves mean "open space" and "sunshine." Hence an attitude of leisure creates an opening that allows the sunshine in. Conversely, the Chinese character for busy is also composed of two elements, which by themselves mean "heart" and "killing." This character points out that for the beat of one's heart to be healthy, it must be leisurely.[21]

"Cluttered rooms and complicated schedules interfere with our ability to treasure the moment," writes Victoria Moran in her book *Shelter for the Spirit*. "Ironically, our houses and apartments—where some of our best moments can be—seem to attract clutter and complication like a magnet." Even if we lack the inherent ability for simplifying and culling the inconsequential from the basic necessities, she insists that we can all learn to do so. Such discernment is the way intentionally to create a home and a life that nurtures our spirit, a life that separates the essential from the nonessential—and leisure is essential.

We tend to think of leisure, according to Brother David Steindl-Rast (a Benedictine Monk), as the privilege of the well-to-do. "But leisure," says Brother Steindl-Rast, "is a virtue, not a luxury. Leisure is the virtue of those who take their time in order to give to each task as much time as it deserves... Giving and taking, play and work, meaning and purpose are perfectly balanced in leisure. We learn to live fully in the measure in which we learn to live leisurely,"[20] a sentiment echoed by Henry David Thoreau: "The really efficient laborer will be found not to crowd his day with work, but will saunter to his task surrounded by a wide halo of ease and leisure."

Living leisurely was a trait of the Shoshonean People, who arrived in what is now Death Valley, California, about 1,000 AD.[21] The Shoshonean People were the seed gatherers of the desert. Much of the year they lived among the sand dunes in simple shelters of brush where they harvested mesquite beans. But when the seed of the piñón pine ripened, they camped in the nearby Panamint Mountains for the harvest.

They also gathered what other seeds they could and used smooth, flat rocks to grind seeds into flour. In addition to gathering plants, they hunted such small animals as rodents and lizards and ate adult insects and the grubs of beetles.

Although their tools were simple, the people possessed great skill. The ability of these people to find and utilize whatever foods the desert offered was the key to their survival.

The simple society of the Shoshonean People afforded two things that have so far eluded us in modern life—ample leisure time and the peace to enjoy it. Their free time was not devoted to improving their standard of living as is ours, perhaps because that rung on the cultural ladder was unattainable in an environment permitting no cultural revolution, but then perhaps it would not have been perceived as a necessity or even a desire of life had it been possible.

The Shoshonean People thus lived in fullness within the context of the natural cycles of their environment and their lives. Their trust was founded on the natural law of replenishment, just like breathing in and breathing out. But while the environment provided a subsistence that allowed ample time for leisure, it also precluded the luxury of war, an activity that requires its own technology and a perceived abundance of resources to waste. When warlike tribes entered the valley, the residents just slipped quietly away and hid until the intruders left.

This brings me again to the question of when is enough, enough? Was the enoughness of the Shoshonean People imposed on them by their environment or was it an internal sense of contentment and harmony with what they had?

But what about me? Do I want more? I can certainly have more if I want it. But do I want it? If so, why? If not, why not? With all of these questions jousting in my mind, I sometimes wonder what I have learned about enoughness.

In life, I have learned that conscious simplicity—the vehicle of enoughness—is an inner journey that we each must take in our own time. I say this because I am fourteen years older than Zane and, even though we have been married for more than nineteen years and are very close, we are not always in the same place when it comes to making some of the dramatic choices in life. This disparity in our readiness to change was keenly felt when I was younger and wanted to simplify our lifestyle.

Although I was ready to give up much of what we had accumulated, Zane was not, which caused us to have some heated discussions because I thought conscious simplicity, to be valid, had to necessarily manifest itself "across the board" in the outer world. Thankfully, it dawned on me that conscious simplicity is a state of mind, that I could pare down my own things as much as I wished and thus live at peace within, while allowing Zane to be okay just being herself. Then, a few years later, Zane's time to embrace conscious simplicity arrived, although perhaps not with the same degree of austerity that resonates with me. Be that as it may, we are each where we need to be, and our life is fine as it is.

In my garden, I have learned that enoughness allows me to enjoy the fruits of my garden each in its season. So I no longer try to hoard them all for winter, feeling as I used to, a great urgency to preserve each and every grape, lest a grape not stored became a grape wasted.

Although I may have a smaller crop this year than last, I now have enough every year to share with bird and beast and human neighbor, for I now know that I do not and cannot possess things. I can only be in relationship with them. And whatever that relationship is, it is constantly changing and thus "mine" for only a short time, perhaps no longer than the glance of my eye at some beautiful flower. Yet it is the quality of a relationship that holds the value, not the quantity.

In like measure, my thoughts and feelings, which seem to give birth to themselves, arise and pass away, each according to its nature. So it is that one of the greatest gifts I can give the future is to live faithfully and truly the contentment of enoughness, and accept and share in gratitude the bounty each year brings to my garden, however it manifests itself.

Exercise In Conscious Awareness

Although this exercise is related only indirectly to your garden, it is a fundamental way to begin restructuring your thinking on what is sufficient in your life. As your thinking and habits of buying change, the change inevitably shows up in your garden. Since corporate powers attempt to deny us the pleasure of enoughness, we must regain our own sense of personal power and let go the frenzy of consumerism. One way to do this at home is to become aware of the likely staggering number of unwanted catalogs you receive in the mail. Our household was the recipient of a deluge of unwanted, unsolicited catalogs, all seeking to stimulate our senses and feed our inclination to want more and more.

To achieve such awareness, place all the catalogs you receive monthly into a stack. At the end of each month, sit down and consciously go through each one. Notice which catalogs you receive. Did you personally request each of these catalogs? If not, whose mailing list might you be on? Who is making money selling your name to faceless marketers so that they can intrude into your life with catalogs and other stuff you neither want nor need?

When you are finished going through the catalogs, put those that you personally requested into a stack. Next, put the catalogs that you *did not* request into another stack. Compare stacks. How many trees do you think it takes to make the paper in all the catalogs each year that you neither requested nor want? How much of a forest do you think goes into unwanted catalogs if each household in America receives as many as you do?

Now, take the catalogs that you personally requested and go through them carefully. Of these, which ones do you still want to receive? Put them into a separate stack. Go through the catalogs that you did not request and do the same thing.

When you have completed this task, compare the stacks and resolve to regain your personal freedom from the catalog part of corporate America. Of the catalogs you do not want, resolve to call every 800 number and have your name removed from their mailing list, with the admonishment neither to sell nor share your name with anyone else. Then go to the post office and get a handful of their special post cards to send to New York (the postal clerk will give you instructions), requesting that your name be taken off all mailing lists. It takes persistence, hence a handful of cards, but it works. We used to receive twenty to thirty catalogs every month, whereas now receive one or two, and actually have some catalog-free months.

Realize with pleasure the number of trees and other resources that you are saving by making a conscious decision and effort to stop both the catalogs and the temptation to purchase items that you really do not need. Then, if you would like to celebrate your new-found sense of personal power and feeling of enoughness, select a plant in your garden, preferably a perennial, and let it consciously remind you that enoughness and sufficiency are simply a decision, and for a decision, especially a bold decision, to be viable, you must have the courage to act on it.

ACCEPTANCE IS THE KEY TO FREEDOM

Acceptance is seeing each circumstance as it is, untrammeled by conditions, and embracing it wholeheartedly for the personal lesson enfolded within. Our task as human beings is to uncover the lesson; learn it, so it will not repeat itself; and let the circumstance go with thankfulness for the opportunity of personal growth bestowed.

When we accept what life offers, instead of resenting it and fighting circumstances—"kicking against the pricks" in the words of the Bible—we are free to focus on what we have, rather than what we think we lack. We are free to focus on circumstances as they are, rather than as they are not. It takes great learning, *A Course in Miracles* explains, "to understand that all things, events, encounters, and circumstances are helpful."

The true spirit of acceptance is captured by the haiku poet who wrote:

The barn has burned down!
Now at last I can enjoy
the sight of the moon.

A strong gust of wind came up while I was working in my garden the other day and, unbeknownst to me, broke off at its base a huge, magnificent white snapdragon in its prime. I was at first saddened to see it lying in a heap on the ground wilting. Then I thought: "Well, it's broken. I can't fix that. So what can I do with it?"

I took it in inside, where Zane and I enjoyed it for days as part of a bouquet. We transformed an apparent misfortune into a gift of color and beauty. ". . . one who enjoys sweets but can drink a bowl of something bitter," attests Pir Vilayat, "that person has reached mastery."

The snapdragon is admittedly a simple example, but then a principle is a principle, and there is no degree of difficulty associated with it outside of our thinking. To this end, there is a video about Mother Teresa in which she talks about acceptance. She says that if God puts you in a palace, to accept being in the palace. If God puts you in the street, to accept being in the street. But, she admonishes, that you are not to put yourself either in a palace or in the street; you are simply to accept whatever God gives you at the present moment. In this context, unconditional acceptance is knowing with a certainty the wisdom of the Universal Laws.

Acceptance, simple acceptance of what is, is perhaps the most difficult lesson with which we daily struggle. This struggle is necessary, however, in order to reach a state of knowing that whatever happens brings with it an opportunity for a deeper, truer quality of consciousness. Acceptance, then, is radical trust.

The circumstances of our lives, the experiences we daily encounter, are not the prison house. The prison bars through which we stare with sunken, lifeless eyes are the products of our conditioning, our opinions and impulses, and of our insistence on having life as we want it, so that discomfort and uncertainty are held in abeyance. Acceptance, on the other hand, is the key to freedom from our attachments to our likes and dislikes, which form our prison bars.

In the instance of the snapdragon, for example, the unexpected gust of wind freed me from my wanting the snapdragon to be as I had last seen it, upright and healthy. This was an opportunity disguised as loss, an occasion for me to realize that everything ultimately has a positive resolution, if I am but willing to yield and accept.

In Buddhism, Buddha Consciousness is the ability to yield to and accept the conditions of life in such a way that one can firmly declare, "I have overcome conditioning." The Buddha calls this accepting attitude "the freedom of determinism." It is the freedom in the present moment to undergo adversity with equipoise and know the result will be an increased self-awareness and thus self-rule in the here and now.

Acceptance also allows us to transcend a purely emotional state of mind and reach an integrated point of logic. In so doing, we can define the problem and in turn transcend it with the "evenness" of mind that Meister Eckhart urged us some centuries ago to adopt. Because acceptance of a problem must come before resolution is possible, it would behoove us to practice evenness of mind when first confronted by an uncomfortable circumstance, such as change.

Why do we fear unwanted, uncontrollable change so much? We resist such change because we are committed to protecting our existing conditioning and belief systems. Even if they are no longer functional or valid, they represent the safety of past knowledge in which there are no unwelcome surprises. We erroneously get lulled into believing we are on *terra firma* and, therefore, will not be swept away in a sea of change.

Eknath Easwaren has found, however, that people are terrified of change because they are disconnected from the "changeless ground of the Universe," where indeed the inner substratum is firm, infinite, and immovable. We lose touch with the perspective that beyond the world of time and space is revealed the unity behind the seeming multiplicity, or as the Sufis would say, that our everyday, unreal world veils the truth of the "Divine Oneness," the "Unchangeableness."

When confronted with change, we try to control the thoughts of others by accepting what to us are "approved" thoughts and rejecting "unapproved" thoughts, again aimed at trying to prevent unwelcome surprises. We see such control as a defense against unwanted change that casts us into the unknown. But as author George Bernard Shaw candidly revealed, "my own education operated by a succession of eye-openers each involving the repudiation of some previously held belief." Few of us, however, willingly relinquish control of treasured beliefs, and even fewer are able to admit that change is always helpful, although sometimes only realized in hindsight.

Change may require the death of an accepted, "tried-and-true," once functional belief system through which we have coped with life, and which has become synonymous with our identity and therefore our security, hence our comfort zone. When we get too comfortable with our belief systems, we might, as I said earlier, think of the turtle, for which only two choices in life exist—pull its head into its shell, where in safety it starves to death, or stick its neck out to move and risk finding something to eat and live.

We have the same two choices the turtle does. While we cannot control a circumstance, we can choose to control how we respond to the circumstance, what our attitude will be, and in that choice lies our freedom from fear. By giving up trying to control things outside of ourselves (which we *cannot* control), we are in better control of ourselves (which we *can* control) and thereby can choose how we want to respond to any given circumstance. We can then begin the process of intentionally discerning between what is truly valuable to us and what is valueless.

Here a passage from the *Daily Word* seems especially helpful as we each strive to choose inner control:

> I no longer try to change outer things. They are simply a reflection. I change my inner perception and the outer reveals the beauty so long obscured by my own attitude. I concentrate on my inner vision and find my outer view transformed. I find myself attuned to the grandeur of life and in unison with the perfect order of the universe.

My garden is often the most poignant interface between theory and down-to-earth, pragmatic application of the principles of circumstance, choice, and acceptance. In my garden, I am afforded an infinite variety of opportunities to apply one of the vital tenets from *A Course in Miracles*: "We are all teachers who teach what we need to learn over and over again until we have learned it."

To illustrate, late one January, we had an unseasonably warm spell, which stimulated our roses to begin growing. We then had a sudden hard freeze, which killed the tender new growth and some of the established parts of the roses as well. The same thing happened in March. As the weather finally warmed towards the beginning of May, the roses cautiously began to grow again. Then we unexpectedly had two surprising nights of severe freezing that killed some of our roses outright. What could we do? The freeze of death and change was upon us.

We could rant and rail against the freezing as though it had been a personal affront sent by the demons of darkness to thwart the survival of our roses just to spite us. Or we could, as St. Paul exclaimed in Romans 5:3 of the Bible, "… rejoice in our sufferings, knowing that suffering produces endurance." In other words, we could accept the freeze as Nature's course that year, be grateful for those roses that survived, and replace those that did not. We chose to be at home with this opportunity to reevaluate our bed of roses and purchase those varieties of old-garden roses Zane had longed to have grace our garden.

"Dispose of all things according to your will and judgment," councils mystic Thomas a Kempis, and "you will always find that of necessity you must suffer somewhat, either willingly or against your will; and so you shall always find the cross." The way to life *is* the way of the cross, which is a prerequisite for both wisdom and the liberation it brings.

In the last analysis, we have a choice. We always have a choice, and we must choose. If we don't like the outcome of our choice, we always have the choice of choosing again. We are not, therefore, victims of our circumstances or of the cross, but rather products of the consequences, of our choices. Although we are continually reaping the harvest of our past sowing, we cannot always choose the timing of events, such as the freezing of our roses. Yet, *A Course in Miracles* tells us that "the time will be as right as is the answer."

I was not taught, however, that I was a product of *my* choices; I was taught that I was somehow a product of outside choices, such as my father's or a punishing God's. I was, for example, taught as a youngster in Sunday School to pray by asking God for the things I wanted to have or to have happen. Over the years, as I have visited various churches in different countries, I noticed that people tended to ask to have things made easy for themselves, rather than asking to be strengthened and to be made worthy of that which they desired by earning it, whatever "it" was.

But how, you might ask, do you know when your prayer has been answered? That's easy. The tests begin. Why? Because, as poet William Blake pointed out, that is when the "contraries" make themselves known. If, for instance, I ask for patience, I am given all manner of things to try my patience, obstacles against which to practice. It is not by accident that patience and passion both come from the Latin *passior*, meaning suffering or endurance, the encounter with the cross Thomas a Kempis spoke of. After all, practice does move me toward the perfection of my patience. Thus, whenever I ask for anything, I am given ample opportunities in the "acceptable time of the Lord" to practice that which I would learn, but first I must accept that which I am given.

Here the word "acceptance" is paramount. By acceptance, I do not mean "complacency, resignation, apathy, inertia." I mean to actively embrace and participate in whatever circumstance life in its perfect timing puts before me. This can be quite interesting because the circumstances I am given are the contraries I need as sparring partners from which to

learn that which I desire, but they are seldom either what I had anticipated or what I would have chosen. The old saying, "what is for you will
not pass you by," is the promise of a whole coin, both the side that seems
a curse and the side that is a blessing.

That notwithstanding, the contraries I am given are the contraries
with which I must work, be it a small army of slugs eating their way
through my newly outplanted lettuce seedlings, a late freeze that kills
Zane's roses, or a thoughtless neighbor filling our early morning slumber
with dissonant noise. Regardless of what a particular contrary is, the
lesson is the same—patience. Acceptance and patience each operate as
the flip-side of the other, be it in my garden or at international nego-
tiations in Geneva, Switzerland. Patience, which is
based on acceptance, is an intuitive part
of those who trust. In the end, acceptance and patience unite
in the positive emptiness of
spiritual fulfillment.

L. EDGINGTON

Exercise In Conscious Awareness

Here is an example of the dynamics of nonacceptance. I heard a story from a friend about a woman who was disheartened and dismayed that a small grove of willow trees at her library was slated to be cut down. She was so torn by emotion and agitation that she literally made herself physically sick. She became so upset at the mere mention of the removal of the trees that she instantly became angry and accusative. In her irrational state of passion and uncontrolled emotion, she was unwisely dissipating her precious energy. Having said this, I do not mean in any way to minimize the genuine distress she experienced over the loss of her sacred grove of trees, which she looked forward to seeing every time she went to the library.

This story is meant to illustrate only that her perception of the event and how she chose to respond to it was what caused her the terrible suffering and bout of sickness. Her energy was indignantly aimed at what she could not change, instead of what she did in fact have control over, namely her attitude, her reaction, and her validation of her own feelings of grief. Then, at some point, she would have naturally moved to a position of acceptance, because she would have attended, by turning the searchlight inward, to what she was really angry at and not the misdirected target.

The reason the library decided to remove the fast-growing willows was they had been planted too close to the buildings and their roots had invaded the plumbing system, where they were beginning to cause considerable damage. The trees were not arbitrarily taken out. But in the turmoil of her emotions, the woman lost her rationality, because she felt out of control and did not want to have to cope with the change brought about by the loss of her tree friends, so she did not for some time learn the reason for their removal.

For many of us, the pain of loss and grief and its terrible suffering is an exceedingly difficult, scary state to encounter in its rawness. So much so, that we often remain unconsciously stuck in anger and a sense of victimhood, rather than moving to a deeper layer, where our intense feelings reside, as well as our healing.

Our initial reaction to such a traumatic event is what sounds good, what appears good on the surface, but in truth, we are unwilling to do the hard inner work of uncovering what we are truly feeling and reacting to and why. If we were honest with ourselves, we would inevitably discover that the object onto which we project our anger and blame is not the real source of our suffering. We have to get down to the true source of the pain because only there does permanent healing occur.

Non-acceptance is an energy-draining, stuck place. It is an environment of stagnation. Unfortunately, many of us spend a lot of our time, thoughts, and existence there. We exist in our resistance and nonacceptance to whatever it might be that we do not have control over and do not want to change. How many people realize that undisciplined and uncontrolled emotions, for whatever reason, disturb their bloodstream and glandular system, and this eventually produces minor, or even major, ailments? On the other hand, acceptance is letting go of the wear and tear of resistance, and is a choice that detoxifies the whole system of turmoil, negativity, and stuckness.

Go now into your garden, sit quietly, and remember clearly an incident in which something happened that you did not like. How did you react? Was the reaction mild or strong? Did your heart start pumping faster and your face flush red with anger? Looking back, what was it like being held captive in that state? Was it pleasant or unpleasant? Did you react to something you actually had any control over? How long did you exist as a prisoner in that state, mulling it over, returning to it again and again in your thoughts and feelings? What does it make you feel like to re-trigger the incident and be in it once again? Did you ever resolve your feelings and move on to the freedom of acceptance?

Be aware over the next few days of your reactions to incidents that engender strong feelings. Are you reacting without thinking? Do you spend much time reacting to things you have absolutely no control over? Make an inventory of the things you react to and what your feeling is. If you rate yourself on a scale of one (non-acceptance and strong reactiveness) to ten (acceptance, evenness of mind, and equanimity), where do you most often come out on the scale of your reactions to the incidents of your life? Acceptance is the essence of the Serenity Prayer, which is attributed to Sir Thomas Moore:

God grant me the serenity to accept
the things I cannot change,
courage to change the things I can,
and wisdom to know the difference.

In Emptiness is Spiritual Fulfillment

Emptiness is letting the chatter of the mind die away and productive hands be idle. In emptiness one accesses the law of Wu Wei, which literally means "without doing, causing, or making." It is understanding that in the emptiness of inner solitude, where one melds in consciousness with the heartbeat of the Universe, there is nothing to do, hence nothing left undone. In this place of "effortless effort," of utter stillness and inner silence, one hears the great universal sound, the Voice of the Divine. It is here that all sages and saints have stood and received the Grail.

When I walk through the gate of the high cedar fence surrounding my garden, I enter into a secluded place, a sanctuary of the soul, wherein worldly knowledge, incessant noise, frantic motion, aggrandized stimulation, and competitive ambition fall away. "If a man can be absolutely quiet" a Chinese teacher once told his students, "then the Heavenly Heart will manifest itself." Here, in the solitude of my garden, is the heartbeat of the Universe palpable.

It beats in the rustling of dragonfly wings about my pond and in the cold North Wind blowing far from its Arctic home; it is felt in the rain coming off tropical currents of the Pacific Ocean and is seen in the twinkling light from distant stars. It is in the howling fury of a winter storm and the silence of a summer's day when the world hangs limply in relentless heat. In this "wise silence," as Emerson termed it, is the eternal center, "the still point of the turning world," which is best expressed in the Sanskrit word *purnata*—a stillness that is completely full.

The antithesis of my garden's hush is the disenchanted outer world, where it is absolutely imperative to get somewhere and produce something. Yet, as Thomas Moore explains in *The Re-enchantment of Everyday Living*, time spent in a garden gets us nowhere.[22] "A garden," he says, "entices us to slow down and stop," which, he adds, is an important dynamic of the soul, for anything of the soul requires time and a lowering of productivity and effort.

Gardening is thus a monk's way of nurturing the soul, which Moore calls a "fruitful silence," where movements of the soul are amplified. A life that honors solitude is a requisite for self-mastery, living with a sense of direction, and discovering the true song of one's own soul.

When thus I enter into my garden I am on holy ground at the center of the Universe, for all relationships begin and end therein as they are gathered up and given forth from the spirit of my being, which is diffused throughout the cosmos. In Muslim countries, the old part of their cities was called *medina* or "holy place." And so it is when you enter into your garden or *medina*, the center of the Universe is everywhere and nowhere.

One of the great classics of the East states that "the universe turns upon the axis of silence." It moves when we move and rests when we rest. If therefore, I am simply content to be in the moment, I am filled with the vast emptiness of inner solitude, which I long ago experienced in the deserts of Egypt when I was too young to understand.

There is a silence in the deserts of Egypt that wraps like a cloak around the heat by day and the cold by night, when the wind is still and not a grain of sand stirs. On such a day in the Nubian Desert east of the Nile, one piece of iron stone dropped upon another can be heard by a Dorcas gazelle a mile away.

It is there, in the silent splendor of the desert, that the early Christian monks went to live that they might find emptiness. This is the contemplative life to which monks are called. The word "contemplative" means to cut out a space for divination, to set apart space for sacred use, for the building of an inner temple, as noted by Thomas Moore in *Meditations*.[23] "Contemplation," explains Moore, is the primary work of the monk if he or she is to achieve the necessary emptiness in all things.

The early Christian monks, according to Moore, were experts at doing nothing and tending the culture of that emptiness. Their existence denoted a complete absence of drivenness. In the exact measure to which they were empty so were they in like measure full, for emptiness, instructs Brother David Steindl-Rast, is the necessary condition for fullness in all its forms.

One evening in that long ago, I sat down to rest on a large boulder of iron stone. As I surveyed the enfolding magnificence of the Nubian desert, watching the waves of heat dancing in the distance, I had a profound sense of company. Looking around, I discovered that I was sitting on the same rock on which a Paleolithic man sat more than 15,000 years ago as he chipped hand axes from the iron stone. One of them lay at my feet.

Picking it up, I discovered the tip was broken. I could almost feel his frustration at breaking the tip just when he thought he had a finished ax. I felt a kinship with this artisan of antiquity and intuitively knew that time was only an intellectual construct that trapped my worldly mind, that behind the veil of illusion, in complete stillness, was the omnipresent unitive state. Because I so keenly felt the ancient one's presence, I also felt the roots of all humanity embodied in and passing through the craftsmanship of one man stored in the seemingly timeless silence of the desert.

As I sat where my Paleolithic brother had sat and pondered his countenance and frame of mind, I knew that I somehow stood on the shoulders of what he had learned and passed on when, to me, time seemed younger and the world seemed newer and more innocent. In that moment, I entered the emptiness of eternal solitude as one liberated in timelessness. All that existed for me was the presence and the touch of my Paleolithic brother.

I had thus entered an alternative place of being, which the mystics have called a retreat or *vacatio*—an emptying of ordinary life, which affords the opportunity for a different kind of experiencing. In the emptiness of this "lucid stillness," the mystic is able to live on a deeper level in order to be keenly attentive to messages that come from God, as Thomas Merton puts it.

Before you can experience the "lucid stillness," however, you must empty yourself, as a university professor discovered when inquiring about Zen from Nan-in, a Japanese Zen master. Nan-in served tea. He poured the professor's cup full and kept on pouring. His visitor watched the overflow until he could no longer restrain himself: "It is overfull. No more can go in without overflowing."

Nan-in replied, "like this cup, you are full of your own opinions and speculations. How can I show you Zen unless you first empty your cup?"

Some years ago, I read about the Buddhist concept of the "Nothing" from which everything comes and into which everything returns, but I did not understand it. That night, I had a vivid dream in which I actually entered the Nothing and found everything, a reality I am not sure I can explain, but I will try.

In my dream, I passed gently through some kind of border or boundary and found myself without form in a formless gray, the color being more of a sense than an actuality. Blending into the formlessness as pure energy, I had ceased to exist in the morphological shape of a human being. I felt totally at peace, a kind of peace that permeated everything, that merged seamlessly into and through me, leaving room for nothing but itself and so became everything.

I awoke the next morning with an incredible sense of peace and without fear of losing my identity beyond the veil because, when one has absolute peace, there is nothing else of value and so one has everything.

To this day, when I still my intellect, I can enter the Nothing and, for the eternity of an instant, find everything in the amorphous, seamless feeling of peace.

Trying to explain the Nothing calls forth the memory of an Emperor in a far away land who, wanting to adorn his palace with a new and original painting, held a contest in which the greatest painters of the day were commissioned to paint a flock of geese just taking wing. Although many great painters presented the Emperor with works of delicate beauty, he chose for his palace the painting by a Taoist whose canvas was blank except for the upper right-hand corner, which held the foot of the last goose to take flight.

Thomas Merton, the Trappist Monk, conveys the nothingness a little differently: "At the center of our being is a point of nothingness which is untouched by sin and by illusion, a point of pure truth, a point or spark which belongs entirely to God, which is never at our disposal, from which God disposes of our lives, which is inaccessible to the fantasies of our mind or the brutalities of our will."

In the thinking of German poet Johann W. von Goethe, emptiness has an invisible power from which patterns emerge, much as a vase on a potter's wheel forms itself around the active presence of a hollow, without which the vase could not exist. The vase is simply the external shell of a specifically shaped void, which holds emptiness within itself.[25] From India, the *Heart Sutra* adds:

> ...form is no other than emptiness,
> Emptiness is no other than form;
> Form is exactly emptiness, emptiness exactly form,
> ...all phenomena are emptiness/form.

I am myself such a vase, and life is the wheel upon which the Master Potter is molding and emptying me. And it is my singular goal in life to serve the still small voice within; thus, I must learn to empty myself of myself. And if I can find within a single-minded purpose, then I might also find complete emptiness or self-forgetfulness, and achieve both fullness and fulfillment, in keeping with the Sanskrit word *apuruamanam*, which means "ever-full."

Although I began as a solid lump of clay, I am discovering little by little what in life is valuable and what is not, and I am discarding the latter with no desire to fill the space left empty by the sorting out and relinquishment. "Give up what you do not want," suggests *A Course in Miracles*, "and keep what you do." Each time I discard the valueless, I find that spiritual peace not only abides within but also fills the emptiness to the exclusion of all else.

As I mature in spirit, and the sorting continues, I find, as Thomas Merton wrote, that to be truly silent, one must let go the yearning for recognition and cease worrying about making the right impression.[18] Spanish mystic St. John of the Cross adds, in verse that has a Zen flavor:

> In order to arrive at having pleasure in everything,
> Desire to have pleasure in nothing.
> In order to arrive at possessing everything,
> Desire to possess nothing.
> In order to arrive at being everything,
> Desire to be nothing...

Finally, when one is filled with and enveloped by total peace and the desire for anything worldly becomes a foreign country, one abides in Divine emptiness, with its stillness and silence, in which there is nothing—and everything of lasting value is contained. Now when I go into my garden and simply sit with it, there are moments when the material world fades and I enter once again into the Nothingness of my dream, into the fulfillment of Divine emptiness, within which absolute peace overcomes the self and becomes the Self.

Exercise In Conscious Awareness

White Eagle, the spiritual teacher, once said: "If you read the account of John the Baptist in the Gospels, you will notice that the place in which he dwelt is described as a wilderness—the wilderness of the world, the chaotic condition of man's collective soul. We are all in a wilderness within until we begin to discipline ourselves and turn our soul-wilderness into a beautiful garden. The term 'wilderness' in fact stands for the state of chaos, loneliness, and unhappiness which is the lot of the soul before it is awakened [or emptied of the little outer self]."[24] The conquest of oneself and the overcoming of egotism was the central aim of all the mystery schools of the past.

Through the ages, self-emptying has been a central theme of mystics and has been called by many names: self-naughting, self-extinguishing, being unselfed, self-forgetfulness, self-achieved submission, being self-slain, and self-abnegation. For instance, Sri Krishna, in talking to Radnu about his flute said, "Look, it's completely empty so I can fill it with my divine melody." Radnu represents the human soul longing for union with the Divine.

"Knowth when you learn to lose yourself, you will reach the Beloved," continues Sufi mystic, Ansari of Herat. "There is no other secret to be learnt, and more than this is not known to me."

The process towards self-transcendence is meant to transcend the mortal life of fears, worries, opinions, and wants for spiritual realization. Death of the ego is the purpose of all disciplines of the spiritual life, which is a letting go of the overshadowing worldliness. It has been called the "second death" in the Biblical Revelations, where one must die-to-self or die away from the self. Meister Eckhart terms this second death "a mighty upheaval."

People of today, when confronted with the concept of renunciation of self-will and dying to their separateness and selfishness, immediately believe they will lose their personal identity and freedom of choice. They believe they risk losing their independence and autonomy, but what they actually lose is the sense of self as a small, limited personality of the physical life, as the above mystics clearly attested. Carl Jung plainly describes this moment of realignment as the relocation of the center of gravity of the personality, from the ego as one's center to a center greater than one's self.

With this as a context for the value of relinquishing some of the outer self, begin now as you are sitting comfortably in your quiet place to shift your awareness from the clutter and clatter of the outer world to the peace and quiet of your inner garden. You may notice, when first arriving in your garden, that you are making too much noise with the busy activity of your mind to see, hear, or experience its peace and quiet. As your shoulders relax, feel all the cares and tensions melting away. Let go now any mental and physical tightness or strain in your body; be still and comfortable. A soothing relaxation is spreading through your entire body.

Notice that your breathing has become more quiet and peaceful. Feel its comfortable, serene rhythm as you begin to experience the feminine Nature of life, where the less you make of yourself, the more you are. The wisdom of the feminine is in opening and letting go in order to become. The greatness of the feminine comes from knowing within the center of your being how to empty yourself of your ego's will and become receptive to unconditional service.

Feeling so pleasantly relaxed, you find you are being gently led through the now familiar gateway of your inner garden. You have once again entered the special place of your own creative imagination. Open your senses to the full array of sights and sounds. With each breath, feel the transforming power of Nature's original innocence.

You feel most drawn to the center of your garden to the still pool of azure water. Remember the absolute peace and refreshment here as you sit comfortably beside the pool. A soft breeze caresses the trees and the birds sing about the harmony of all life. You feel the all-satisfying fullness and richness of divine life here beside the pool.

Again you notice that on the still water floats a pure-white water lily. White is the perfect blending of all colors of the rainbow, and the lily is the symbol of surrender and relinquishment. You realize, as you gaze at the lily gently unfolding in the sunlight, that each part of life in this garden exists in a perfect state of resonance with every other part. The longer you gaze at the lily, the more you become the lily through the joyful emptying of self-forgetfulness. Now your little self is simply open to the will of your higher Self, the Will of the Divine. When you are empty of yourself, you are completely full of that upon which you dwell.

Now, thoroughly empty of the self-will of the ego, your soul merges gently, softly into the union of cosmic life. Empty of the ego, you have traveled a long way on the path of spiritual fulfillment and liberation, the path of self-transcendence to Self-realization.

Remain here for as long as you wish, breathing in the purity and the fragrance of the white lily as you bask in the gentle, golden sunlight. You feel as empty and yet as full and satisfied as you have ever felt. When you are ready and want to return to outer life, walk slowly, softly back through your spacious garden of lawn and vibrant flowers. Retrace your steps through the gateway.

Slowly and gently breathe your way back to the consciousness of your room, your body, and the greater world about you. Be aware of the sense of harmony and well-being you may feel.

If you want to know how empty you are of your ego's will and how filled you are with the Will of God, go one day without using the personal pronoun *I*. Keep track on a piece of paper of every time you use *I*. At the end of the day, you might think of this simple prayer for your soul's journey: *Thy will, not my will, be done that I may serve selflessly in life wherever I can do the most good.*

Finding Peace in My Garden

Peace already exists in the world as a condition of its being.
I cannot, therefore, create peace. I can only discover it,
recognize it, and hold fast to it, which is perhaps
my greatest spiritual task.

It is all too easy to get caught up in the seductive, social trance of collective beliefs and thereby remain a counterfeit person in a conforming world. Trapped in these collective beliefs, it is easy to become overwhelmed by the sheer frenzy of motion and constant noise in our increasingly hectic and loud society, where haste and worry are the perpetual entrees on the daily menu. Yet, few people realize that a hectic lifestyle equals a hectic mind, which inevitably results in "time sickness."

Worry, hectic's close companion, is a weakening of the self as it gives way to fear of the in-between times when the enemy has no face, when the mind enters its great hall of past emotional entanglements or potential disasters and everywhere skulk dark possibilities that taint and dim our view of the future. These fearful possibilities caused Franklin Delano Roosevelt to observe that "the only limit to our realization of tomorrow will be our doubts of today." Worry, the marauding "Darth Vader" of the mind, chokes creativity, stifles and drains energy, exaggerates potential problems before they exist, and steals confidence by overshadowing positive thought and action to dwell chronically on fear.

Worry comes to us from the Old English *wyrgan*, which means to strangle, through Middle English *worien*, which means to seize by the throat, harass. Worry is a strangling or seizing of the mind by dis-eased thoughts. It is, as nineteenth century writer Anna Robertson Brown declared, a "spiritual nearsightedness, a fumbling way of looking at little things and of magnifying their value." When instead of worrying, a person focuses his or her mind continually on the present moment, the tormenting internal conflicts of the past are loosened and eventually evaporate. Hence, the anxiety and fear that derive from projecting into the future also expire. In the language of the mystics, a person is delivered from the debilitating burden of time into the *eternal Now*.

Contemplating the *eternal Now* reminds me of a passage I read somewhere, which said in effect that I can't do anything about the past, but I can ruin a perfectly good present by worrying about the future, because it is my reaction in the Now that creates my future. As my past thoughts and deeds have brought me to my present set of circumstances, so my present thoughts and deeds are the seeds I sow that will shape my tomorrow when it becomes my today. If, therefore, I focus first and foremost on happiness, love, trust, and respect, I have those kinds of thoughts, make those kinds of decisions, and sow those kinds of seeds—and vice versa if I sow negative thought pollution, such as unhappiness, hate, distrust, and arrogance. All life begins with thought, and all thoughts produce effects consistent with themselves.

As I partake in society today, I wonder what thoughts people have, because as I look about I see the lines of worry and hurry etched into the faces of young and old, of man and woman, regardless of nationality, race, or creed. The deep grooves of soul-worriness and soul-weariness sculpt people's faces, bodies, and demeanors. And, I am often asked where peace is to be found.

Peace already exists in the primordial germ of Nature. Peace underlies all manifestation. There is nothing we can do to create peace, but there is much we can do to avail ourselves of it.

Chinese philosopher Lao-Tzu says it simply, that "when everyone goes along with the Tao [the natural flow of things], the world is at peace and everyone is happy." That which we focus our attention on—peace—is real, and those things from which we withdraw our attention, worry and hurry, cease to exist.

Unfortunately, we usually hide, even destroy, our own chances of discovering peace because many of us live perpetually out of sync with the Tao. Peace, however, both *resides* within us and so *comes from* within us.

Even as we individually hide from or destroy our chances of finding peace in our personal lives, we keep looking to this government or that to make peace among their own people, or to broker peace with their neighbors, or at least to keep the peace they promised. But governments cannot make peace in the first place; they can only control violence to some extent.

Be that as it may, peace exists in my garden; it is already there—inherent and available in the present moment. "No peace lies in the future," wrote medieval monk Fra Giovanni, "which is not hidden in this present instant."

Although peace was there when my garden was nothing but a patch of weeds, I could not find it because I did not know where and how to look for it. I had heard the world's cry of "seek but do not find." Even though I did not know what peace in a society was, I found it in the high mountains of my youth as described by John Muir: "Nature's peace will flow into you as sunshine into flowers; the winds will blow their freshness into you and the storms their energy, and cares will drop off like autumn leaves."

Now as I work in my garden, I am increasingly aware of the peace with which life flows in the Tao through death into life again in an unending cycle of creative novelty. When I am peaceful in one sphere of life, tending my garden for instance, I am able to kindle peace everywhere I reach. It is the law of life. I now see peace as the unconditional acceptance of what is and the willingness to embrace it unconditionally for the intrinsic value of the personal lesson it has to teach.

I have learned that peace is an inner state, which can only be reflected outwardly, that true peace in the world is the collective inner peace of individuals—not the so-called "political peace" of nations. Because peace is secreted within each of us, the degree to which each person responds to his or her own inner peace enhances the peacefulness of the world. Our common global bond is that, regardless of creed, color, sex, religion, social status, or national heritage, we all face the same inner search for peace and the same inner obstacles to finding it and recognizing it when found.

People in Western industrialized society, however, seemingly find it necessary to look outside of themselves for the causes and solutions to most of their problems. "We rage against 'forces' over which we have no control," says Joseph Chilton Pearce, former humanities professor and author. "But control would require effort, and our efforts go to self-comfort, personal benefit, and living the good life." It often makes people angry to hear the truth, to know that, at least in part, emotional and psychological healing is up to them in their search for peace.

When people come to grips with the fact that they always have a choice of thought and behavior, that any serious reformation of character has to begin with transforming the thought process itself, two things will happen. First, they will begin asking themselves: What am I doing physically, mentally, emotionally, and spiritually to cause my inner turmoil? Second, they will discover hope and begin to seek the self-knowledge and determination that will enable them to heal toward inner peace.

I note here with interest that the word "Islam" means peace, that *jihad* or holy war originally referred to our own personal, *inner* struggles to become masters of ourselves and our passions, so that we eventually would become established in a deep, abiding peace. Mystics call this war within the conflict between that which is spiritual in us and that which is selfish.

But without doing the inner work necessary to find one's own peace, world peace is certainly not possible, because peace is based on one's being defenseless, which demands great inner strength and courage. It is not danger that comes when defenses are laid down, but rather safety, peace, joy, and a remembrance of God, says *A Course In Miracles*. Defenselessness takes enormous discipline, the discipline of individuals who are staunchly committed to finding and retaining inner peace.

For peace to be experienced in the world we must each learn: (1) the only true peace is within us as part of Nature's endowment, (2) our task is to find peace and hold fast to it, and (3) peace in the world is the outer manifestation of the inner peace of individuals and is possible only through the collective thoughts and actions of an ever-increasing number of such peaceful people because the infectious nature of peace is peace.

Is peace in the world possible? Emphatically yes! The great irony, however, is that neither governments nor nations can make peace, although they spend much time talking and posturing about it. They can only limit violence within acceptable social standards, because peace is a state of consciousness—not of politics. General Omar Bradley, in his now-famous words, put it thusly: "We have grasped the mystery of the atom and rejected the Sermon on the Mount. ... The world has achieved brilliance without conscience. Ours is a world of nuclear giants and ethical infants. We know more about war than we do about peace, more about killing than we know about living."

Thus, by the thoughts we each sow daily through our actions, we collectively reflect to a greater or lesser degree either the light of inclusive peace into the world or the darkness of fear, separateness, and violence. And the degree to which we individually find peace is the collective degree to which peace in the world is possible. In this connection, the UNESCO Constitution explicitly urges us to consider the following: "Since war is born in the minds of men [and occasionally women], it is in the minds of men [and women] that we have to erect the ramparts of peace."

Beyond our individual peace, as we grow toward self-realized wholeness, we must embrace one of the ultimate tests of human beings, that of *justly* sharing the labors and fruits of society because the things we do always become part of the things we are. To share the best society has to offer, we must offer the best we have to society by learning to work together as equals, as one another's keepers and learning partners.

"… I think each of us is put here to dilute the misery in the world," said Dr. Karl Menninger. "You may not be able to make a big contribution, but you can make a little one, and you've got to try." Centuries earlier, St. Francis de Sales said, "great occasions for serving God come seldom, but little ones surround us." Even if your contribution is a "little one," in the long run the smallest ingredient can be the most powerful, and the slightest act may be the most potent.

If you wonder about the impact of your service, remember that the saints of old did not set out to become saints; they simply set out to serve with love. Only through our own little acts of joyful service can we achieve a collective vision for the future that is inclusive, responsible, and yet simultaneously allows and protects the sacred space and autonomy of each individual.

As we serve others, we build peace and contentment in our hearts. As we build peace within our hearts, we build peace in the world. By building peace in our hearts—where the only true peace can reside—we create a healed society and a healed Earth. As peace grows, it becomes evermore a hologram, which Gandhi knew when he said, "Peace between countries must rest on the solid foundation of love between individuals." But first we must find the courage to struggle within ourselves, because courage is the price of peace, which, after all, is only a choice, a choice based on love.

I remember some years ago when I found a butterfly in my garden. It was a tiger swallowtail freshly out of its chrysalis, with wings still wrinkled and wet. I put it on the sun-drenched limb of a tree. As its wings gently unfolded, I marveled at its fragility and small size compared with the grandeur of its color, form, and function. With wings dried, it floated lightly on the warm, summer air, until it finally landed on a thistle blossom, where it began to drink nectar.

It helped me to understand that a weed, such as a thistle, which appears drab with little outward beauty, becomes more beautiful when visited by a butterfly. And I realized that there are times in most people's lives when they feel like a prickly, unapproachable thistle growing unwanted in a wasteland. These are the times when the gentle touch of love, like the brush of a butterfly's wing, makes beautiful the thistle no matter where it grows, for love is a gift we bestow on one another.

Love is the sweet-scented elixir that transforms life, removing all that is ugly and unwanted. Love is the foundation of peace.

Peace in the world starts with each and every one of us. As I find my own inner peace, I manifest peaceful relations in the world outside of myself in like measure. Thus, the peace in my garden is a measure of my harmony, which comes from within but may be felt from without by friends and strangers who enter my garden. The same is true for you and your garden.

From our own inner peace, we become emissaries of peace among the people with whom we daily interact, from a small group of family and friends, to casual acquaintances, to our various communities. As communities become more peaceful, cities and states become more peaceful. As cities and states become more peaceful, nations become more peaceful. As nations become more peaceful, the world becomes more peaceful. And it all begins with our own search for inner peace, one person at a time.

L. Edgington

As we each struggle along our sometimes dimly lit path toward inner peace, we are a procession of candles in the night. A candle is but a tiny flame piercing the darkness. Though it is delicate, faltering at times perhaps, it has a strength beyond our understanding, because a candle is not diminished of its light by lighting another candle. Its light only grows stronger, brighter, and clearer. And we must dare to share our light, for peace in the world can be lighted only by candles of the human spirit— one, by one, by one—beginning with me and with you.

Thus, can we each sow the seeds of kindness and peace in the world, one individual at a time, one thought at a time, one decision at a time, one action at a time, one day at a time. The choice belongs to us in the present. The consequences of our decisions, however, belong to the children. It is wise, therefore, to be ever-mindful that the kind of world they will inherit and inhabit may well depend on the thoughts we entertain and the actions we commit while working in the privacy of our gardens.

Exercise In Conscious Awareness

Sit comfortably poised with your back supported, relaxing, and letting any tension fall away from your shoulders. Breathe gently and a little more deeply, more slowly but with no strain or extra effort, being aware of the gentle rhythm of your breath. Breathe in slowly, feeling more and more relaxed, at peace, releasing the little knots of held-in tension from your body. You become more aware of your now-familiar, inner garden unfolding as you feel more serene, more tranquil. You feel safe and richly cared for in your sacred spot.

As you gradually become aware of your inner garden in all its splendor, you see a pathway that leads through the colorful array of flowers and vegetation. You realize that Nature is the prime source of the spiritual life. You may be aware of being accompanied by your own guardian angel and your guide-teacher.

As you stand looking at your garden, it begins to expand, urging you to walk toward the East. After some time, you realize that you are in the center of a beautiful valley dancing with wildflowers and ringed by snow-clad mountains, for your garden has become the world. As peace continues to permeate your being, you gradually become aware of a most beautiful tree in front of you.

The magnificent tree is strong, steadfast, and tall, growing as it does from the richness of Mother Earth. You are aware that this great tree is sending out peace and enfolding you in loving care, as it does with all life. You are drawn closer to the tree, which rises up and up into the sky towards the sun, with great sweeping branches spreading almost beyond your sight. It shelters and succors many beneath its beautiful green branches.

You gaze upon the tree for a long while. Something inside tells you this is the great White Pine of the Confederacy of Nations, the Tree of Peace, which spreads a fine net of white roots of peace and unity over the whole Earth. As you stand gazing upon the tree, become aware of the peoples of all nations, all races, and all faiths being drawn together in peace, unity, and goodwill under the loving protection of this great White Pine with a oneness of life, which includes the very fundamentals of creation: Earth, Air, Fire, and Water.

Not only are the peoples coming together in harmony and sharing but also all animal life is drawn within. Birds are singing as they rest upon the branches, serenading the whole gathered company with a heavenly melody. This vision of peace, unity, and joy, of which you are a part, gives you a deep feeling of reassurance and comfort, knowing you can take with you the accord of the great Tree of Peace and share it in your own environment and the outer world. You too can nurture the white roots of peace and unity in your thoughts, words, and acts of kindness and gentleness.

Rest here for as long as you like. As you rest, realize that the white roots of peace spread in all directions for all individuals. Know that if a person is searching for peace, all he or she has to do is find even the tiniest white rootlet and begin diligently to follow it toward its ever-increasing larger end. As the root increases in size, it imparts peace in like measure. Each root, no matter its size, will inevitably lead to its source, to the Tree of Peace. You know, without a doubt, that each person has both the choice and the opportunity to follow any root of peace back to the Tree.

When you are ready, retrace your steps as your garden resumes its familiar size. Come gently back along the pathway that leads you through the colorful array of flowers and vegetation, through the gate, and back into everyday consciousness in your quiet spot. Become firmly aware of your breath and your physical body, and of the room in which you are sitting. When you do move, move slowly and gently, savoring the quiet and relaxation you have just experienced. Take with you in your heart the music of the great Tree of Peace, where all life is one. Peace be with you. Be the peace in your relationships and in your world.

AFTERWORD

"Each person," says writer Maya Angelou, "deserves a day away in which no problems are confronted, no solutions searched for. Each of us needs to withdraw from the cares which will not withdraw from us."

Go, therefore, into your garden, where peace abides and the emotional weeds of worry can be plucked from amidst the beds of bright possibilities. Again, I say go into your garden. Kneel there before the Master Gardener that you may learn how to weed and thus learn how to plant, for it is in planting that you sow your future and it is in weeding that you keep it pure and bright. Inasmuch as you create in the garden of your soul the world as you would perceive it, that shall you see reflected in the garden you share with Nature, for a garden is a private bridge of endless prayer between you and the Eternal Mystery.

Go therefore. Find peace. Become a center of peace and share it with the world through your daily thoughts, words, and actions. Go into the garden of your soul and be still in the quiet of the Perfect Moment.

One who plants a garden plants happiness.
Chinese Proverb

INSTRUCTIONS FOR GUIDED MEDITATION

THERE IS, IN ADDITION TO THE OUTER GARDEN of your home in everyday physical life, a perfect and beautiful garden within your creative imagination, which is found when you withdraw from the outer world into inner quietness. This is a unique garden created in the safety and peace of your own thoughts, which are the basis of all your outer creations. The inner garden of your imagination, which is not susceptible to the ecological fragility of the outer material world, is a manifestation of the highest aspiration and purest thought within you, that which captures your concept of the perfection of Nature. You are that which you visualize, and, through your own visualization, you create beauty and harmony.

In creating a garden in your inner imagination, you have wide choice and artistic freedom in selecting the setting, its contents, and the season. By way of example, it may be the awakening of spring that speaks to you in your garden, or the height of summer with all its vibrant color and hum of life. Your garden may be set in a perfect landscape with majestic, wise, old trees, with flowering shrubs and herbaceous borders. Yours may be a carefully sculpted oriental-style rock garden with a trickling brook of pure, clear water, where stones sparkle like jewels and fish of iridescent colors may be seen. In the center of your garden might be a still pool with water lilies or a lake of crystal blue-green water, where you can rest in total peace. Here, in your special garden, you are awakening your inner senses of sight, sound, smell, taste, touch, and intuition, and you are as free as your imagination to fly beyond the physical limitations of the outer world.

The following is an example of an inner garden that you may either adopt as your own or merely use as a template from which to create your own. To help pass into your own garden, which is a journey of spiritual awareness, this exercise is a guided visualization to help you withdraw from the hectic activity and turmoil of the outer world to a quiet, inner garden of peace and renewal.

The turning inward is to see with your mind's eye through your imagination, with your inner vision, instead of your physical eyes. By using your power of visualization, your awareness will gradually arise from the heart rather than as a strictly mental picture. The intent of this exercise is to find within a place of quiet and silence, where your true Self may be known. Indeed, this is what poet William Blake meant when he wrote: "If the doors of perception were cleansed everything would appear as it is, infinite."

The following are practical recommendations for beginning your guided visualization:

1. If you do not already have a place or room that you use for meditation and inner withdrawal, choose a quiet spot, where you will not be disturbed. It may be called your "quiet place." If you have a small room that you can devote solely to this purpose, it will be a great advantage.

   Whichever place you choose, reserve it for meditation and spiritual reading only. As you begin to associate your special place with meditation, you will find your mind starting to become quiet as soon as you enter. If you find it helpful, put up an image of a spiritual figure or beautiful garden that inspires you; otherwise keep your special place simple, austere.

2. Make sure you will be warm enough by using a shawl or wrap, because your body temperature drops when you shift your awareness inwardly and begin to relax completely.

3. A little lamp or lighted candle is helpful to create an initial point of focus and to establish a quiet center of reflection.

4. Soft, soothing music is also a useful adjunct.

5. Have a comfortable place to sit, either in a chair or on the floor with a pillow, and sit comfortably upright with your spine erect, so that your body is perfectly poised and balanced. Make sure your posture allows your body to be relaxed and at peace, so all tenseness and tightness may be released.

6. As you begin to relax and prepare, notice your gentle rhythmic breathing. Let it be slightly deeper and slower than usual, but without strain. The breathing must remain calm and peaceful with a gentle, easy, soft inhalation and exhalation. Watch your

breath with its slower, soothing in and out rhythm.

7. When you are ready, quietly breathe your way back into the physical consciousness and your physical surroundings. Become well and truly grounded. Remain for a few moments savoring the peace, and when you get up, do so slowly and without any sense of haste.

The following is a possible example of how you might prepare yourself to relax and open as much as you are able:

Sit as comfortably but as upright as you can, poised and relaxed. Sit so that you are well balanced, with your spine as erect as you can comfortably manage. Actually, there is a ninety degree angle between your spine and your thighs, where you are properly balanced upright, and this place of alignment and balance is an important place for you to find. Remember, your spine is a channel of light and its uprightness and straightness will help you to make a gentle, quiet inner contact.

Now consciously relax your shoulders downward, as well as any other areas of tension or tightness you may notice in your body. Let your shoulders sink, and in so doing, let go all tension. Stretch the back of your neck gently upwards. Feel your shoulders being relieved of all the responsibility and worry they normally carry.

Focus your mind on the place where your neck meets your shoulders. Imagine and consciously feel a gentle, warm hand pouring a ray of golden light into your spine, which is relaxing your shoulders and warming that entire part of your body as all your cares, worries, tensions, feelings of hurry and challenge of your everyday world fade quietly away. Notice the lovely feeling of warmth, comfort, and peace—a sense of total well-being—beginning to envelop you.

Your awareness is drawn to the natural rhythm of your breath as you breathe a little more deeply, a little more gently and easily, a little more quietly and softly. Make no effort to alter or control your breath. Each time you breathe in, your lungs are being filled with the Divine essence within the air, called *prana* in the East, the breath of life and of healing. With every breath you take, the cells of your body are recharged through this healing essence.

Become more and more aware now of the feeling of peace and tranquillity you are experiencing. You feel restful, content, and comfortable as your awareness has gradually shifted from your outer surroundings to your quiet, still inner world. Your breathing is slower, slightly deeper, and very relaxed. You rest peacefully and gently, feeling safe and ready now to venture through the arched gateway into your inner garden—the garden of your own creative imagination.

Withdraw, now, from the senses of the outer world and move through the arched gate into your beautiful sunlit garden within. Little by little, you become aware of just how lovely your garden really is. All is quiet and peaceful here—"the peace that passeth all understanding." As you breathe in the sweet pure air, you feel the warm sunlight bathing you with comfort in the perfect temperature. The sky is the softest blue and is swept clean by an occasional white billow of cloud touched with shades of rose pink and sunshine as it drifts by from distant snow-clad peaks.

There are flowering honeysuckles and gardenias and a soft carpet of green grass intermixed with many tiny perfumed flowers. Your feet do not even crush these delicate blooms as you walk because of the joy in your heart. The flowers and roses are the colors of the rainbow and the softest hues imaginable. Touch the sensitive petals of a flower if you like, and see their iridescence. Inhale the perfume and absorb the flower's delicate essence. The flowers are ministered by hummingbirds and hosts of butterflies, each dotting the warm, gentle afternoon with a bit of winged color. You may also catch a whiff of the warm fragrance of aromatic herbs, such as rosemary, thyme, and sage growing among the stones.

Be very still in your innermost being and listen deeply to all the sounds of Nature. Listen to the quietly flowing water, the sound of little creatures, the hum of bees and the trill of crickets, the familiar songs of birds, and the soft movement of gentle breezes among the leaves of the trees. Notice the various kinds of animals in their free state; see and feel their gentleness. You feel safe and secure in their presence.

There is a unity of life in your garden, a deep underlying peace and calm. It is the peace of eternity, the active stillness of the Universe. Here you may sense and feel the very heartbeat of the Earth, rhythmic and harmonious.

In the center of the garden is a peaceful blue lake with crystal clear water. It reflects the sky, flowers, and trees, and the reflection makes the garden even more tranquil and lovely. Rest here, if you like, on the grass by the lake and bask in the life-giving sunshine, absorbing the revitalizing essence of its light. Rest serene in your innermost heart. Time does not exist here. You are enfolded in peace …peace … peace. In your heart, you know all is well.

When you feel refreshed and renewed, walk leisurely back through your garden, absorbing with all your senses the wonder and harmony of this special place filled with the healing vibrancy of Nature. Take its essence with you and realize you can return anytime you desire for rest and peace of spirit.

When you are ready, walk back through the arched gate of your inner garden. Gradually and gently bring yourself back to the consciousness of the world around you, of your physical body, feeling well and truly earthed. You have withdrawn your attention now from the inner world and are once again firmly focused and functioning with your outer mind in your everyday world. Feeling absolutely at peace and rejuvenated, you are ready to return once again to physical life, taking with you in your heart the beauty and harmony of your inner garden and the at-one-ment of life therein.

NOTES

1. Manly Palmer Hall, *Self-unfoldment by Disciplines of Realization* (Los Angeles: The Philosophical Research Society, 1946), 221.

2. Witter Bynner, *The Way of Life According to Laotzu* (New York: The John Day Co.), 76.

3. *The Holy Bible, King James Version* (Iowa Falls, IA: World Bible Publishers), Numbers 35:34.

4. The discussion of the formation of soil is taken from the following: (1) Mark Ferns, "Geologic Evolution of the Blue Mountains Region, The Role of Geology in Soil Formation," *Natural Resource News* 5 (1995): 2-3,17; (2) Rob Marvin, "The Earth Churns, Moans, Breathes, and the 'Living Rocks' Keep Rollin' On," *The Oregonian* (Portland, Or.): April 18, 1991; (3) James L. Clayton, "Processes of Soil Formation," *Natural Resource News* 5:4-6; (4) David D. Alt and Donald.W. Hyndman, *Roadside Geology of Oregon* (Missoula: Mountain Press Publ. Co., 1978), 268; (5) Elaine R. Ingham, "Organisms in the Soil: The Functions of Bacteria, Fungi, Protozoa, Nematodes, and Arthropods," *Natural Resource News* 5 (1995):10-12, 16-17.

5. Steve Newman, "Earthweek: A Diary of the Planet," *Corvallis Gazette-Times* (Corvallis, OR.): September 6, 1998.

6. W.C. Lowdermilk, "Conquest of the Land Through 7,000 Years," *Agricultural Information Bulletin No. 99*, (Washington D.C.: U.S. Department of Agriculture, Soil Conservation Service, U.S. Government Printing Office, 1975): 30.

7. David Suzuki, "Native Values," *Resurgence* 178 (1996):12.

8. Wendell Berry, *Sex, Economy, Freedom, and Community* (New York: Pantheon Books, 1993).

9. Calvin S. Hall, Gardner Lindzey, John C. Loehlin, and Martin Manosevitz, *Introduction to Theories of Personality* (New York: John Wiley & Sons, 1985), 657.

10. Kirk Talbott, *Central Africa's Forests: The Second Greatest Forest System on Earth* (Washington D.C.: World Resources Institute, 1993), January.

11. David Orr, "Conservatives Against Conservation," *Resurgence* 172 (1995):15-17.

12. OSU News Service, "Researchers Trace Causes of Prejudice Against Illegal Aliens," *Corvallis Gazette-Times* (Corvallis, OR): May 14, 1996.

13. *The Holy Bible, King James Version* (Iowa Falls, IA: World Bible Publishers), Leviticus 16:21-22.

14. James Allen, *As a Man Thinketh* (New York: Grosset & Dunlap, 1981), 72.

15. Robert A. Johnson, *She: Understanding Feminine Psychology* (New York: Harper & Row Publ. Inc., 1976), 72.

16. Austine Roberts, *Centered On Christ: An Introduction To Monastic Profession* (Still River, MA: St. Bede's Publications, 1977), 169.

17. The discussion of the "shadow" is based largely on the book by Robert A. Johnson, *Owning Your Own Shadow* (San Francisco: Harper, 1991), 118.

18. Thomas Merton, *Cistercian Life* (Spencer, MA: Cistercian Book, 1974).

19. Ralph Blum, *The Book of Runes* (New York: Oracle Books, St. Martin's Press, 1987), 149.

20. Brother David Steindl-Rast, *Gratefulness And The Heart of Prayer: An Approach to Life in Fullness* (Ransey, NJ: Paulist Press, 1984), 224.

21. William D. Clark, *Death Valley, The Story Behind the Scenery* (Las Vegas:KC Publications, 1981), 45.

22. Thomas Moore, *The Re-enchantment of Everyday Living* (New York: HarperCollins Publishers, 1996), 396.

23. Thomas Moore, *Meditations* (New York: HarperCollins Publishers, 1994), 107.

24. White Eagle, *The Path of the Soul* (New Lands, Liss, Hampshire, England: The White Eagle Publishing Trust), 79.

25. James Hillman, "Growth Revisited," *Resurgence* 176 (1996): 8-10.

ABOUT THE AUTHORS

CHRIS MASER has spent more than 25 years as a research scientist in natural history and ecology. He lectures internationally on sustainable community development and facilitates environmental conflict resolution. A consultant in forest ecology and sustainable forestry practices, Maser has published more than 270 articles, including 20 books.

ZANE MASER has been involved with the spiritual healing work of the Church of the White Eagle Lodge. The Masers live in Corvallis, Oregon.